Rosa
Luxemburg

ROSA LUXEMBURG

REFLECTIONS AND WRITINGS

EDITED BY PAUL LE BLANC

Humanity
Books

an imprint of Prometheus Books
59 John Glenn Drive, Amherst, New York 14228-2197

This book is dedicated to my friend

Carol McAllister

whose fine work as a cultural anthropologist and ethnographer,
whose feminist and political sensibilities, and whose personal qualities
have contributed much to my own outlook and life.

Published 1999 by Humanity Books, an imprint of Prometheus Books

03 02 01 00 99   5 4 3 2 1

Library of Congress Cataloging-in-Publication Data

Rosa Luxemburg : reflections and writings / edited by Paul Le Blanc.
        p.   cm. — (Revolutionary studies)
    Includes bibliographical references.
    ISBN 1–57392–729–5 (pa. : alk. paper).
    1. Luxemburg, Rosa, 1871–1919. 2. Socialism. 3. Women communists—
Germany. 4. Women revolutionaries—Germany. I. Luxemburg, Rosa, 1871–1919.
II. Le Blanc, Paul, 1947–   . III. Series.
HX273.L83R585   1999
335.43'092—dc21   99–42498
                                                                                    CIP

Printed in the United States of America on acid-free paper

CONTENTS

5

INTRODUCTION

Paul Le Blanc

In this period of crisis, reevaluation, and renewal within the Left, the ideas of Rosa Luxemburg assume a greater vitality and relevance than ever before. The present volume provides a representative sampling of Luxemburg's luminous and often exciting writings that, however, have generally not been among those commonly anthologized. That she had a powerful impact on every generation of the twentieth century is documented in the accompanying essays that draw the reader into "discussions"—in one case a loving reminiscence, in some cases scholarly reflections, in others comradely arguments—that a number of intellectuals and activists have had with this vibrant thinker. It is important that new generations make her acquaintance.

Although common wisdom in the 1990s has been that "socialism is dead," what actually died had little to do with what Luxemburg represents. The socialism that animated Rosa Luxemburg as a thinker and revolutionary activist involved a vision of a society in which our economic resources would be socially owned, democratically controlled, and utilized for the benefit of all people, a goal that she was convinced could only be realized through the struggles of the working-class majority. The defining principle of what it means to be "on the left," after all, had originally been *popular sovereignty*, rule by the people, democracy. In the decades following Luxemburg's 1919 martyrdom, this truth got lost. Stalinist totalitarianism came to dominate the Communist movement. At the same time, the reform-oriented movement of social democracy displayed its commitment to practical compromises with the market economy and capitalist power, flavored with a "modernizing" technocratic elitism. The turn-of-the-century bankruptcy and collapse of both the bureaucratic-authoritarian and the bureaucratic-reformist variants of "socialism" suggests the relevance of Luxemburg's revolutionary-democratic alternative.

Nor does the triumphal "globalization" of the capitalist economy demonstrate the irrelevance of this keen observer of the market economy's voracious economic expansionism. The growing inequalities between countries; the degradation of the many millions of men, women, and children in the "less-developed" regions; the assaults on working-class living conditions and dignity everywhere—all of this is consistent with the understanding that Luxemburg developed through a tough-minded application of Marxist theory to the realities of her own time. Her theoretical orientation in the first two decades of the twentieth century had already begun to touch on issues dominating the final two decades: the increasing obsolescence of national sovereignty (not to mention of democracy) thanks to the global reach of immensely powerful multinational corporations; the degeneration of nationalism into sometimes murderous ethnic conflicts; and the increasingly lethal threat posed by bourgeois "progress" to the natural environment of the entire planet. "Socialism or barbarism," she insisted, was the choice facing humanity. The history of our century validates the somber plausibility of this challenge.

In order to live, Rosa Luxemburg needs those of us who will bring her voice alive in ourselves and in our own times. It may be the case, too, that we will need to listen to that voice, and respond to it with our own life-activity, if we and future generations are also to live.

I

Rosa Luxemburg (1871–1919) was born in Poland (then divided under German and Russian domination), into a fairly well-to-do and cultured family that enabled this exceptionally bright daughter to pursue an education in Warsaw and then Zurich. By the early 1890s she was active in the Polish revolutionary movement, moving to Germany shortly thereafter in order to play a more substantial role in the massive and internationally influential German Social Democratic Party. Here she took the lead—with her polemic *Reform or Revolution*—in opposing the reformist dilution of Marxist theory and politics that was being spearheaded by the "revisionist" spokesman Eduard Bernstein. Bernstein had concluded that some of Marx's predictions about the inevitability of capitalist crisis had been wrong, that the struggle between workers and capitalists would not need to culminate in socialist revolution, and that instead the progress of capitalism could be transformed in a socialist direction through an accumulation of more modest reforms.[1]

The struggle against "revisionism" was joined by the "pope" of Marxist orthodoxy, Karl Kautsky, editor of the authoritative theoretical journal *Neue Zeit*. Kautsky and the prestigious old "warhorse" of German Social Democracy August Bebel believed that the well-organized German socialist workers' movement—seen by socialists around the world as a model that was destined to realize the revolutionary hopes expressed by Marx and Engels in the *Communist Manifesto*—had no need to revise its theoretical perspectives. At first delighted with the brilliance and eloquence of this young revolutionary from the east, Bebel and then Kautsky eventually began to draw back as she challenged their party's "tried-and-true" routinism that seemed to be yielding increasing successes in the realms of membership growth, electoral support, securing reforms, and expanding influence. Luxemburg was concerned that the bureaucratic organizational apparatus of the German Social Democracy would—despite a formal adherence to Marxist "orthodoxy"—fail to reach out to working people in a manner that would facilitate the development of the revolutionary energy that she felt was latent within them. This highlights the importance of her insistence that Marxism must not be allowed to stagnate. It also helps to explain her well-known negative reaction to the organizational perspectives of a prominent revolutionary Marxist in Russia, V. I. Lenin. Lenin's emphasis on organizational centralism in Russia seemed to smack of the bureaucratic orientation that Luxemburg was combating in Germany, although—in the wake of the 1905 wave of strikes and workers' uprisings throughout eastern Europe—she and Lenin soon found themselves standing closer together. By contrast, the 1905 experience compelled Luxemburg to write her 1906 classic, *The Mass Strike, the Political Party, and the Trade Unions*, which criticizes the bureaucratic conservatism permeating much of the German Social Democracy. It also analyzes the actual dynamics of revolutionary situations that are animated by spontaneous upsurges of largely unorganized masses unexpectedly swept into motion. Luxemburg's opposition to those who stood for "business as usual" in the trade unions and party placed her unambiguously in the revolutionary wing of German Social Democracy.

Refusing to occupy a "safer" and marginalized position as a women's spokesperson in the socialist movement, she nonetheless had a vibrant sense of the interpenetration of women's liberation and working-class liberation. In 1902, she wrote that "with the political emancipation of women a strong fresh wind must also blow into [the socialist movement's] political and spiritual life, dispelling the suffocating atmosphere of the present philistine family life which so unmistakably rubs off on our party members too, the workers as well as the leaders." Many older male comrades believed that "a woman's place is in the home" (despite pioneering work for women's rights by such respected leaders as Clara Zetkin and party-founder August Bebel), and Luxemburg's whole life constituted a conscious and powerful challenge to such sentiments.

More than this, there was the painful process of self-definition as she ended her intimate involvement with her first great love, Leo Jogiches. A master at developing and maintaining revolutionary organizational structures that were especially important for the necessarily clandestine situation of the Polish workers' movement, Jogiches has been well described by Hannah Arendt as "a very remarkable and yet typical figure among the professional revolutionists," combining a strong masculinity with an incisive analytical mind and a deep life-commitment to strongly held values and beliefs. There were few men Luxemburg respected, Arendt tells us, "and Jogiches headed a list on which only the names of Lenin and Franz Mehring could be inscribed with certainty. He definitely was a man of action and passion, and he knew how to do and how to suffer." Luxemburg's intense, sometimes consuming intimacy with Jogiches lasted amid all the stresses imposed by two strong personalities and by the fluctuating, often tense and difficult conditions of revolutionary struggle from 1892 until 1907. When it finally broke apart—angrily, stormily, and not without some personal destructiveness for them both—Luxemburg nonetheless maintained a comradely working relationship as a political equal with him. As Raya Dunayevskaya has perceptively suggested, "it was there, *just there*, that something new was emerging." It is highly significant, and appears to set her off from the norm, that (although she continued to have comradely ties, close friendships, and sometimes erotic liaisons) her "further self-development was reaching new heights without leaning on Jogiches" or any other man. Dunayevskaya stresses: "Luxemburg needed to be free, to be independent, to be whole. . . . Her greatest intellectual accomplishments occurred after the break." It is interesting to note that Luxemburg herself felt that "the character of a woman shows itself not where love begins, but rather where it ends."[2]

The focus of Luxemburg's political and theoretical work, however, was on issues such as the development of capitalism into a new imperialist phase that threatened to bring about a devastating world war. Her major economic work, *The Accumulation of Capital* (1913) was followed by a more practical and tragic political critique of 1915, *The Junius Pamphlet: The Crisis of German Social Democracy*. This was written from a prison cell because of her opposition to the German war effort—while a majority of the de-radicalized, bureaucratized Social Democratic Party rallied to "the fatherland."

Both "orthodox" and "revisionist" Marxists had been inclined to have faith in the progressive upward swing of History, which—with the spread of capitalist industry—would create a working-class majority that one way or another would inevitably bring about a socialist democracy. Instead, there was a seemingly inexorable spread of imperialism and militarism, accompanied throughout Europe by the intensification of chauvinistic, racist, superpatriotic forms of nationalism. This was especially true in Germany, where "uneven and combined development" had resulted in an explosively contradictory mix of rapid industrialization and capitalist modernization with the preservation of old traditions and power relations. A conservative political synthesis had consequently been forged: a strong monarchy, a powerful military, an elaborate state bureaucracy, and a rather stunted parliamentary democracy. While this political reality increasingly frustrated the hopes of the worker-based Social Democratic Party, it more or less successfully blended the interests of the aristocratic land-owning elite and the urban business classes, together with the "middle sectors" made up of small farmers plus many upwardly aspiring white-collar employees and professionals. If the bulk of the German labor movement in 1914 had not been swept along by the wartime patriotism, it would have been jolted onto a violent collision course with the government, the upper classes, and a myriad of ultranationalist currents among the "middle sectors." (Over the years, nationalism had also become a growing influence within the Social Democratic Party—not only among the open revisionists—and also within some of its working-class base, eroding the party's traditional anti-imperi-alist and antimilitarist orientation.) The colossal devastation and defeat brought on by World War I, however, would wreck the German political synthesis, win many workers to a deeper and angry rejection of militarism and the old status quo, and create new opportunities for revolutionaries—but it would also unleash a brutal right-wing countercurrent that eventually brought Adolf Hitler to power and set the stage for the Second World War. Grasping such dynamics, Luxemburg warned that things could end badly—that a failure by a revolutionary working class to move forward to a socialist democracy would result in humanity's downward slide into barbarism.

While the war still raged, Luxemburg joined with a relative handful of revolutionary Marxists to organize the oppositional *Spartakusbund* (Spar-tacus League). When kindred spirits in Russia—led by Lenin's Bolshe-viks—brought about a workers' revolution in 1917, she was elated. Although critical of some of Lenin's and Trotsky's policies in Russia, she nonetheless strongly identified with what they represented, and she helped form the German Communist Party at the end of 1918. The monarchy had just collapsed—to be replaced by the Weimar republic and a moderate Social Democratic government—in the wake of the devastation and defeat of World War I. Amid the chaos and revolutionary ferment, masses of workers were rallying to the orientation with which Luxemburg was iden-tified. But her enemies (including the Social Democratic bureaucracy) were spreading vicious and provocative slanders about "Red Rosa," and right-wing paramilitary units were being organized to combat insurgent workers and kill revolutionary militants. An abortive uprising in early 1919 was used as a pretext to murder Luxemburg, Karl Liebknecht, Jogiches, and others.

II

Did being a woman enable Rosa Luxemburg to develop a Marxist orientation animated by qualities often beyond the reach of her male counterparts? She was an "outsider" who became a powerful force in the predominantly male milieu in the inner circles of the German, Polish, and Russian left-wing workers' movement, which may have helped her perceive connections less easily visible to others. There were other unusual dimensions of her thought as well.

She proved herself as a brilliant political analyst and a pioneering economic theorist, a fine writer, an inspiring teacher, a powerful speaker, and a revolutionary leader who displayed both courage and insight. But to all of this she brought something different, something special, soaring like an eagle (as Lenin once put it) above most of the others. There was a sensuousness that was an integral element in how she saw things and expressed them—brushing aside artifice and laughing at posturing, connecting with what was real and dynamic, reaching deep into her own emotional reserves in a way that deeply touched the emotions of others, consistently moving beyond abstractions, nourished by an amazing awareness of the infinite and ever-renewing threads that connect all living things, unashamed of valuing beauty and emotion and nurturing, uncompromisingly honest.

She proudly embraced the "scientific socialist" doctrines of Karl Marx, while openly dismissing the vulgar-Marxist notion that "economic development rushes headlong, like an autonomous locomotive on the tracks of history, and that politics, ideology, etc., are content to toddle behind like forsaken, passive freight wagons." Of course, other mature Marxists had made much the same point—yet this passionate revolutionary consciously fused thought and feeling in an insistent manner that was unusual for the prominent theoreticians who dominated the socialist movement. "Unrelenting revolutionary activity coupled with boundless humanity—that alone is the real life-giving force of socialism," she wrote amid the storms of crashing empires and working-class insurgency in the wake of the First World War. Such expressions were typical of her, but set her apart from many of the more "worldly" personalities on the left. Many years before, she had explained to a jaundiced Polish comrade, in regard to the massive Social Democratic Party of Germany, which she had recently joined, that

"I do not agree with the view that it is foolish to be an idealist in the German movement. To begin with, there are idealists here too—above all, a huge number of the most simple agitators and from the working masses and furthermore, even in the leadership," but what's more, "the ultimate principle" in all of her revolutionary activity "is to remain true to myself without regard for the surroundings and the others"—thus, "I am and will remain an idealist in the German as well as the Polish movement."[3]

Her uncompromising idealism was focused on pushing the German workers' movement to remain true to its original revolutionary perspectives: to win the battle for democracy through an uncompromising struggle by the working class against its oppression (and against all forms of oppression)—finally taking state power and bringing the economy under the control of the working-class majority. Considerable lip service was given by the Social Democratic Party to such socialist goals, but "when you look around, the Party looks damn bad—completely headless. . . . No one leads it, no one shoulders the responsibility." The result: a drift toward routinism; a pull toward piling up reforms as a substitute for revolutionary struggle; the rising influence of trade-union bureaucracies and of the party's vote-chasing electoral apparatus; in short, policies involving an opportunistic adaptation to capitalism. She had little patience, however, for the ultraleft elements of "supposed orthodox 'radicalism' . . . attacking each of the opportunist imbecilities and submitting it to a garrulous exegesis . . . [and] who endlessly find it necessary to bring the stray lamb, the Party, back into the safe fold of 'firmness of principles' without realizing that these negative proceedings will not get us ahead even one step." Instead, as working-class support for the German Social Democratic Party shifted from hundreds of thousands to millions of people, "we ourselves must move ahead, *develop* our tactics, *reinforce* the revolutionary side of the movement," which she believed would become possible—and effective—in the revolutionary storms that would soon transform "the stagnant waters of the movement" into "a strong fresh current." This indeed came to pass in the mass strikes and revolutionary upheavals that swept eastern Europe in 1905–1906. As historian Gary Steenson has commented, "it was her willingness to act . . . that gave legitimacy to her position; unlike others in the SPD, Rosa Luxemburg was neither an armchair revolutionary not a firebrand who expected others to carry out the real struggle in the streets."[4]

With the temporary abatement of the revolutionary upsurge, the forces of moderation and opportunism became stronger than ever in the German party. A cautious trade unionism had become predominant, and trade union leaders indignantly dismissed the mass strike concept with the comment that "the general strike is general nonsense." Rather, as historian John Moses explains, the union leadership "advocated the patient adaptation to existing forces with the ultimate aim of winning piecemeal concessions from both government and management." This was matched by an increasingly moderate parliamentary strategic orientation, in part because the labor bureaucracy had sought to make the Social Democratic Party—in the satisfied words of trade union head Karl Legien—into "the representative of the political interests of the trade unions." In addition, the party apparatus itself, as scholar Richard N. Hunt has noted, had been "created during a long period of social stability and economic expansion, [and] it was hired to run election campaigns, handle finances, disseminate the press, and do everything possible to attract new voters." Party functionaries were not inclined "to mount barricades or overturn existing society, but only to work within it for the attainment of a socialist [electoral] majority." For this they preferred "a moderate, easy-to-sell program appealing to the widest possible audience," enabling the party to become a sufficiently powerful force in parliament to pass beneficial social legislation. Even if this was justified with "orthodox Marxist" rather than "revisionist" phrases, it added up to a reformist orientation that Luxemburg saw as evolving into an accommodation to an oppressive capitalist status quo.[5]

Yet Luxemburg was convinced that "the masses, and still more the great mass of comrades, in the bottom of their hearts have had enough of this parliamentarism," as she wrote to her cothinker Clara Zetkin in 1907. "I have the feeling that a breath of fresh air in our tactics would be greeted with cries of joy. But, still they submit to the heel of the old authorities and, what's more, to the upper strata of opportunist editors, deputies, and trade union leaders." Economic and political developments were transforming the realities facing the German workers' movement, opening up new opportunities, creating new moods within the working class, but also highlighting inadequacies in the increasingly bureaucratized apparatus of the German social democracy. By 1910, Carl Schorske has noted, "the mood of the social-democratic rank and file waxed stormier as the hopelessness of reform from the top grew more apparent from week to week," and it was Luxemburg "who took the intellectual leadership of the movement to drive on to more radical action." Yet time was running out. "We are approaching the time when the Party masses will need a leadership that is aggressive, pitiless, and visionary," she commented in 1912, but noted that "our higher leadership cadres, the party paper, parliamentary group, as well as our theoretical organ" threatened to "grow shabbier and shabbier, more cowardly, more besotted with parliamentary cretinism."[6] Within two years, her warnings were confirmed more disastrously than even she had expected, when the bulk of the socialist leadership led the party into an accommodation with imperialism and militarism—abandoning the traditional clarion call, "workers of all countries unite," in order to embrace patriotism and support the German war effort in World War I.

The influence of nationalism and the success of prowar "patriotic" appeals within much of the working class—utilized by some Social Democrats to explain part of their own support for the war effort, and pointed to by other comrades as a bitter disappoint of the Marxist principles of working-class internationalism and proletarian revolution—was seen by Luxemburg from a different perspective. Her view of the interplay between the masses of the working-class and revolutionary leadership is marked by a striking dynamism:

> There is nothing more mutable than human psychology. The psyche of the masses like the eternal sea always carries all the latent possibilities: the deathly calm and the roaring storm, the lowest cowardice and the wildest heroism. The mass is always that which it *must* be according to the circumstances of the time, and the mass is always at the point of becoming something entirely different than what it appears to be. A fine captain he would be who would chart his course only from the momentary appearance of the water's surface and who would not know how to predict a coming storm from the signs in the sky or from the depths. . . . The "disappointment over the masses" is always the most shameful testimony for a political leader. A leader in the grand style does not adapt his tactics to the momentary mood of the masses, but rather to the iron laws of development; he holds fast to his tactics in spite of all "disappointments" and, for the rest, calmly allows history to bring its work to maturity.[7]

Related to this was the firm belief that when and where the German socialist movement was strong and effective, the German working class had learned that "socialism is not only a question of the knife and fork, but of a cultural movement and a great and proud worldview." Although Marx and Engels themselves had proclaimed that "the German proletariat has become the heir of classical German philosophy, . . . since their terrible collapse in the world war, the inheritors look like miserable beggars, eaten alive by vermin." But as Luxemburg wrote to her friend Franz Mehring, "the iron laws of the historical dialectic . . . will force these beggars to stand up and turn into proud and tough fighters" animated by "the spirit of socialism."[8]

Hardly viewing history as the inexorable movement of impersonal forces bringing about hoped-for revolutionary results, Luxemburg believed in the importance of what people like herself did or failed to do. Revolutionary leadership meant putting forward clear ideas that would help masses of workers as they sought to make sense of the realities of which they were part. It meant winning people to a revolutionary pro-gram—a fighting strategy and practical tactics—that could bring the working class to power. *How* one advanced this orientation could be deci-sive in moving forward the class struggle and the revolutionary process.

"Do you know what keeps bothering me now?" she once wrote in an 1898 letter. "I'm not satisfied with the way in which people in the party usually write articles. They are all so conventional, so wooden, so cut and dry." In the opinion of the twenty-seven-year-old revolutionary Marxist, one must do better:

> Our scribblings are usually not lyrics, but whirrings, without color or resonance, like the tone of an engine-wheel. I believe that the cause lies in the fact that when people write, they forget for the most part to dig deeply into themselves and to feel the whole import and truth of what they are writing. I believe that every time, every day, in every article you must live through the thing again, you must feel your way through it, and then fresh words—coming from the heart and going to the heart— would occur to express the old familiar thing. But you get so used to a truth that you rattle off the deepest and greatest things as if they were the "Our Father." I firmly intend, when I write, never to forget to be enthusiastic about what I write and to commune with myself.[9]

By the time she was in her mid-forties, she confessed to an intimate friend that "in theoretical work as in art, I value only the simple, the tranquil and the bold. This is why, for example, the famous first volume of Marx's *Capital*, with its profuse rococo ornamentation in the Hegelian style, now seems an abomination to me (for which, from the Party standpoint, I must get 5 years' hard labor and 10 years' loss of civil rights)." She hastened to add that Marx's economic theories were the bedrock of her own theoretical work, but also emphasized that her "more mature" work was in "its form . . . extremely simple, without any accessories, without coquetry or optical illusions, straightforward and reduced to the barest essentials; I would even say 'naked,' like a block of marble." Delving into theoretical questions—explaining the economic expansionism of imperialism that arose out of *the accumulation of capital*, which became the title of her 1913 classic—was a creative labor through which "day and night I neither saw nor heard anything as that one problem developed beautifully before my eyes." The process of thinking—as she slowly paced back and forth, "closely observed by [her cat] Mimi, who lay on the red plush tablecloth, her little paws crossed, her intelligent head following me"—and the actual process of writing combined as an experience of trancelike and profound pleasure.[10]

Luxemburg's gifts were hardly restricted to the realm of study and the written word. As a public speaker similar qualities came through. "An untamed revolutionary force was alive in this frail little woman," an admiring Max Adler later commented. "It was characteristic of her, however, that her intellect never lost control of her temperament, so that the revolutionary fire with which she always spoke was also mingled with cool-headed reflectiveness, and the effect of this fire was not destructive but warming and illuminating." And in personal interactions, as well, Luxemburg's student and biographer Paul Frölich tells us, her "large, dark and bright eyes . . . were very expressive, at times searching with a penetrating scrutiny, or thoughtful; at times merry and flashing with excitement. They reflected an ever-alert intellect and an indomitable soul." Her "fine-toned and resonant" voice "could express the finest nuances of meaning," and her slight Polish accent "lent character to her voice and added a special zest to her humor." More than this, Frölich tells us, the sensitive revolutionary was by no means full of herself but knew—when with another—that sometimes one must remain silent or listen, and be able to talk "in a natural, down-to-earth, and spirited way" about everyday life. "All this made every private moment with her a special gift."[11]

As the brutalizing First World War dragged on, Luxemburg commented that "although I have never been soft, lately I have grown hard as polished steel, and I will no longer make the smallest concession either in political or personal intercourse." In almost the next breath, she added: "Being a *Mensch* [a person] is the main thing! And that means to be firm, lucid and cheerful. Yes, cheerful despite everything and anything—since whining is the business of the weak. Being a *Mensch* means happily throwing one's life 'on fate's great scale' if necessary, but, at the same time, enjoying every bright day and every beautiful cloud."[12]

Luxemburg's powerful personality and intellect derived, in large measure, from the fact that she refused to narrow herself—for example by an exclusive focus on political conflicts—believing that "such one-sidedness also clouds one's political judgment; and, above all, one must live as a full person at all times." For that matter, although she had more than once suffered from anti-Semitism, she rejected what she viewed as a fixation on "this particular suffering of the Jews," insisting that it was in no way worse than the often murderous oppression of other peoples by European imperialism. "The poor victims on the rubber plantations in Putumayo, the Negroes in Africa with whose bodies the Europeans play a game of catch, are just as dear to me," Luxemburg wrote to a friend. "Do you remember the words written on the work of the Great General Staff about Trotha's campaign in the Kalahari desert? 'And the death-rattles, the mad cries of those dying of thirst, faded away into the sublime silence of eternity.' " Indignant over the murderous arrogance and smug eloquence of the poetic imperialist, she concluded: "Oh, this 'sublime silence of eternity' in which so many screams have faded away unheard. It rings within me so strongly that I have no special corner of my heart reserved for the [Jewish] ghetto: I am at home wherever in the world there are clouds, birds and human tears."[13]

Of course, the violence and inhumanity visited on those victimized by colonial oppression in "faraway lands" of Asia and Africa became a murderous backdraft which exploded into Europe with the imperialist slaughter between 1914 and 1918. Luxemburg concluded that humanity stood at a crossroads: either forward to socialism or a downward slide into barbarism. She and her comrades in the newly formed Spartacus League (soon to become the German Communist Party) warned:

> The great criminals of this fearful anarchy, of this chaos let loose—the ruling classes—are not able to control their own creation. The beast of capital that conjured up the hell of the world war is not capable of banishing it again, of restoring real order, of insuring bread and work, peace and civilization, and justice and liberty to tortured humanity.
>
> What is being prepared by the ruling classes as peace and justice is only a new work of brutal force from which the hydra of oppression, hatred, and fresh bloody wars raises a thousand heads. . . .[14]

This certainly turned out to be true. The "war to make the world safe for democracy," the "war to end all wars," generated catastrophic aftershocks. Luxemburg herself, and some of her closest comrades, were destroyed by these—which, in turn, helped to undermine the new revolutionary possibilities that she had identified. It is impossible to measure the loss of this vibrant and magnificent person. The intellectual legacy that she left, however, sheds light not only on the quality of this individual, but also on the times in which she lived, and on the twentieth century as a whole—and perhaps also on the dynamics and possibilities of the twenty-first century.

III

It is worth reflecting on the fortunes of Luxemburg's reputation as recounted in a classic 1966 essay by the decidedly non-Marxist political theorist Hannah Arendt, who blended profoundly conservative and radical perspectives in her own fascinatingly idiosyncratic philosophical outlook and yet was among the most insightful admirers of this revolutionary Marxist. Her comments were aimed not simply at the Stalinized Communists whom she detested, but especially at de-radicalized "democratic socialists" that completely dominated the socialist and labor parties of twentieth-century social democracy after the 1919 murder of Luxemburg:

Shortly after her death, when all persuasions of the Left had already decided that she had always been "mistaken" (a "really hopeless case," as George Lichtheim, the last in this long line, put it in *Encounter*), a curious shift in her reputation took place. Two small volumes of her letters were published, and these, entirely personal and of a simple, touchingly humane, and often poetic beauty, were enough to destroy the propaganda image of bloodthirsty "Red Rosa," at least in all but the most obstinately anti-Semitic and reactionary circles. However, what then grew up was another legend—the sentimentalized image of the bird watcher and lover of flowers, a woman whose guards said good-by to her with tears in their eyes when she left prison—as if they couldn't go on living without being entertained by this strange prisoner who had insisted on treating them as human beings. . . .

It took a few more years and a few more catastrophes for the legend to turn into a symbol of nostalgia for the good old times of the movement, when hopes were green, the revolution around the corner, and most important, the faith in the capacities of the masses and in the moral integrity of the Socialist or Communist leadership was still intact. It speaks not only for the person of Rosa Luxemburg, but also for the qualities of this older generation of the Left, that the legend—vague, confused, inaccurate in nearly all details—could spread throughout the world and come to life whenever a "New Left" sprang into being. But side by side with this glamorized image, there survived also the old cliches of the "quarrelsome female," a "romantic" who was neither "realistic" nor scientific (it is true that she was always out of step), and whose works, especially her great book on imperialism (*The Accumulation of Capital*, 1913), were shrugged off. Every New Left movement, when its moment came to change into the Old Left—usually when its members reached the age of forty—promptly buried its early enthusiasm for Rosa Luxemburg together with the dreams of youth; and since they had usually not bothered to read, let alone to understand, what she had to say they found it easy to dismiss her with all the patronizing philistinism of their newly acquired status. . . . Nothing Rosa Luxemburg ever wrote or said survived except her surprisingly accurate criticism of Bolshevik policies during the early stages of the Russian Revolution, and this only because those whom a "god had failed" [i.e., embittered ex-Communists who from the late 1940s onward had become Cold War anti-Communists] could use it as a convenient though wholly inadequate weapon against Stalin. . . . Her new admirers had no more in common with her than her detractors. Her highly developed sense for theoretical differences and her infallible judgment of people, her personal likes and dislikes, would have prevented her from lumping Lenin and Stalin together under all circumstances, quite apart from the fact that she had never been a "believer," had never used politics as a substitute for religion . . .[15]

Things were no better within the Communist mainstream, where from the mid-1920s onward, Luxemburg's stature as a revolutionary was increasingly denigrated. Leading a strong ultraleft current that helped to "Bolshevize" the German Communist Party, Ruth Fischer denounced Luxemburg's continuing political influence in her organization as "syphilitic," and by 1930 Joseph Stalin himself warned against the "utopian" and "semi-Menshevik" errors infesting Luxemburg's thought that were "seized upon by Trotsky . . . and turned into a weapon of struggle against Leninism." Nonetheless, she and Liebknecht continued to be enshrined as revolutionary martyrs in the pantheon of German Communism. In 1932 the staunchly Stalinist leader Ernst Thaelmann proclaimed: "We have no intention of diminishing the importance of Rosa Luxemburg, Karl Liebknecht, Franz Mehring, and the other comrades who formed the left radical wing of prewar social democracy. . . . Rosa Luxemburg and the others belong to us, belong to the Communist International and the KPD [German Communist Party], to whose founding they contributed." Yet most of those who had been closest to her had by then been pushed aside—either expelled from or marginalized within the Communist movement. And the worst was yet to come. By the end of the decade, her former student, comrade, and biographer, Paul Frölich, commented on "the desecration of her memory committed by those who should have been the first to preserve her political heritage," and his elaboration was bitter:

Whilst pursuing, for reasons of prestige, a dishonest cult with her name and that of Karl Liebknecht they waged a fierce and unscrupulous campaign against something called "Luxemburgism," created by perverting her ideas and misrepresenting her political work. They disparaged her role in the working-class movement, outlawed her followers, many of whom had founded the party with her; and placed obstacle after obstacle in the way of any publication of her works. And finally, many of her close collaborators, and in particular her Polish comrades in arms, lost their lives in the Lubianka and other prisons as victims of Stalin's campaign of extermination against the Old Guard of the revolution.[16]

All of this stands in marked contrast to the reaction of Lenin to the posthumous publication of Luxemburg's sharp critique of the policies for which he and the other Bolsheviks were responsible in 1918. She had been critical (a) of the Bolsheviks giving land to the peasants rather than nationalizing it, (b) of what she considered to be a mistaken catering to "outdated" nationalist sentiments, and (c) of the dissolution of the Constituent Assembly in the name of a higher form of "soviet democracy." Even historians sympathetic to Luxemburg have granted that these points are at least debatable. More than this, however, she issued a profound warning, which proved devastatingly accurate, against the repressive "temporary expedients" (and the no less dangerous theoretical justifications for these expedients) that were carried out in the early phases of the Russian civil war:

> In place of the representative bodies created by general popular elections, Lenin and Trotsky have laid down the soviets [democratic councils] as the only true representation of the laboring masses. But with the repression of political life in the land as a whole, life in the soviets must become more and more crippled. Without general elections, without unrestricted freedom of press and assembly, without a free struggle of opinion, life dies out in every public institution, becomes a mere semblance of life, in which only the bureaucracy remains as the active element. Public life gradually falls asleep, a few dozen party leaders of inexhaustible energy and boundless experience direct and rule. Among them, in reality only a dozen outstanding heads do the leading and an elite of the working class is invited from time to time to meetings where they are to applaud the speeches of the leaders, and to approve proposed resolutions unanimously—at bottom, then, a clique affair—a dictatorship, to be sure, not the dictatorship of the proletariat, however, but only the dictatorship of a handful of politicians . . .[17]

Lenin's 1922 response to this critique by no means read Luxemburg out
of the revolutionary movement. Instead he expressed his disagreement
while immediately adding: "not only will Communists all over the world
cherish her memory, but her biography and her *complete* works (the publication of which the German Communists are inordinately delaying . . .) will
serve as useful manuals for training many generations of Communists all
over the world."[18] His incapacitating illness in the following year, and death
in 1924, prevented Lenin from helping to ensure that an immersion in Luxemburg's ideas would become part of every Communist's education—and
those who came to dominate the movement afterward, as we have seen, had
a qualitatively different attitude toward the martyred revolutionary.

It is instructive to consider Hannah Arendt's explanation that Lenin
"despite all his mistakes still had more in common with the original peer
group [of Luxemburg and her close comrades] than did anyone who came
after him." This "peer group" consisted of a cluster of professional revolutionaries, initially in her native Poland, who had "no conventional prej-
udices whatsoever, and had developed, in this truly splendid isolation, their
own code of honor" consisting of "mutual respect and unconditional
trust, a universal humanity and a genuine, almost naive contempt for
ethnic and social distinctions." They also had "a violent contempt for the
careerists and status seekers" in the working-class movement, since "such
things as ambition, career, status, and even mere success were under the
strictest taboo" among those infused with a determination to alter the circumstances of the world that offended their sense of justice and freedom.
Such a peer group was duplicated in the clandestine *Spartakusbund* which
she and Jogiches helped organize in wartime Germany, and one can also
find precisely such qualities in the early Russian revolutionary movement
described by Lenin, Trotsky, and others.[19]

The deep longing for such heroism and idealism in many parts of the
world, and the deepening crises of our time, may give Luxemburg's life
and ideas a powerful resonance among growing numbers of people who
seek a more positive meaning in life than can realistically be provided by
either business or politics "as usual."

There remains a question, however, of to what extent Luxemburg's
heroism and idealism—and her revolutionary ideas and commitments—
might have constituted more than simply a beautiful gesture in the face of

the immense and destructive forces that overwhelmed her. About this there is no agreement among historians. A. J. Ryder speaks for many in asserting that "the Spartacist cause won few adherents: in a time of fierce nationalism its somewhat abstract internationalism had little appeal, and few German workers were willing to run the risk of defeat for the sake of world revolution." On the other hand, William Pelz argues that "by war's end, Spartakus had grown into an organization of thousands with influence in numerous working class areas." Given the fact that Pelz has inquired more carefully than most into the nature and dimensions of this movement that Luxemburg led, it is worth considering more of what he has to say:

> Struggling underground, the Spartakusbund was able to grow, propagate its ideas and develop linkages with like-minded revolutionary groups and individuals, based heavily in urban industrial areas. Thus, Luxemburg, Liebknecht and the other Spartakusbund leaders directed what was the heart of a growing revolutionary workers movement. Young, active and concentrated in the most modern vital sections of the economy, Spartakusbund members were to prove the revolutionary voice within the ideological vacuum [that the bureaucratized leadership of the German] Social Democracy labored to maintain.[20]

To the extent that Pelz's account is accurate, it suggests that what Luxemburg was doing had practical implications that—if her luck had run somewhat differently—might have profoundly altered the course of history. If such people as Luxemburg, Liebknecht, Jogiches, and Eugen Leviné had survived the abortive uprising of 1919, it seems not unlikely that around them a powerful, self-confident, increasingly experienced leadership core would have crystallized to lead a growing German Communist Party to victory in, say, 1920 or 1923—rescuing the Russian Revolution from the isolation that would soon generate Stalinism, and at the same time preventing the possibility of the rise of Hitlerism.[21]

Regardless of the relevance of Luxemburg's example and ideas for her own time, there is the separate question of how relevant such things will be for the twenty-first century. The answer to this question lies beyond the reach of this essay. But there is little doubt that what she was, what she did, and what she said pose a challenge for our own time no less than for hers.

IV

In 1966 Hannah Arendt noted that most of Luxemburg's works translated in English were only available in hard-to-get pamphlets published by Trotskyists in Ceylon (now Sri Lanka). Fortunately, as the bibliography of the present volume demonstrates, that is no longer the case.

The selection of writings by Rosa Luxemburg in this volume was guided by several criteria. One was a desire not to duplicate materials contained in another volume which I produced—*From Marx to Gramsci: A Reader in Revolutionary Marxist Politics*. This includes selections from the following works: "Stagnation and Progress of Marxism"; *Reform and Revolution*; *The Mass Strike, the Political Party, and the Trade Unions*; *The Junius Pamphlet*; and "Women's Suffrage and Class Struggle." These are key texts, and should be read by anyone interested in Luxemburg's ideas. In this sense, and in others, *From Marx to Gramsci* and *Rosa Luxemburg: Reflections and Writings* can be seen as companion volumes; the first (in particular the substantial introductory essay, I would hope) helps to illuminate the context of the second, while the present volume allows for a deepening and elaboration of aspects all too briefly touched on in the earlier work.

There are also presently three substantial English-language collections of Luxemburg's writings in print: *Rosa Luxemburg Speaks*, edited by Mary-Alice Waters; *Selected Political Writings of Rosa Luxemburg*, edited by Dick Howard; and *The Letters of Rosa Luxemburg*, edited by Stephen Eric Bronner. Presently out of print is Robert Looker, ed., *Rosa Luxemburg: Selected Political Writings*. Here, too, an editorial decision was made to avoid duplication of easily available texts—in the few cases where this rule was violated, the included text appears only in one of the volumes edited by Waters, Howard, or Bronner. All of these books are highly recommended, as is Paul Frölich's indispensable biography, *Rosa Luxemburg: Her Life and Work*, and a superb collection of critical essays by Norman Geras, *The Legacy of Rosa Luxemburg*; the perspectives of these two volumes have prodoundingly influenced my own understanding. The desire of the editor was to produce a volume containing representative writings by Luxemburg that could stand on their own but could also be a useful addition to both personal and institutional libraries containing the aforementioned works.

Another unique feature of this volume is that it contains a diverse sampling of informative and in some cases provocative essays about Rosa Luxemburg. Not all of these writers agree with each other, nor should readers be expected to agree with all that they have to say, but each engages with Luxemburg's life and work in ways that may add to our understanding of what she was and move forward our thinking on the issues with which she was concerned. It is to be hoped that this volume will help readers to benefit from, but also perhaps contribute to, a rich and continuing collective evaluation and utilization of this passionate revolutionary's life and thought.

Notes

1. This initial section of the introduction reproduces and somewhat expands the biographical summary presented in Paul Le Blanc, *From Marx to Gramsci: A Reader in Revolutionary Marxist Politics* (Amherst, N.Y.: Humanity Books, 1996), pp. 161–62. A valuable, more detailed biographical overview by Stephen Eric Bronner can be found in *The Letters of Rosa Luxemburg*, New Edition (Amherst, N.Y.: Humanity Books, 1993), pp. 3–52. (Also, one could do worse than view Margarethe von Trotta's moving 1986 film *Rosa Luxemburg*, which is available in video.)

2. Bronner, ed., *The Letters of Rosa Luxemburg*, pp. 90, 163; Hannah Arendt, "Rosa Luxemburg, 1871–1919," in *Men in Dark Times* (New York: Harcourt, Brace and World, 1968), pp. 45–47; Raya Dunayevskaya, *Rosa Luxemburg, Women's Liberation, and Marx's Philosophy of Revolution* (Urbana: University of Illinois Press, 1991), pp. 92–93.

3. Bronner, pp. 60, 77–78.

4. Ibid., pp. 75, 94–95; Gary P. Steenson, *"Not One Man! Not One Penny!": German Social Democracy, 1863–1914* (Pittsburgh: University of Pittsburgh Press, 1981), p. 221.

5. John Moses, "Socialist Trade Unionism in Imperial Germany, 1871–1914," in Roger Fletcher, ed., *Bernstein to Brandt: A Short History of German Social Democracy* (London: Edward Arnold, 1987), p. 31; Richard N. Hunt, *German Social Democracy, 1918–1933* (Chicago: Quadrangle, 1970), pp. 166, 59.

6. Bronner, pp. 121, 149; Carl Schorske, *German Social Democracy, 1905–1917* (Cambridge: Harvard University Press, 1955), p. 181

7. Bronner, 179.

8. Ibid., pp. 294–95.

9. Quoted in Paul Frölich, *Rosa Luxemburg: Her Life and Work*, trans. Johanna Hoornweg (New York: Monthly Review Press, 1972), pp. 39–40.

10. Bronner, pp. 185, 204.

11. Frölich, pp. 197, 182.

12. Bronner, pp. 172, 173.

13. Ibid., 179–80.

14. "Spartacus Manifesto," in Anton Kaes, Martin Jay, and Edward Dimendberg, eds., *The Weimar Sourcebook* (Berkeley: University of California Press, 1994), p. 38.

15. Arendt, pp. 36–38.

16. Peter Nettl, *Rosa Luxemburg*, Abridged Edition (New York: Oxford University Press, 1969), p. 470; J. V. Stalin, "Some Questions Concerning the History of Bolshevism, Letter to the Editorial Board of the Magazine *Proletarskaya Revolutsia*," in *Problems of Leninism* (Peking: Foreign Languages Press, 1976), pp. 566–67; Eric D. Weitz, *Creating German Communism, 1890–1990: From Popular Protests to Socialist State* (Princeton: Princeton University Press, 1997), pp. 183, 195; Paul Frölich, *Rosa Luxemburg: Her Life and Work*, trans. Edward Fitzgerald (London: Victor Gollanz, 1940), p. 336; a somewhat revised but no less bitter formulation can be found on page 302 in the previously cited 1972 edition of Frölich's biography.

17. "The Russian Revolution," *Rosa Luxemburg Speaks*, ed. Mary-Alice Waters (New York: Pathfinder Press, 1970), p. 391.

18. V. I. Lenin, "Notes of a Publicist [1922]," excerpted in *Rosa Luxemburg Speaks*, p. 440. For discussions of Lenin's perspectives on the national question and how they contrast with Luxemburg's, see Horace B. Davis, *Nationalism and Socialism: Marxist and Labor Theories of Nationalism to 1917* (New York: Monthly Review Press, 1967), and Kevin Anderson, *Lenin, Hegel, and Western Marxism, A Critical Study* (Urbana: University of Illinois Press, 1995); on the peasantry, see Esther Kingston-Mann, *Lenin and the Problem of Marxist Peasant Revolution* (New York: Oxford University Press, 1983); on questions of democracy, see John Rees (with Sam Farber and Robin Blackburn), *In Defence of October, A Debate on the Russian Revolution* (London: Bookmarks, 1997); for an attempt at a balanced discussion of Luxemburg's critique, also see Frölich (1972 ed.), pp. 243–52.

19. Arendt, pp. 54, 40, 41, 43, 44, 38, 46; Paul Le Blanc, *Lenin and the Revolutionary Party* (Amherst, N.Y.: Humanity Books, 1993), pp. 15–54.

20. A. J. Ryder, *Twentieth-Century Germany: From Bismarck to Brand* (New

York: Columbia University Press, 1973), p. 171; William A. Pelz, *The Spartakus-bund and the German Working-Class Movement, 1914–1919* (Lewiston, N.Y.: Edward Mellen Press, 1987), pp. 286, 287, 289.

21. Among the studies that suggest such a possibility are Evelyn Anderson, *Hammer or Anvil: The Story of the German Working-Class Movement, 1875–1945* (London: Victor Gollancz, 1945); Ossip K. Fleichtheim, "The Role of the Communist Party," in Fritz Stem et al., *The Path to Dictatorship, 1918–1933: Ten Essays by German Scholars*, trans. John Conway (Garden City, N.Y.: Anchor Books, 1966); and Chris Harman, *The Lost Revolution: Germany, 1918 to 1923* (London: Bookmarks, 1982).

PART ONE.

REFLECTIONS

1

REMEMBERING ROSA LUXEMBURG

Luise Kautsky

Luise Kautsky was one of Luxemburg's best friends and has written a classic biographical memoir. Wife of the prestigious Marxist theoretician with whom Luxemburg would eventually cross polemical swords, Luise Kautsky's loving appreciation of her friend's personal and political qualities shines through this fine and fair-minded essay first published in 1923.

Rosa Luxemburg was born in 1870. She was the daughter of a Warsaw merchant who was fairly well-to-do, and who gave his children a good education. As long as Rosa lived she spoke with special affection of her father, while the memories of her mother seem to have been more or less relegated to the background. Yet of her, too, she spoke in loving terms, albeit a note of good-natured compassion seemed at times to accompany her references to her.

I have the impression that her mother was one of those self-sacrificing women whom one often finds in Jewish families, who center their whole being upon husband and children, and in their concern for them give up

From *Letters to Karl and Luise Kautsky from 1896 to 1918*, ed. Luise Kautsky, trans. Louis P. Lochner (New York: Robert M. McBride Co., 1925).

their own identity, yes, fairly obliterate it, so that the memory of their existence easily becomes a hazy one. Nevertheless her mother must have been well read and educated—which fact was disclosed to me by a casual remark of Rosa's. We were once discussing Schiller and his literary works, and Rosa spoke rather deprecatingly of him as of a second-rate poet. When I warmly defended him and insisted that she, a revolutionary, ought especially to take to him as a revolutionary poet, she replied, thoughtfully: "Well, perhaps I took an instinctive dislike to him because my mother was so crazy about him. By that very fact he was labeled as old-fashioned and sentimental as far as I was concerned."

However that may have been, in any case her father was more congenial to her, and it is from him that she seems to have inherited her strong intellect, her energy, in short, her sense of "the earnest conduct of life."

She must have developed very early and thirsted for knowledge even as a child. That is borne out by the nature of her reading-matter, with which she busied herself from earliest childhood on. Hardly sixteen years old, she already occupied her mind with the most difficult problems,—not only with the origins of humanity, with the right to motherhood, the history of tribes and clans, but also and especially with all problems connected with the modern labor movement, with the history of revolutions, the theory of surplus value, etc. Morgan, Bachofen, Lubbock, Kowalewski, and other sociologists, besides Marx and Engels, constituted her chief reading.

At the *gymnasium* or high school which she attended she soon gathered about her a circle of like-minded fellow students, whose spiritual leader she forthwith became. Although the youngest in the group, she was looked to from the beginning as an undisputed authority. Whenever there were difficulties the others said confidently, "Oh well, Rosa will know it all right; Rosa will help us." With flushed faces the girls debated for hours, and in this clash of minds the youthful faculties were sharpened. Soon, however, these meetings, which czarism rightly suspected to be the centers of plots, aroused the suspicions of the political police and of its stool pigeons. If Rosa and those of like mind with her did not want to see their studies rudely ended and their life at school exchanged for one in the prison that was but too eager to receive revolutionary students, they must needs leave Warsaw as quickly as possible. Still wearing the garb and apron of a high-school student, the sixteen-year-old Rosa fled to Switzerland, there to begin the life of intensive study for which she yearned. There was no lack of Russian and Polish companions from her native land, for the universities of Berne and Zurich were filled with large groups of revolutionary countrymen of hers, who like herself had fled to Switzerland to escape the czaristic police.

At Zurich, where she settled, she found in her compatriot, Leo Jogiches, a young man but a few years older than herself, a guide and leader with whom she was associated until her death in an abiding friendship. Her fiery spirit caught flame from his; in him she saw the type of representative of revolutionary thought who was worth emulating, for while still quite young he had already learned to know the terrors of Russian prisons and of banishment to Siberia. Besides, he was a master in the art of plotting, the romanticism of which cast an irresistible spell upon Rosa's impressionable mind.

Rosa plunged head over heels into her studies. Her ardor knew no bounds, and as she comprehended with the utmost facility, she was tempted to go into all branches of human knowledge. But she finally decided to specialize in political science, economics, and jurisprudence, as these studies gave promise of supplying her with the best weapons for the struggle to which she intended to devote her life: the struggle for the rights, now trampled upon the ground, of the workers, the poor, the dispossessed. In Zurich, too, she soon became the recognized spiritual head of her fellow students, and was rated by her professors as the keenest-minded and most gifted of all.

For Rosa this period was a very happy one. Freed from the unbearable political pressure from which her Russified native land suffered, she breathed deeply the free air of Switzerland. And even though hunger was more than once the guest of the students from the East, who were none too well supplied with earthly goods, and though, despite the mutual aid freely extended to each other, the rebellious stomach insisted in the midst of discussions upon being appeased with large quantities of tea and a little sugar and less bread, yet these university days constituted the high spot, in Rosa's memory and she always spoke of them with a sort of happy emotion.

Besides her studies, the problems of the working-class movement, then under discussion in the German "Arbeiterverein" at Zurich, interested her keenly, and she took an active part in the debates. In addition, she had begun to write quite early, and even before she came up for her doctor's examination her name had appeared here and there in the columns of socialistic organs. At first this was true only of the Polish periodicals which were published abroad on account of the Russian censorship; soon, however,—as the first letters in the present collection show— also of the most important organ of the socialist Internationale, the *Neue Zeit*, published in Germany. This was the scientific organ of the German social democracy. It was founded in 1883 by Karl Kautsky and edited by him continuously up to the year 1916.

After Rosa finished her studies and, decorated with two doctors' degrees—of philosophy and of jurisprudence—left Switzerland, she went to Paris for further study and for the purpose of obtaining first-hand knowledge of the political and party conditions there. She came in close contact with the socialist leaders, Guesde, Vaillant, Alemane, and the emigrés there. She was charmed by the temperament of the French, felt very much at home in French surroundings, and remained true to the friendships there formed throughout her life. Her feeling for the *doyen* of the French labor movement, Edouard Vaillant, was one of reverence. Her stay in Paris widened her viewpoint very much. She who had come out of the East now became intimately acquainted with the West, and thus felt at home in both civilizations. Warsaw—Zurich—Paris—this combination certainly afforded a good basis for her internationalism! But her greatest yearning was that for the German labor movement, which at that time, after the collapse of the antisocialist law promulgated by Bismarck, had grown tremendously.

To work in the German movement, not as an outsider but as a full-fledged, equal comrade, was her most passionate desire. As this would never have been possible under the laws then existing in Germany—she being a Russian—she seized upon the device of which Russian students often availed themselves in order to force the state to yield certain rights to her: she decided to enter upon a sham marriage with a German national, by which fact she automatically became a German citizen. Gustave Lübeck, son of an old German comrade who lived in Zurich and of a mother who, like Rosa, hailed from Poland and was an intimate friend of hers, was picked by the two energetic women to help Rosa to obtain German citizenship by marriage. After the "wedding" had been performed the "young couple" separated at the very doors of the marriage license bureau. Rosa had achieved what she was after: she was now a German citizen and was entitled to join the German social democracy as an active member; she was now enabled to devote her strength to the German movement and directly to influence the German proletariat by speech and written word—that is, insofar as the state's attorney did not set limits to her activities, a thing that could happen but too easily in Prussianized Germany. Prussian censorship, after all, did not differ much from Russian! But Rosa never knew fear, and in high spirits she arrived in Germany, the scene of her future activities, in the spring of 1899. She found plenty of work immediately—work of a nature that well suited her keen mind and her sharp tongue.

For, at the end of the last century the fight between the old radical tendency and the new "revisionism," as it was called, was in full progress in Germany.

This new tendency, which had for its object to exercise sharp criticism of the Marxian principles thus far adhered to by the social democracy, to modify them, tone them down and "revise" them, had found its spiritual leader in the person of Eduard Bernstein, then living in exile in London. Bernstein had somewhat lost contact with German conditions and, under the influence of the milieu of England, bad been swerved from his former, very revolutionary standpoint to one that was strongly reformistic. Among those who rallied to his side were Edward David, M.P., whose specialty was the study of the agrarian question, Max Schippel, also a member of parliament, who specialized in colonial and tariff questions, and a whole circle of publicists, who conducted a spirited fight against the old radical movement in their revisionistic organ, *Socialist Monthly Review*.

The leader of the old radical movement was Karl Kautsky. His organ, *Die Neue Zeit*, was conducted strictly along Marxian lines. Together with August Bebel and others he opposed the "revisionists" sharply, and Rosa, who had meanwhile joined this group of radicals, boldly jumped into the fray as an esteemed associate editor of the *Neue Zeit*. The rest of her time was devoted chiefly to agitation and discussion, and soon she stood out as one of the propagandists best hated by the bourgeoisie, who scornfully dubbed her "bloody Rosa."

In 1904 she was destined for the first time to make the acquaintance of a German jail. She was sentenced to several months' imprisonment for *lese majesté* and for inciting to class war, and started to serve her sentence in Zwickau in Saxony. The death of the king of Saxony, however, and the general amnesty granted to political offenders upon the new ruler's assumption of the reins of government, led to a shortening of her prison term, much to her own discomfiture. She left prison under protest, for she found it incompatible with her revolutionary principles to accept any sort of present from the king.

Another year passed amid industrious educational and propaganda work, when suddenly the storm bell of revolution began to toll in the East. By the end of 1905 we see her on her way to Warsaw, and early in 1906 she begins that feverish underground activity, concerning which the letters of that period can best inform the reader. For two months she succeeds in avoiding the czar's spies; then, however, fate overtakes her and she is dragged, first into the prison of the Warsaw city ball and later into the Warsaw citadel. Gripping descriptions of her experiences in Poland are contained in the letters from Warsaw dated March and April 1906. Set free at last after half a year's incarceration, because nothing could be proved against her, she spends two more months of intensive work in Warsaw and then proceeds via St. Petersburg to Finland, in order to strengthen herself and rest up in the seclusion and quiet of that country and to commit her experiences and impressions to paper.

The problem of the general strike, especially, now occupied her mind and became the center of her whole thought and action. In Warsaw as well as in Moscow she had seen the principle of the general strike translated into practice, and hereafter the question was uppermost in her mind as to how the experiences gathered and the results achieved in Russia might be applied to Germany. In Finland she wrote a pamphlet about the lessons of the general strike, which she published immediately after her return to Germany in September 1906. Even at that time she came in conflict with Kautsky, with whom she had thus far been wholly of one mind. Rosa defended the Russian standpoint while Kautsky argued that in Germany different conditions demanded different tactics. Every time the two met they debated the question of the general strike heatedly and earnestly. Yet, despite the heat of the argument there was never even the suggestion of a breach in their friendship.

Then came the contest over the elective franchise in the Prussian parliament. The question of whether or not the socialists should participate in the elections had been one of the most hotly contested problems in the party. Rosa had joined Kautsky in favoring the party's participation, and their point of view had carried the day in the party.

When it came, however, to carrying out the decision of the party convention, there was sharp division of opinion as to tactics. Rosa developed a feverish activity as agitator. She called for general strikes throughout Prussia as a measure for demonstrating the power of the masses. According to her plans, the masses were to organize street demonstrations everywhere; and, wherever possible, general strikes which, in her opinion, alone could bring victory, were to be arranged. Kautsky was of the opposite opinion and defended it in a much-discussed article in the *Neue Zeit* entitled "What next?" in which he vigorously opposed Rosa's views. It was then that Rosa for the first time publicly took issue with him. It now became evident that insurmountable divergencies of opinion separated them and that even the most intimate of personal friendships could not let them forget the factional differences between them. There resulted an estrangement which grew worse as time went on and which finally led to a complete break. In keeping with her fiery, inspiring personality, she soon rallied about her a following from the ranks of the radical elements within the socialist party, who in every way tried to hasten the *tempo* of the revolutionary development. It became evident soon that a left and a right wing were forming in the group thus far associated with Kautsky. Or, to put it more concisely, Rosa and her followers now constituted the extreme left wing of the German movement. Kautsky was thus forced into the center, while the right wing retained its revisionist-reformist character unchanged. From now on Rosa no longer fought side by side with Kautsky, as in former years, but began to go her own way politically. There remained, nevertheless, many points on which she could arrive at a friendly understanding with Kautsky, all the more so since both parties were anxious, in view of their long friendship, to remain as well disposed toward each other as possible. Kautsky especially did everything possible along this line, as the following incident will show:

In view of its constant and rapid extension, the German Social Democratic Party had felt the crying need of pressing into the service as many functionaries, or organizers, as possible and to equip them in the best manner possible. To give these functionaries a proper education seemed an indispensable necessity. The party therefore planned to found a party school, and began to look about for teachers. When Karl Kautsky was approached with the suggestion that he conduct the courses in economics, he declined as far as he was concerned, but suggested Rosa in his place, whereupon she was promptly chosen. This meant that she had been given the highly complimentary task of instilling in the rising generation within the party—and in the best spirits among them at that, for the various districts sent to this institution, which was looked upon as a party college, only the most gifted and carefully chosen members—the fundamental principles upon which their whole future work in the party was to rest. Rosa thus entered upon an entirely new field, but one in which she was destined to display unusual ability. After but a brief period of teaching she earned the unanimous opinion that she had excellently mastered her problem. Indeed, although the other courses were taught by able, even exceptionally gifted teachers, Rosa was unquestionably looked upon as the spiritual head of the institution. Her pupils adored her. For, not only did she possess the faculty of explaining the subject under discussion in such a manner that it was easily comprehended and understood, but she also inspired them, awakened the love of scientific study, gave life to subjects that had heretofore been looked upon as dry, spurred her listeners on by her own enthusiasm and thirst for knowledge, and filled her pupils with that same sacred fire with which she herself was aflame.

The symphony of Rosa's rich life reechoes from the pages of her letters. The whole gamut of scales is touched, depending upon her frame of mind, her whims, and the particular situation in which she chanced to find herself. At all times, however, she is *herself*—a genuine personality— whether in the strong *forte* of her work, or the soft *pianissimo* of tenderest emotion, during her *andante* as well as her *allegro*, or when, divinely cheerful and happy, she forgets all cares in a gay *scherzo*.

Hers was the ability to enjoy life as few persons could, to drink in its beauties and find ever new pleasure in them. Whether she was busy at some creative task, or whether she was assimilating the results of other people's investigations—everything meant enjoyment and happiness to her. In July 1918, despite an endless imprisonment that shattered her nerves, she writes me nevertheless: "We shall get out of this mess despite everything and never forget gratefully to enjoy the least of the beautiful things that are left to us."

The thing that characterized her before everything else, and that gave her whole being such buoyancy, was just this: while at work or at leisure, whether stirred by the emotions of love or of hate, she was always at the same white heat; in fact, one of her favorite sayings was, "One must be like a candle that is burning at both ends." And this white heat that radiated from her proved contagious to her entire surroundings. She was a wizard in the art of winning persons over, provided, of course, that she cared about winning them.

The most fossilized Prussian bureaucrats, the most brutal janitors and prison guards were devoted to her and handled her far more tenderly than they did their other prisoners. In the jails of Wronke and Breslau she had the good fortune of finding persons among the officials in charge—both the civil and the military—who caught a breath of her spirit, who showed her the greatest deference, and who counted it a pleasure and an honor to chat with her now and then. With one of the officials, who through his chivalrous behavior toward her alleviated many a hardship of her long detention, she continued to correspond after her liberation.

When, immediately after her death, I called at the Moabit jail for a young girl who had been arrested on the false suspicion of having conspired with Rosa, one of the higher officials there expressed words of the greatest regret, yes of mourning for Rosa when I introduced myself to him as a friend of hers, saying that he had known her and held her in highest esteem.

The secret of the magic effect of her personality was partly this: she was able, as few persons were, to interest herself in other human beings in a perfectly human way and to treat them humanely. She possessed the rare gift of listening with concentrated attention, and just as her ear was accessible to every complainant, so also her heart went out to every human being in distress.

That the word friendship was not a mere conception to a character of her type is self-evident. Despite the complicated nature of her being the simple words of the old poet Siman Dach, of which she was very fond, seem as though written to apply to her:

> To man there is no finer,
>   No more peculiar charm,
> Than to be counted faithful
>   In friendship ever warm.

To have anybody doubt her friendship grieved her deeply, unless, indeed, in consonance with her ironical nature, she made fun of such doubts as being absolutely senseless. The reader will find various passages in substantiation of this point, e.g., the letter of January 20, 1916, written from the prison in Barnim Street, Berlin, ". . . and 'trifles' don't exist for me as far as you are concerned; everything is important and of the greatest interest." Again, the letter from Breslau dated December 16, 1917: "How is it, you sheep, that you still doubt my friendship from time to time? I was surprised, since I know that our relation is already founded as upon a rock . . ."

There was one field or sphere, however, where all love of her fellow men and all friendship counted for nothing in case she felt herself misunderstood or even suffered disappointment: that was the realm of politics. For, artist though she was, she was politically minded through and through. To think and act politically was a necessity to her; politics was the element in which she disported herself as a fish does in the water. However tolerant she might be to her *personal* friends, acquaintances, and relatives, however good-naturedly she might laugh at and make fun of their weaknesses, which she detected with a sharp eye and exposed with a sharp tongue, in the case of her *political* friends she would stand for no joking. With reference to conflicts within her political party, especially, she regarded considerateness as lukewarmness, readiness to yield as weakness, willingness to meet the opponent halfway as cowardice, and compromise as treason. Her passionate nature led her to go straight at the center of an issue, without circumlocution. Concessions even to her closest political friends were anathema to her. Inflexible and unyielding as she herself was in these matters, she demanded a similar attitude from her political friends and closer comrades at arms, and in case she was not able to bring them unreservedly over to her own point of view, she did not hesitate to break with them. "Whosoever is not for me, is against me" was her political *leitmotif*.

Those who know the history of the party during the last two decades are aware how her relation to Karl Kautsky underwent a change and how the most intimate personal friendship gradually changed over into one of bitterest, political opposition.

During the year 1896, as a comrade almost unknown in German circles, she addressed herself for the first time to the editors of the *Neue Zeit*, a periodical which at that time enjoyed a splendid reputation, and which was personified in the figure of Kautsky. The leading spirits in the international socialist world at that time counted it an honor to contribute to its columns.

With a certain respect, though not always without objection, she submitted to Kautsky's editorial suggestions. Even here, however, one is struck by the self-assurance of this young woman of hardly twenty-six, as well as by her masterful diction, the keenness of her argumentation, the depth of her thinking, the wealth of ideas. In short, a new Pallas Athene, sprung from the head of Zeus, she stood before us, resplendent in her armor.

Notwithstanding the respect that she evinced toward her "beloved teacher," her "master," she felt herself as his peer and had the faculty of defending her standpoint. Her strong feeling of self-reliance is strikingly shown in the first eight letters; and as I was anxious to show this side of her character also, I overcame my original misgivings on this point and, at the risk of turning away this or that reader not interested in politics, I have placed these letters, which have to do with purely editorial matters, at the beginning of the collection, where indeed they belong chronologically. This increasing self-reliance is, by the way, emphasized even more sharply in the letter to Kautsky, written in 1901 after the Lübeck convention of the party.

After about three years of correspondence Rosa came to Berlin in March, 1899, and soon written communication was superseded by active personal intercourse. Residing at first in the student section of Berlin, she moved to the suburb of Friedenau as early as the fall of 1899 and rented a flat on the same street on which we lived.

Hardly a day now passed which did not see her at our home. At first, of course, her visits were intended solely for the party comrade, editor, and theoretician Kautsky, with whom she loved to discuss things untiringly. As for myself, I proved a great disappointment to her, used as she was to the ways of the Russian students. Laughingly she herself later confessed this to me:

"Karl Kautsky's wife wears an apron!!"—what a surprise, what a terrible discovery! She, too, nothing but one of those narrow-minded German housewives! Or, according to Rosa's own terminology of that period, "a foolish hen, a cow!"

The apron was not destined long to separate us. After but a few weeks she was so accustomed to it as well as to its wearer that she declared, "All my wants are cared for in the Kautsky home."

With the *pater familias* she embarked upon politics, with me upon everything that makes life more beautiful, with the three boys upon the maddest tomfoolery, and with our faithful domestic fairy, Zenzi, she even ventured, ambitiously and just like a little housewife, upon the mysteries of cooking, on which occasions she at times did not even scorn—an apron!

For, her versatility was quite as surprising as were her mental elasticity, her readiness at repartee and her ability to adapt herself immediately to every person and to every situation. Supposing she had just gone deeply into the most difficult theoretical problems with Kautsky—the very next moment she could be found romping about with the boys like a wanton schoolgirl, or sitting with our second son and engaging with him in friendly rivalry at drawing (she was extraordinarily gifted at painting and sketching, of which fact one finds many a proof in the letters). Or, she appeared in the kitchen department and listened with the most earnest expression in the world to Zenzi's wise maxims concerning the culinary art, delivered in the broadest Suabian brogue; in fact, she herself hinted, rather shamefacedly, that she was no stranger to Lucullian secrets, and waxed eloquent about a certain legendary "husar's roast" which she knew how to prepare in an unrivaled manner.

Christmas would have been unthinkable without Rosa, and it was a joy to observe with what zeal and devotion she played with the children, especially with the youngest, Bendel, then about six years old. The toys which she brought him were always selected with thoughtfulness and good sense. Usually they consisted of pretty, movable objects created by Arno Holz's* imaginative mind and offered for sale on the Potsdamer Platz. It was at her hand that the nodding little mule and the creeping crocodile

---

*[A modern German poet of distinction, who for many years was so poor that he had to invent children's toys to earn his living.—Trans.]

made their entry into the House of Kautsky. Her greatest and most enduring success was achieved, however, with a little cart that, sliding down a winding trestle, in ever accelerating motion brings its passengers down to the ground. With glowing cheeks she could for hours kneel down with the boys and enjoy these wondrous things. It was only with difficulty that she tore herself away from them when the children had to go to bed. After that she would chat and argue for a long time with Kautsky until he, too, withdrew. My hour had now arrived, for I accompanied her home, and measureless is the distance that we traversed, as we brought each other again and again to our respective doors. Tired of boarding-house life, she had soon rented a flat of her own in Cranach street, New Friedenau, about ten minutes away from our home. These minutes usually grew into hours, for there was no limit to the things we had to tell each other. Then, too, Rosa was in the habit of constantly forgetting her "Dricker," as she called all keys for short, and almost every night we stood before her house, waiting for the night watchman to open the portal. The incident always furnished the occasion for unrestrained mirth. She was also fond of giving vent to the revolutionary urge within her by singing aloud in the stillness of midnight, and many a time we were sternly reprimanded by the guardians of law and order in Friedenau, who lacked the necessary artistic appreciation of arias from *Figaro*, or songs by Hugo Wolf, or the *Marseillaise* or the *Internationale*. One stout police sergeant especially, named Maier, whom the young folk, to the infinite delight of Rosa, disrespectfully nicknamed the Fat-eye of the Law, "had it in" for us. To outwit him was Rosa's greatest earthly joy.

In two passages of her letters she refers to nightly escapades of this sort. Her overbubbling spirit knew no bounds, and she was as though intoxicated by her effervescent cheerfulness, which had a contagious effect. During such moments I felt instinctively what has since then become perfectly clear to me, namely, that hers was a poetic nature which was drawing upon a fountain that was practically inexhaustible. To use her own words, it seemed on such occasions "as though we had drunk champagne, and life pricked us in our fingertips."

Thus our friendship became an ever faster one, and to all of us, not least to our boys, she had soon become the indispensable friend, who had to take part in everything affecting our house, whether in days of joy or of sorrow. She was never absent from the Sunday evening "at homes," when a circle of devoted friends came to us, and half seriously, half in mockery she called herself the "Sunday Supplement of the *Neue Zeit.*"

Gladly and without much fuss she also joined us when, as was often the case, we were invited to dinner at the Bebels. It did not disturb her in the least to appear there in a simple housedress even if she suspected that a more formal party was in store. Thus she was very fond of wearing a certain olive green morning frock of velvet, which I had given her as a birthday present, and with which she was so unwilling to part that I presented her with similar goods on all festive occasions thereafter.

Her relations with Bebel were likewise most cordial and she was very fond of teasing him. For instance, during the party convention at Lübeck, where she was especially overbubbling and full of temperament, she stuck an anonymous slip of paper one morning at the hotel into the shoes standing before his door. The following words were written upon it: "Aujust, ick liebe Dir."* He on his part reciprocated this affection and always enjoyed her breezy humor and her readiness at repartee. When at times she had possibly overshot the mark and had been exceptionally biting and aggressive against acknowledged "big guns" in the party, so that the older party members could not find words strong enough to express their indignation at her insolence, he merely observed, smiling indulgently: "Just you leave my Rosa alone. It's a mighty good thing to have a wolf like her in our sheepfold."†

When my husband and I went to Paris in the spring of 1900, where Kautsky was to sift the papers left by Karl Marx at the home of his son-in-law, Paul Lafargue, Rosa acted as mother to our boys and helped them with their lessons at school. It must be admitted that, according to reports from both parties concerned, a pretty hot time ensued, and the two grammar-school students, Felix and Karl, are said really to have succeeded in putting the fearless fighter to rout—an unusual triumph!

---

*["August, I love you." In ordinary high-German the phrase should read, "August, ich liebe Dich." But the Berliners speak a dialect as different from standard German as the New York dialect is different from college English. Just as the New York dialect is characterized by "oi" sounds, so the Berlin dialect substitutes "j" (pronounced like "y") for "g" and "ck" for the soft "ch."—Trans.]

†[Literally "to have a pike like that in our carp-pond."—Trans.]

In this connection I want to recall a pretty episode, since it unrevealed to me a certain human and lovable trait in her character: Rosa was at that time on intimate terms with the meritorious socialist writer, then editor of the *Leipziger Volkszeitung*, Bruno Schönlank, an ingenious man and the father of our poet, Bruno Schönlank. One day she surprised us with an invitation to have dinner with him at her rooms, which were at that time located in the apartments of a certain Mrs. Klara Neufeld, an extremely capable lady of Friedenau whom we all esteemed very highly. The invitation had been extended with such solemnity that I donned my evening clothes to honor Rosa, although Karl's mother declared, "Why should you bother to make a big fuss about Rosa!"—My instinct had served me well, however. When she opened the door and, looking me over with a quick, critical glance, discovered that I was in evening dress, she fell upon my neck and declared with deep gratitude and emotion, "I thank you for having taken me seriously."

The evening was a stimulating and harmonious one, Rosa proved a charming little housewife, who took her duties as hostess most seriously, yet who dominated the conversation by her wit and repartee.

Gradually she drew all of her friends then living in Berlin into our circle: Adolf Warschawski and Julian Marsehlewski, two Polish socialist writers now in the Communist Party of Russia, were among our regular guests, and whenever Leo Tyschko (Jogiches) turned up, meteor-like, we had the pleasure of entertaining him, the shy conspirator, also in our house.★

Her relation to Jogiches was a very special one, but I never presumed to speak to her about it. Nothing, perhaps, cemented our friendship so firmly as the circumstance that I never put questions to her, but let her do as she pleased, without every prying into her feelings or investigating her coming and going. For, despite her vivacity, her communicativeness and her apparent frankness she was, after all, of a reserved, taciturn nature, wanted to live her life all by herself and not be pursued by obtrusive curiosity. She was fond of weaving a thick veil of secrecy about herself,

---

★[Leo Tyschko, or Jogiches, was Rosa's intimate friend, a distinguished Polish revolutionary socialist, who found his death in the German revolution a few weeks after Rosa and in the same beastly way as she: he was shot from behind by reactionary soldiers.—Trans.]

which was to guard her against inquisitive eyes; and a modicum of conspirator's romanticism was indispensable to her if life was not to seem too
flat and "petty bourgeois" to her. However anxiously she sought and even
demanded to know all emotions and experiences of her friends—about
which, by the way, she was able to keep silent with a model sense of dis-
cretion—, just as little was it possible for her to reveal herself unreservedly.
I recall certain moments when I knew her to be involved in difficult conflicts of the soul or of the heart. She could then sit with me for a long
time, her hand clasped in mine, and evidently struggle for words with
which to tell me of her distress. Usually, however, nothing more resulted
than that she uttered a few doleful sounds, a few disconnected sentences.
After that she told me with a helpless shrug of the shoulders, "I can't"—
placed her head against my shoulder and remained silent. In situations of
this kind she merely craved quiet understanding and sympathetic tender-
ness. To press her hands or to fondle her gently was quite sufficient to
restore her cheerfulness and to bring back her customary equilibrium.

In this connection I should like to make a sort of correction on my
own behalf: In the spring of 1919 a member of the Belgian commission
in Berlin, M. Maurice Berger, visited us to make Kautsky's acquaintance,
since he was engaged in writing a book about the "new" Germany. In the
course of the conversation the activity and death of Rosa Luxemburg
were also touched upon. M. Berger evidenced the greatest interest in her
and was most anxious to devote a chapter of his book to her. He pressed
me for data concerning herself, laying special stress upon her private life
and the circumstances accompanying her death. He finally persuaded me
to write him an appreciation of her character and a sketch of her life *as a
politician*, though at the same time I declined emphatically to give any
other information. In addition, I made it an expressed condition of my
imparting this information, that the whole chapter be submitted to me in
French translation before it went to press.

Imagine my surprise when, a while later, a bound copy of a book
entitled *La Nouvelle Allemagne* reached me from Brussels, containing, in
addition to the section approved by me, several pages derived from a
source entirely unknown to me, which gave a detailed report about Rosa's
"amours" and her sensational death!

I protested immediately by letter and by telegram against this misuse of my name, but obtained no further satisfaction than that the author apologized politely, stating that, while the personal data brought at the end of the sketch had "been told him by another source," he had nevertheless incorporated them in my article and published them under my name "for literary reasons and in order to round off the sketch." At the same time he authorized me to publish this explanation. The whole incident, transpiring as it did during days that were in themselves full of excitement, almost made me sick, for I trembled at the thought that the French and Belgian comrades might look upon this publication as an indiscretion, and possibly even as an attempt to be sensational, though nothing had been further from my thoughts than that. But no unfavorable comment came from them, so that I gradually calmed down, all the more so as I had to say to M. Berger's credit that he had done his job not only with tact and literary taste, but even with feeling and from a full heart, so that he had succeeded in placing Rosa in a very sympathetic light before foreign readers.

While Rosa had given conclusive proof of her unusual abilities in all the fields in which she had been active, it began to seem as though her greatest ability lay along educational lines. She possessed all the prerequisites of a pedagogue: not only was she gifted and thoroughly educated, but she also possessed the self-confidence and self-assurance that a teacher needs in order to impress his students. She found great satisfaction in teaching and, while in her former positions, such as editor of the Dresden *Volkszeitung*, of the Berlin *Vorwärts*, etc., she had not shown particular stick-to-it-iveness, the teaching profession seemed permanently to fascinate her and her enthusiasm seemed to kindle anew with every succeeding semester. Then came the war and with it an abrupt end to her activity. The school ceased to exist and Rosa was confronted with new problems.

The outbreak of the war was terrible to her. Still more terrible did the attitude of the German Social Democracy seem to her; in fact, as she herself admitted, she was brought to the verge of insanity and almost committed suicide. The granting of war credits by the social democrats was the signal for her to part company once and for all with her former comrades from whom she had already felt herself estranged for a long time, and with a little band of like-minded followers to begin the underground work of propaganda among German workers that found expression in the so-called *Spartacus Letters*, which, of course, had to be issued secretly because of war censorship. Besides containing propaganda against the war, its pages were filled chiefly with the most biting criticism of the right wing and of the center of the German Social Democratic party. Through hundreds of channels the *Spartacus Letters* found their way into the factories, the shops, the armies of the reserve, and even out to the front.

Rosa was able to carry on this underground propaganda for but a few months, when the "band of justice" was laid upon her. She was arrested and sentenced to a year in prison for a speech delivered before the war, on September 25, 1913, near Frankfort-on-the-Main, on "The Political and Economic Situation and the Task of the Proletariat." Her address to the court on the occasion of her trial on February 20, 1915, in defense of her action has become quite famous, and has appeared in print. She spent a full year in a woman's prison in northeastern Berlin. This did not keep her, however, from continuing her activities with undaunted courage, and from speaking to the outside world with the aid of friends and like-minded comrades, who undertook to smuggle out not only the *Spartacus Letters* but also the celebrated *Junius Pamphlet*. In the latter Rosa attacked the war and her former comrades even more boldly than in the *Spartacus Letters*. This pamphlet, written in prison in April 1915, and distributed secretly, achieved unparalleled success with all opponents of war in Germany and, in so far as it could pass the frontiers, also abroad. The wealth of ideas, the boldness of speech, the beauty of diction, and the truly revolutionary content characterize this work as one of the weightiest documents against the crime of war.

Upon leaving her cell in February 1916, she plunged at once into the maelstrom of events. Above all she sought contact with the "left" elements in the party, especially with Karl Liebknecht, to whom she had been very close ever since parting company with Karl Kautsky. Liebknecht was at that time in Berlin on furlough. Like herself, he had suffered terribly under the outbreak of the war and had been the only member of parliament to vote against granting war credits when the government demanded them the second time. From then on Rosa felt herself in complete accord with him. Together with Liebknecht she now planned a bold public action, for the slow, underground propaganda, the results of which could not become apparent very quickly, tried the patience of these two fiery spirits too sorely. They decided to call out loudly and audibly into a world paralyzed by terror and fear what they had thus far dared to say only secretly and surreptitiously to the masses of the workers. No matter how dire the consequences might be for them personally, they hoped by their self-sacrifice to stir up the sluggish spirits or at least to hurl a *mene tekel* at the ruling powers.

They summoned all their followers to the busy Potsdamer Platz on May 1, 1916. It was impossible to organize a May-day celebration on a large scale then, since most men were at the front and military control was unusually severe at that time. Nevertheless a crowd of faithful followers had gathered, from whose midst Liebknecht stepped forth upon the street and with a voice that resounded afar cried out, "Down with War." He was surrounded immediately by police in uniform and in plain clothes; Rosa and several of his followers, who clung to him, were shoved aside, and he was dragged off to prison. His courage, to be sure, challenged the admiration of all free spirits, but he failed to achieve the far-reaching result that he had hoped would follow upon his action. The time was not yet ripe and people's minds were still too much bound by the tradition of war for his rallying cry to awaken the right sort of echo. Oddly enough, Rosa had been permitted to return home unhindered, and for about four more months she was at liberty. She used this respite to conduct incessant educational propaganda. On July 10, 1916, however, she was taken into "Precautionary arrest" upon the orders of the military—an arrest that differed in no way from regular imprisonment.

At first she was brought into the same prison on Barnim Street in northeastern Berlin in which she had served previously; soon thereafter, however, to the citadel of Wronke in the Province of Posen, and after another half year, to the prison at Breslau.

The letters of that period furnish eloquent testimony as to how she, the great specialist in the art of living, knew how to make her life, even in that place of severe confinement, a reasonably human one, yes, and even to draw more satisfaction, not to say a greater measure of happiness out of that life than the rest of us succeeded in gaining from our life of freedom. These letters best give us an idea of the richness of her spirit and the greatness of her soul. If it is true that we tried through our letters and gifts to relieve the lonesomeness and enliven the monotony of the cell for her, the prisoner cut off from life, it is also true that her letters carried forth from this solitude light and color, joy and sunshine for our troubled spirits.

These letters of hers from prison reveal her from her most beautiful human side. Every one of them shows how a strong mind can triumph over all outward adversities, how a noble soul can rise above even the terrors of incarceration. Whenever her health threatened to give way under the exhausting monotony of her long imprisonment, whenever her fiery temperament was arrested by the bars of her narrow prison cell, again and again her studies and her work as well as her mental superiority constituted the magic remedy that sustained her and enabled her to suffer in patience. And infinite patience was indeed necessary! The grandiose drama of the Russian revolution in October 1917, the seizure of power by the Russian bolsheviks, many of whom had been her former companions in arms—events which, as they transpired, made every fibre of her being tremble and awakened the yearning in her to participate actively in them—all this she had to let pass by her, condemned as she was to be inactive and to play the part of an impotent bystander. Who can adequately gauge the magnitude of her grief, the pain of her impatience, the anguish of enforced passivity! Who can feel adequately what emotions shook her frail body!—And yet, not a word of complaint, of lamentation! Perfectly composed, proudly and even stoically she bore the hard fate that was hers until finally, at last, the hour of liberation struck for her, too.

The German army was defeated. Its glorified leader, Ludendorff, had run away in shameful flight, while the emperor himself had withdrawn from the world's stage in no less despicable a manner. During the first days of November 1918, first the sailors at Kiel and later the soldiers at Berlin had refused to continue to serve, had fraternized with the people and had ended the military dictatorship at one blow. The prisons were automatically opened for political offenders. Liebknecht was set free and triumphantly received, and soon thereafter Rosa, too, appeared in Berlin, after she had addressed the masses on Cathedral Square, Breslau, immediately after her liberation. Not a moment for quiet reflection was given her. Though still weak and wan from her long confinement, though still unused to the bustle of life after the stillness of her prison cell, the gigantic wave of events carried her right into the midst of the whirlpool of life, where not a moment for thought or even for hesitation was given her, and in the midst of which she had to fight, lest the waves of counterrevolution that were rising threateningly engulf her.

Rosa Luxemburg and Karl Liebknecht were still members of the Independent Socialist party which had split off from the old Social Democratic party over the war issue. But the gulf that had begun to separate the majority of the party from the Spartacus group in recent years became wider and wider, and all attempts on the part of the late Hugo Haase, leader of the Independents, and his followers to bridge the chasm were doomed to failure because of the obstinacy of the Spartacists. Thus it happened that there were sharp differences between the two factions at the convention of the party in Berlin in the middle of December, and that a definite split occurred by the end of December. The group thus far known as Spartacists organized the Communist Party and decided to publish its own organ, the *Rote Fahne*, which was to take the place of the *Spartacus Letters* thus far issued.

Although the masthead of the new organ gave the names of Rosa and Karl Liebknecht as founders, it was evident that Rosa from the beginning held views contrary to those of many of her followers and co-workers. Like the sorcerer's apprentice in Goethe, she had conjured up many spirits whom she was no longer able to hold in check and who in following their own ideas went far beyond what Rosa had mapped out as a goal capable of immediate attainment.

Thus, for instance, she differed with most members of her party on the important questions of participating in the coming elections for the Constituent Assembly. Rosa deemed participation essential and categorically demanded it. But this advocacy brought her her first defeat at the organization congress of the communists, and she had to realize that she was powerless against the comrades who were rushing headlong blindly. Many a thing she had to let happen with which she did not at all agree. Out of a revolutionary uprising against the military state there had developed, because of these differences within the proletariat and among their leaders, the bloodiest kind of civil war. The bourgeoisie was concerned about reestablishing the spirit of the old system under the slogan "Peace, order, and security," by which it meant the domination of capitalism over the workers. The communists were determined at any price to "carry the revolution on." And the right-wing, moderate socialists, fearing an economic breakdown for Germany if this were to result, looked upon the extremists among the radical elements as constituting the greatest danger.

They made use of the military apparatus, such as still existed, and of the officers of the old regime, on the erroneous assumption that they could control them and employ them to hold down the extreme left wing, at the head of which were Rosa and Karl Liebknecht. The military was under the command of Gustav Noske and his staff of old generals. Skirmishes were fought for weeks with extreme bitterness and it was not long before a final catastrophe ensued. In the streets everywhere there were bloody encounters daily, and whatever happened in one quarter of the city was reported in a wildly exaggerated manner in the other sections. The fury of the misguided soldiery was directed mainly at Rosa and Liebknecht and their followers, in whom they saw the instigators of the daily recurring attacks upon the troops. They therefore tried in every manner to apprehend them, and both were constantly forced to flee, were constantly compelled to hide, and were prevented from going to their own homes on pain of failing into the hands of their military captors. For several weeks they succeeded in keeping in hiding. But, either because they had been made too bold by their success so far, or else because they tired of being forever pursued, they became very careless in their last abode in the western part of Berlin, where they stopped with sympathizers. They openly took up quarters in the fashionable house of some friends, and soon the other bourgeois tenants became aware of the unwelcome company living under their roof.

It was not long before someone reported them, and the military were quick to throw themselves upon their victims. Under strong cover the two were brought to the Hotel Eden, where the staff of the Reinhard Brigade had its headquarters.

It is hardly to be supposed that Rosa fully appreciated what was in store for her. Although she was undoubtedly familiar with the thought of death, which threatened her daily either in an open street fight or by a treacherous bullet, yet she seems to have thought about this last seizure that, as so often previously, it was merely a case of being brought to prison so that she might be made harmless for a while. Evidence of this is the fact that she took with her a little bag with books and laundry when the soldiers led her away. In the best of spirits she bade farewell to her hosts, in the best of spirits she started off on the journey that was destined to be her last.

As to what the officers of the Reinhard Brigade discussed with Rosa, and as to what they negotiated with her, the public has never learned the facts with certainty. Judging from later events one may assume that these "gentlemen" heaped vile insults upon the defenseless, delicate woman, in order to wreak their anger upon their hated adversary and to let her feel their power. But even though they may have preserved the semblance of an orderly procedure, the fact is that these murderers seemed to have determined in advance not to let Rosa leave the building alive. Altogether too willing tools were found who undertook to carry out the bestial deed. As she left the building and stepped out upon the street, a noncommissioned officer named Runge struck her down with the butt of his gun, causing her to fall to the ground in a swoon. She was then picked up and thrown into a waiting automobile and, as she gave signs of still being alive, one of the "heroes" present shot a bullet through her head. Runge, the hired assassin, who afterwards quarreled with his noble employers, later described the gruesome scene in all its ghastly detail before the court. Nevertheless, there is still much in this drama that remains to be explained.

The courageous officers, however, were not yet completely satisfied with their deed. They feared Rosa even though dead and dreaded her influence upon the proletarian masses. The problem therefore was for them that of getting the corpse out of the way and of making up a story about her resistance and flight, so as to deceive the public and to divert the fury and revenge of the angered masses from themselves. As is characteristic of assassins, they added cowardice to their bestiality and dared not stand by their deed. The corpse disappeared, and those who had participated in the cowardly murder would tell nothing but fantastic lies. According to one version Rosa was supposed to have been dragged out of the automobile and lynched; according to another, Rosa's dead body was seized by her murderers and taken into hiding. Then, too, some persons claimed to have seen her body thrown into the water. For months no exact details about the whole affair were known, and already the proletarian masses began to weave legends about the memory of their martyr. Also, they did not cease to hope that she might turn up unexpectedly some fine day and again march at their head as their leader.

This state of uncertainty continued until, several months later, Rosa's distorted corpse was found floating in the water and every doubt was silenced by the gruesome reality. As to just how she died, we shall probably never learn with absolute certainty. That she was fearless and courageous and faced death composedly, of this the letters written shortly before her death give every assurance. That she faced death consciously on behalf of the cause sacred to her is proven by the fact that she remained in Berlin and never thought of fleeing to another country.

For us who outlive her the thought is terrible that her last glance fell upon the brutalized faces of paid assassins, and that she, who believed so firmly in the good within each human being and faced death fighting on behalf of this faith, should have been surrounded by such scum of humanity during her last hours. But although the circumstances attending her death helped to intensify the grief over her loss among her friends, yet not one of them denied to himself that this sacrificial death, despite its gruesomeness, constituted a fitly solemn close to a life rich in sacrifices.

"Enshrined within the great heart of the working class," Rosa Luxemburg's memory will continue to live among the millions of oppressed and dispossessed throughout the world, for whom she fought, suffered, and lived. And the name of Rosa Luxemburg will remain engraven upon the brazen tablets of history upon which are recorded the heroes of humanity.

2

Rosa Luxemburg:
The Dialectical Method
Against Reformism

Lelio Basso

*Lelio Basso was a militant and theorist in the left wing of the Italian
Socialist Party, and a founder of the Italian Socialist Party of Proletarian
Unity (PSIUP). For years he sought to utilize Marxist theory to indicate
a revolutionary path to the mass Italian workers' movement, amid the pulls
and tugs of Stalinism and social-democratic reformism. This was a task that
naturally drew him to expound upon the works of Rosa Luxemburg. Basso's
writings were among the early influences on the international "new left" of
the 1960s, and his work on Luxemburg was meant for younger activists as
well as older comrades.*

When Rosa Luxemburg arrived in Germany in 1898, the discussion of revisionism set off by Bernstein's writings was at its
peak. Up until then, Luxemburg had largely limited herself to the internal
affairs of Polish socialism, particularly to the national problem, and her
participation in the Bernstein discussion marked her entry into the quite
restricted circle of the most respected students of Marxism. Indeed, her
reply to Bernstein is still today a model of Marxist methodology, clearly

First appeared in *International Socialist Journal* 3, no. 16–17 (November 1966).

superior to the criticisms of Bernstein penned by Kautsky, Plekhanov, Mehring, etc. during the same period.[1]

If we accept Lukács' idea that the principal value of Marxism is its dialectic method,[2] an idea with which Luxemburg would have fully agreed, we can easily appreciate the importance of her contribution toward the elaboration of a modern Marxist strategy.[3]

Luxemburg's efforts were in fact directed toward making the dialectical method a living part of the class struggle. In her mind the dialectical method was not merely a tool for historical interpretation and analysis of contemporary society, but also a method for the making of history, to be applied to the action of large masses and to the conscious building of the future. As few other Marxists, she saw reality and history in the light of the dialectic, and in her own words, she conceived of the historical dialectic as "the rock on which the whole teaching of Marxian socialism rests,"[4] or as "the specific mode of thought employed by the conscious proletariat," and "the intellectual arm with the aid of which the proletariat, though materially under the yoke of the bourgeoisie, is yet enabled to triumph over the bourgeoisie. For it is our dialectical system that shows to the working class the transitory character of this yoke, proving to the workers the inevitability of their victory, and is already realizing a revolution in the domain of thought."[5] It was the dialectic that allowed Rosa Luxemburg to see the socialist future already existent in the capitalist present. And this entailed the recognition of the contradictory, but indivisible, aspects of contemporary reality and of the historical process that these contradictions produce. It also meant the realization that we can grasp the real essence of any historical moment only if we consider this moment as an integral part of the continuity of history. And when we say history, we must intend the totality of the historical process. We can no more separate the various aspects of reality from the general context of which they are a part and within which they mutually condition and influence each other than we can artificially separate chronologically various moments in the stream of history.

Whatever phenomenon or event she was considering, Rosa Luxemburg always adopted the point of view of the totality, and it is this point of view that Lukács, under her influence, considers the essential factor in this Marxist method.[6] I am naturally using the word "totality" in the sense intended by Lukács, or to be more exact, in the sense intended by Marx and Luxemburg, of a concrete totality, an organic system of relationships in which everything is referred to the whole and the whole takes precedence over the part, although this whole itself is not static and unchangeable but in constant transformation. From this point of view, every separation between politics, economics, legal systems, morals, etc. is arbitrary, since they appear as different aspects of the same process. As such, these aspects can be distinguished, but they cannot be abstractly separated. Any clear-cut separation of various periods and phases within the historical process is likewise arbitrary, since each of them bears within itself the seed of successive developments and the reason for its own extinction. No less arbitrary are attempts to interpret isolated facts apart from the whole of reality, as if each fact, each action, each movement, each phenomenon were not a link in an infinite chain of reciprocal actions and reactions. Only a person who is aware of this totality can understand the various forms in which it presents itself, seeing the mutual relationships and intrinsic contradictions between them and their line of development. Only a person who does not attempt to create artificial compartments can study and analyze individual phenomena.

Rosa Luxemburg was constantly aware of the totality in her analysis of social phenomena, and in her polemics with her adversaries she had frequent occasion to point out their tendency to isolate facts and lose the sense of the whole. In her polemic with Bernstein, which as we have said is a lesson in method, this accusation is a constant refrain: "when he abandoned scientific socialism he lost the axis of intellectual crystallization around which isolated facts group themselves in the organic whole of a coherent conception of the world,"[7] or again: "even though we should fail to take into account the erroneous character of all these details of Bernstein's theory we cannot help but be stopped by one feature common to all of them. Bernstein's theory does not seize these manifestations of contemporary economic life as they appear in their organic relationship with the whole of capitalist development, with the complete economic mechanism of capitalism. His theory pulls these details out of their living economic context. It treats them as the *disjecta membra* [separate parts—Ed.] of a lifeless machine."[8] This same emphasis on the sense of totality in the evaluation of phenomena is present in almost all her polemics; both against Lenin ("However, to separate these phenomena, which arose on a concrete historical base, from their context, making them into abstract models having universal and absolute value, is the greatest of sins against the 'Holy Ghost' of Marxism—namely, against its historical-dialectical mode of thought"[9]) and against Kautsky who, in order to justify the position of the social democrats during the world war, arbitrarily separated peacetime from wartime, as though "the wars of the present period" were not the result of "the competitive interests of groups of capitalists and in capitalism's need to expand," and as though these causes were not at work "not only while the cannons are roaring, but also during peacetime," confirming Clausewitz's idea that war is "the continuation of politics by other means."[10] And thus against all social democrats who favored the war in the name of the right of self-defense against the Tsarist peril, she replied, "Thus the conception of even that modest, devout fatherland-loving war of defense that has become the ideal of our parliamentarians and editors is pure fiction, and shows, on their part, a complete lack of understanding of the whole war and its world relations."[11] As a militant and leader of two parties, the German and the Polish, at the same time Luxemburg deeply felt and participated in all the activities of the international workers' movement. Her profound sense of internationalism was a part of her sense of the totality: "proletarian policies must be oriented toward an international sense of the whole of the world political situation";[12] or again: "the more we get to know the characteristics of Social Democracy in the entire manifold of its different social milieus, the more we become aware of the essentials, the fundamentals, the principles of the Social Democratic movement, the more the limited horizons conditioned by localism fall away. It is not for nothing that the international note vibrates so strongly in revolutionary Marxism; it is not for nothing that the opportunist modes of thought rings continually in national seclusion."[13]

We can say that the theoretical keynote of Luxemburg's long battle against revisionism and reformism was her reference of everything to the category of totality. This is, indeed, the essence of revolutionary Marxism, whereas the revisionists are vulgar empiricists who isolate individual facts and cannot see the totality of the historical process. When a Marxist understands the totality of the historical process it means that he sees its internal contradictions and the necessity of overcoming them through the victory of socialism. In practice, it means that he never separates the individual phases and objectives of the struggle from the general vision of the struggle itself, nor everyday demands and reforms from the final, revolutionary goal. This unity of the final goal with everyday action is the crux of Luxemburg's strategy of the class struggle. According to her biographer Frölich:

> The significance of Luxemburg's conception of that period can be seen in the fact that even in our own day the working-class movement has to wrestle again and again with the problem of the importance of the small-scale, day-to-day struggles and their relationship to the final objective. Yet in the 1890s already, Rosa Luxemburg produced nothing less than the theoretical foundation of a militant socialist strategy. Such a theory might have been constructed at a pinch from occasional, generally ignored hints left by Marx and Engels. In fact, however, the whole trade union and parliamentary activity of social democracy in Western Europe rested on a purely empirical base, and the dangers of this were to become evident very soon in the revisionist movement. This was an astonishing achievement for such a young woman, who fought against absolutism as a political emigre, in circumstances where romantic ideas luxuriated like weeds. The achievement was the fruit of a serious study of revolutionary theories and of history, but at the same time it was also the expression of a sound political instinct.[14]

Frölich's mention of Rosa Luxemburg's age is in relation to her composition of a report to the International Socialist Congress of Zurich,[15] for the editors of the review *Sprawa Robotnicza*.[16] In this report she affirmed the necessity of a global strategy and an awareness of the final goal. This necessity was reaffirmed with greater clarity in her subsequent report to the London Congress of 1896,[17] in which she emphasized the chaotic situation of the Polish working class in the preceding years (1889–1892), due to the lack of a link between immediate demands and long-term goals. It was, however, in her battle against German revisionism and opportunism that she was able to elaborate and clarify her revolutionary doctrine. Even at the first German Social Democratic congress that she attended (Stuttgart, 1898), the problem of the relationship between the everyday struggle and the final goals was at the center of her argument:

The speeches by Heine and others have showed that a very important point has been neglected by our party: the understanding of the relationship between our final goal and the every day struggle. We have heard that the part in our program dedicated to the final goal is very nice and that we should certainly not forget it, but that it has nothing directly to do with our practical action. There may be a certain number of comrades here who think that the speculations about the final goal are doctrinal questions in the real sense of the word. On the contrary, I feel that for us as revolutionaries and as a proletarian party, no question is more practical than that of our final goal. Let us reflect a moment: what is the specifically socialist character of our movement? Our actual practical action can be divided into three phases: the trade-union struggle, the fight for social reform, and the fight for the democratization of the capitalist state. Are these three forms of our struggle socialist in the real sense of the word? Absolutely not. . . . What is it then that makes us a socialist party in our every day struggle? It is purely the fact that we refer these three forms of practical action to the final goal. Only the final goal forms the spirit and content of our socialist struggle. It is this that makes it a class struggle.[18]

In a later speech at the same congress, she concluded by turning upside down Bernstein's famous proposition that the [socialist—Ed.] movement is everything and the end nothing. "The Kaiser's most recent speech must be answered in this debate. We must say clearly and firmly, like old Cato: 'I am furthermore of the opinion that this state must be destroyed.' The seizure of power is still our final goal, and our final goal is still the heart and soul of activity. . . . The movement for its own sake without regard to the final goal, the movement as an end in itself, is nothing to me, the final goal is everything."[19]

In her two essays against Bernstein, she developed the same theme in depth. Bernstein's concept is mechanical and not dialectical because it does not view society as a framework of organically connected relationships, but as a series of unrelated facts. This permits him to extinguish certain causal relationships, to separate, as Proudhon, the "good" and "bad" sides of society,[20] to consider phenomena that are essential aspects of the process of capitalist development as isolated facts that can be corrected and eliminated. Thus the class struggle is degraded from its fundamental political goal of the struggle for power to a series of unrelated actions aimed at obtaining isolated improvements with no relation to the struggle conceived in its totality. Some twenty years later, illustrating the program of the Spartacist movement, she emphasized its opposition to the [old German Social Democratic Party's—Ed.] Erfurt program on the grounds that the Spartacists connected the final goal and immediate demands.[21]

Lukács observes:

> Seen in this light the revisionist separation of movement and ultimate goal represents a regression to the most primitive stage of the working-class movement. For the ultimate goal is not a "state of the future" awaiting the proletariat somewhere, independent of the movement and the path leading up to it. It is not a condition which can be happily forgotten in the stress of daily life and recalled only in Sunday sermons as a stirring contrast to workaday cares. Nor is it a "duty," an "idea" designed to regulate the "real" process. The ultimate goal is rather that *relation to the totality* (to the whole of society seen as a process), through which every aspect of the struggle acquires its revolutionary significance. This relation informs every aspect in its simple and sober ordinariness, but only consciousness makes it real and so confers reality on the day-to-day struggle by manifesting its relation to the whole.[22]

However, Lukács continues, by seeking to maintain the unity of the final goal, of the "essence" of the proletariat, we run the risk of losing our sense of the concreteness of reality and falling into extremism, the childhood, but ever current, disease of the working class.

Luxemburg was not unaware of this last problem. She had clearly identified the causes of the continual resurgence of opportunism and extremism within the working class as a product of the basic contradiction of capitalist society as reflected in the working class:

> Marxist doctrine cannot only refute opportunism theoretically. It alone can explain opportunism as a historic phenomenon in the development of the party. The forward march of the proletariat on a world historic scale, to its final victory is indeed not "so simple a thing." The peculiar

character of this movement resides precisely in the fact that here, for the
first time in history, the popular masses themselves, *in opposition* to the
ruling classes, are to impose their will, but they must effect this outside
of the present society, beyond the existing society. This *will* the masses
can only form in a constant struggle against the existing order. The
union of the broad popular masses with an aim of reaching beyond the
existing social order, the union of the daily struggle with the great world
transformation, this is the task of the social-democratic movement,
which must logically grope on its road of development between the following two rocks: abandoning the mass character of the party or abandoning its final aim, falling into bourgeois reformism or into sectarianism, anarchism or opportunism.[23]

This passage is of the greatest importance not only for an understanding of the essence of Luxemburg's dialectical thought, but also for an
understanding of the constant and inextinguishable deviations that arise
within the working class towards reformism and towards extremism,
towards opportunism and sectarianism. Luxemburg was undoubtedly aware
of the importance of her observation, for she repeated it almost word for
word several years later in her polemic with Lenin.[24] The sense of the preceding passage is that the worker, living within bourgeois society, partici-
pates in a contradictory manner. He is, at one and the same time, a member
of capitalist society and therefore interested in gaining the best possible
living conditions he can within it and a member of a revolutionary class, of
the class that cannot fully emancipate itself from capitalist exploitation
without overthrowing the capitalist order. Depending on whether individual workers, or various segments of the movement, consider *only* the
every day struggle for improvement or *only* the final goal, they fall into one
or the other of the classical deviations. In the first case they neglect the final
goal, the necessity that every step taken by the movement should carry forward the negation of capitalist society, and thereby they remain entirely
within the framework of that society, on bourgeois ground, and in a subordinate position. In the second case, they deny the usefulness of every day
struggle and worry exclusively about the preparation of the final goals. In
this way, they divorce themselves from reality, abandoning the vital current
of the movement to the point of falling into a maximalist position of "all

or nothing," since the "all" can only be obtained by preparation through that every day struggle that has already been rejected.

Some readers may be surprised that I attribute so much importance to this observation of Luxemburg's, which has been so often repeated as to actually seem banal. Yet anyone who knows the history of the working class knows that it is over this unresolved, much studied, but never fully grasped problem that so many battles have been waged and so many parties split. This same problem is at the root of the progressive degeneration of all the other Western socialist parties. Those revisionists who want to revise Marxism and rid it, according to Bernstein's proposal, of the "atrophic residue" of the final goal, with the pretext of thus giving it scientific unity and freeing it from the dualism between science and utopia, do not realize that the " 'dualism' in Marx . . . [is] the dualism of the socialist future and the capitalist present. It is the dualism of capital and labor, the dualism of the bourgeoisie and the proletariat. It is the scientific reflection of the dualism existing in bourgeois society, the dualism of the class antagonism writhing inside the social order of capitalism."[25] Against the practice of those leaders who at least orally accepting the final goal, tended to arbitrarily separate the political battle from the trade union struggle, Rosa Luxemburg expressed herself as follows: "There are not two different class struggles of the working class, and economic and a political one, but only one class struggle, which aims at one and the same time at the limitation of capitalist exploitation within bourgeois society, and at the abolition of exploitation together with bourgeois society itself."[26]

Luxemburg was not unaware of the fact that, although these abstract distinctions between the political and the economic struggle, between immediate demands and the socialist goal, may be swept away during periods of crisis, they are bound to reappear and even crystallize during periods of tranquillity, when the bureaucratic routine of organizations and the daily activities of the workers themselves (particularly those who have already benefited from better living conditions) get the upper hand over the creative capacity of the masses. She therefore considered opportunism as a permanent phenomenon of the working class. It was one of the two contradictory, but coexistent, Janus-like faces of the movement, the one turned towards today that expressed the direct contact with bourgeois society without understanding it dialectically. This Marxist explanation of

opportunism gives Rosa Luxemburg a preeminent position in the great
Bernstein debate. She did not limit herself to simply correcting Bernstein's
"errors" as Kautsky attempted to do, but explained the class roots of
opportunism. Living within bourgeois society and subjected to the reflection of the contradictions of that society, the working class also presents
contradictory aspects, and one of these—empirical opportunism—implies
the acceptance of bourgeois society and the bourgeois mentality. It indicates the presence of the class enemy within the working class, a presence
that must be combatted, but whose recurrent cause cannot be ignored.

This is why Rosa Luxemburg was, on the one hand, the most radical
opponent of opportunism and Bernstein's revisionism which she considered outside the realm of socialism,[27] and on the other hand, did not enter-
tain delusions about being able to combat opportunism with organizational and disciplinary measures. "It is a totally ahistorical illusion to think
that the revolutionary Social Democratic tactic can be predetermined once
and for all, that the labor movement can be defended once and for all
against opportunist escapades," she wrote in her polemic with Lenin.[28] The
working-class movement must be considered as a continuous process, in
which these deviations, extremism and opportunism, constantly reproduce
themselves. Both are the result of the isolation of the two terms (final goal
and every day struggle), and it is by fighting against these two deviations
and, in the course of the battle, gaining a dialectical consciousness of the
unity of its struggle, that social democracy can succeed in elaborating a
proper strategy. "The proletarian movement has not, as yet, all at once,
become social democratic, even in Germany. But it is becoming more
social democratic, surmounting continuously the extreme deviations of
anarchism and opportunism, both of which are only determining phases
of the development of the social democracy, considered as a process."[29]
The German party had in fact moved from the necessity of combatting the
extremist deviation, the underestimation of the daily struggle and the exal-
tation of the final goal as an end unto itself, to the necessity of combatting opportunistic deviation, the overestimation of the daily struggle and
the practical rejection of the final goal.[30]

But what does unity of the struggle mean? What does it mean when
we say that we seek the final goal, the conquest of power for the socialist
transformation of society in the everyday struggle? It means that both in

its economic and political activity the working class must always be guided by the criteria of effectively shortening the distance between the present situation and the end. In every moment the working class must aim at individual actions, measures, and conquests not for their own value alone, but in relation to the historical process considered as a whole. Thus an economic advantage, such as a wage increase, must be rejected if it must be bought at the price of a political compromise that favors the power of the enemy class or the bellicose projects of imperialism, while a defeat from the practical standpoint, if it reinforces class consciousness, may constitute a step forward and, in the last analysis, turn out to be a success.

If, however, we accept the bourgeois point of view and atomize society, letting ourselves see only things instead of processes and seeking to avoid contradictions by isolating phenomena, if we agree to consider everything only for its own value, separate from the totality, and refuse to recognize the influence these things may have on the historical process, then any sort of bargaining becomes possible even for the working class. But this freedom of bargaining can only be had at the price of giving up the socialist character of the vision of the whole. This was illustrated by the Berlin [Social Democratic—Ed.] deputy [Wolfgang—Ed.] Heine, which went under the names of the theory of "compensation." According to Heine, the socialists should sell their vote in parliament in favor of military credits in exchange for concessions in the field of social policy. The same concept induced another deputy, [Max—Ed.] Schippel, to champion a joint policy between workers and industrialists in favor of tariffs for the "greater development of our industry." Such positions demonstrate complete ignorance of the fact that, in order to obtain some immediate advantage in wages or social policy, the socialists would not only have given a vote in parliament, but would also have contributed to the strengthening of militarism and protectionism, two instruments of capitalist oppression and imperialist development. This was already clear to Rosa Luxemburg, and it should have been clear to anyone who looked below the surface of reality.

Naturally, "if we ignore the irreconcilable contradictions and concentrate our attention only on the fact that proletariat and bourgeoisie live on the same soil, it is not hard to accept the idea of the social-called national interests for the defense of national industry (Schippel at Hamburg), national 'defense' (Schippel on the problem of the militia), the Triple

Alliance (Vollmar at Monaco in 1891), and 'a reasonable colonial policy' (Bernstein in his *Presuppositions of Socialism*)."[31] However, "in this manner, the opportunistic concept, while apparently bringing 'nothing new' into the party, in reality little by little brings about a complete transformation in the physiognomy of the working class. Everything is turned upside down: its program, its tactic, its attitude toward the state, toward the bourgeoisie, toward foreign policy, toward militarism. From a revolutionary and internationalist party, the social democrats are transformed into a national, petty bourgoisie, social-reformist party."[32]

As was to be expected, the opportunists, or at least the admitted opportunists,[33] replied by questioning the basic theoretical foundations of Marxism, "for our 'theory,' that is, the principles of scientific socialism, impose clearly marked limitations to practical activity—insofar as it concerns the aims of this activity, the means used in attaining these aims, and the method employed in this activity. It is quite natural for people who run after immediate 'practical' results to want to free themselves from such limitations and to render their practice independent of our 'theory.' "[34] And unfortunately, as she herself noted, every year, at every congress, the number of advocates of the "gospel of 'practical politics' " increased.[35] But, she added, "not thanks to the gospel of 'practical politics,' but in spite of it, our movement has become great and strong."[36]

In this conflict between the vulgar and opportunistic empiricism of the social-democratic leaders and cadre and Rosa Luxemburg's Marxist outlook, the former won out from the point of view of immediate action, but the events of history have instead tragically confirmed Luxemburg's analysis and predictions. Within but a few years, the slow process of daily corruption brought the German social democrats into the camp of imperialism during the war of 1914 and, after the war, its position served to smooth the road for Nazism. But at the time, it was easy for the short-sighted men to accuse her of being doctrinaire, holding up their vulgar empiricism as practical political "realism," that same small-minded realism that Marx had already condemned[37] and that history has so often refuted, without being able to root out its causes that, as Rosa Luxemburg demonstrated, are inherent in bourgeois society and cannot be destroyed as long as this society lasts.

Notes

1. Bernstein himself admitted that Luxemburg's articles "as far as the method is concerned are among the best written against me." *Voraussetzungen des Sozialismus und die Aufgehaben der Sozialdemokratie* (Stuttgart, 1899), p. 178. Bruno Schonlank also judged them a "masterly blow for the dialectic" and worthy of the "authentic Marx in his best period." Cf. the letter of R. Luxemburg to Leo Jogiches of 17 September, 1898 in *Z pola walki* (1962), no. 1.

2. "Orthodox Marxism . . . does not imply the uncritical acceptance of the results of Marx's investigations. It is not the 'belief' in this or that thesis, nor the exegesis of a 'sacred' book. On the contrary, orthodoxy refers exclusively to *method*. It is the scientific conviction that dialectical materialism is the road to truth and that its methods can be developed, expanded, and deepened only along the lines laid down by its founders. It is the conviction, moreover, that all attempts to surpass or 'improve' it have led and must lead to oversimplification, triviality, and eclecticism." Lukács, *History and Class Consciousness: Studies in Marxist Dialectics*, trans. by Rodney Livingston (Cambridge: MIT Press, 1971), p. 1.

3. "Just as Rosa Luxemburg always taught that the important thing is the Marxist method and not the individual results of Marxist analysis, so we must treat her own writings and teachings. These constitute a school of communism, not because of their individual deductions, but because of their method." Karl Radek, *Rosa Luxemburg, Karl Liebknecht, Leo Jogiches* (Hamburg, 1921), p. 40.

4. Luxemburg, *The Mass Strike, the Political Party, and the Trade Unions*, in *Rosa Luxemburg Speaks*, p. 158.

5. Luxemburg, *Reform or Revolution* in ibid., p. 86.

6. "It is not the primacy of economic motives in historical explanation that constitutes the decisive difference between Marxism and bourgeois thought, but the point of view of totality. The category of totality, the all-pervasive supremacy of the whole over the parts is the essence of the method which Marx took over from Hegel and brilliantly transformed into the foundations of a wholly new science. . . . Proletarian science is revolutionary not just by virtue of its revolutionary ideas which it opposes to bourgeois society, but above all because of its method. *The primacy of the category of totality is the bearer of the principle of revolution in science.*" Lukács, "The Marxism of Rosa Luxemburg," in *History and Class Consciousness*, p. 27.

7. Luxemburg, *Reform or Revolution*, p. 85.

8. Ibid., p. 61.

9. Luxemburg, "Organizational Questions of Russian Social Democracy," in *Selected Political Writings*, ed. by Howard, p. 298.

10. Luxemburg, "Rebuilding the International," in *Selected Political Writings*, ed. by Looker, p. 204.

11. Luxemburg, *The Junius Pamphlet: The Crisis of the German Social Democracy*, in *Rosa Luxemburg Speaks*, p. 308.

12. Ibid. [While it was not possible to find a precise equivalent for the quote offered in Basso's article, on page 305 of above cited work there is the following similar point: "Every socialist policy that depends upon this determining historic milieu, that is willing to fix its policies in the world whirlpool from the point of view of a single nation, is build upon a foundation of sand."—Ed.]

13. Luxemburg, "Organizational Questions of Russian Social Democracy," in *Selected Political Writings*, ed. by Howard, pp. 283–84.

14. Frölich, *Rosa Luxemburg: Her Life and Work* (1972), pp. 20–21. See also Radek, p. 14.

15. *Gericht an den III. Internat. Socialistichen Arbeiterkongress in Zurich 1893 uber den Stand und Verfauf der socialdemokratiechen Bewegung in Russich-Polen 1889–1893, erstattet von Redaktion der Zeitschrift "Sprawa Robotnicza" ("Arbeltersache"), Organ der Social-demokratische Bewegung in Russich-Polen 1893–1896.*

16. The *Sprawa Robotnicza* (Workers' Cause) was founded in Zurich in 1893. The editorial board was composed of Rosa Luxemburg, Leon Tyszko (Jogiches), Adolf Warski, and Julian Marclewski. It soon became the official organ of the SDKP (Social Democracy of the Kingdom of Poland), the party founded in the same year and led by the same persons.

17. *Bericht an den Internationalen Sozialistchen Arbeiter—und Gewerkschafts— Kongress in London uber die Sozialdemokratiche Bewengung in Russich-Polen 1893–96.*

18. Clara Zetkin, Adolf Warski, pub., Paul Frölich, ed., Rosa Luxemburg, *Gesammelte Werke*, III, p. 126.

19. "The Party Conference at Stuttgart," *Marxism and Social Democracy: The Revisionist Debate 1896–1898*, ed. by H. Tudor and J. M. Tudor, p. 283

20. "For him, M. Proudhon, every economic category has two sides—one good, the other bad. He looks upon these categories as the petty bourgeois looks upon the great men of history: Napoleon was a great man; he did a lot of good; he also did a lot of harm. The *good side* and the *bad side* the *advantages* and the *drawbacks*, taken together form for M. Proudhon the *contradiction* in every economic category. The problem to be solved: to keep the good side, while eliminating the bad." Marx, *The Poverty of Philosophy*, in Karl Marx and Frederick Engels, *Collected Works*, vol. 6 (New York: International Publishers, 1976), p. 167.

21. "Our program is deliberated opposed to the leading to the leading principle of the Erfurt program; it is deliberately opposed to the separation of the immediate and so-called minimal demands formulated for the political and economic struggle, from the socialist goal regarded as a maximal program." Luxemburg, "Speech to the Founding Convention of the German Communist Party," *Rosa Luxemburg Speaks*, p. 413.

22. Lukács, "What Is Orthodox Marxism?" *History and Class Consciousness*, p. 22.

23. Luxemburg, *Reform or Revolution*, in *Rosa Luxemburg Speaks*, pp. 88–89. Rosa Luxemburg does not fail to emphasize that the same contradiction is reflected in the individual aspects of the struggle as well. For example: "The role of the social democrats in the bourgeois legislative organs is characterized by an internal contradiction. Our parliamentary delegations face the difficult task of participating in legislative activity, gaining if possible some practical advantage, and at the same time, emphasizing with each move the point of view of an a priori opposition to the capitalist state." Luxemburg, "Nachbetrrachtungen zum Reichstag," *Sochische Arbeiterzeitung* (October 14, 1898).

24. Luxemburg, "Organizational Questions of Russian Social Democracy," in *Selected Political Writings*, ed. by Howard, pp. 304–305.

25. Luxemburg, *Reform or Revolution* in *Rosa Luxemburg Speaks*, p. 68.

26. Luxemburg, *The Mass Strike, the Political Party, and the Trade Unions*, in ibid., p. 208.

27. "The peculiarity of her struggle against revisionism consists in the fact that she so energetically laid bare the political and social content of the problem, directing her offensive against a bourgeois, practical tendency in the working class and not on the basis of theoretical fine points. The mercilessness and the cutting irony of her attack against revisionism was attributed to her volcanic revolutionary temperament. But this was a very superficial judgment. Rosa Luxemburg knew the history of the international working-class movement as few others have known it. For her, this body of knowledge was never simply a collection of stories taken from the lives and theories of the founders of the various socialist systems. The history of the working-class movement had revealed to her how in the working class the battle of ideas always had a profound social basis, and how the struggles over method and tactic were always struggles for the supremacy of one social group or another within the movement, the opportunistic tendency always being represented by the group closest to the bourgeoisie. Rosa Luxemburg saw in revisionism the theory corresponding not only to the practice of the bourgeois

elements which had entered the movement after the abolition of the antisocialist laws in Germany and the parliamentary victories in France and Italy, but also to the politics of a large segment of the working class that had profited from the period of economic prosperity and began to find its place in bourgeois society. . . . When attempts were made to persuade her that the question was only a matter of internal discord within the working class, she replied that it was instead a battle against the bourgeoisie, whose influence had been carried into the working class by revisionism." Radek, p. 13. "But it [the theory of revisionism] is much worse than false: it is the complete negation of all that is social democratic. It is not an erroneous idea of a social democrat. It is the correct idea of a bourgeois democrat who mistakenly think himself a social democrat." Luxemburg, "Nachbetrachtungen," *Gesammelte Werke*, III, p. 159.

28. Luxemburg, "Organizational Questions of Russian Social Democracy," in *Selected Political Writing*, ed. by Howard, pp. 304–305. It is a well known fact that Lenin considered opportunism as the specific expression of certain social strata, the aristocracy of the working class, and denied that it had an intrinsic tie with the masses. It is therefore incorrect to state that Lenin thought he could guarantee the working class against opportunistic deviations once and for all, but it is certain that he considered opportunism a phenomenon originating at the margins of the movement, in the privileged minorities, rather than a necessary dialectical aspect of the movement as a whole resulting from the contradictions of capitalist society in the sense intended by Rosa Luxemburg. It is obvious that, even for Luxemburg, opportunism as the representative of that face of the movement turned toward the present appeals more easily to those segments of the working class most satisfied with the present, but it remains a permanent, latent danger for the whole movement, a sort of recurrent temptation at all times, capable of exploding and extending itself into the entire working class. The history of the European movement seems to have confirmed Luxemburg's point of view which seems to us the most theoretically correct.

29. Luxemburg, *Reform or Revolution* in *Rosa Luxemburg Speaks*, p. 89. The reader should remember that at the time Rosa Luxemburg was writing, the words "social democracy" and "social democrat" had not yet acquired the meaning of opportunistic revisionism that they have today; quite the contrary, they were used to designate the working class movement of Marxist inspiration. Lenin's party, the future Communist Party, called itself in fact the Russian Social Democratic Labor Party.

30. "If at the beginning a wing of the party was inclined to underestimate

or actually deny the utility of the positive every day struggle, the rapid extension of the movement after 1890 necessarily pushed things to the other extreme, that is to an overestimation of positive reform work and opportunistic tendencies. The Erfurt congress constitutes the characteristic phase of transition in which the party had to fight on both fronts." Luxemburg, "Nachbetrachtungen," *Gesammelte Werke*, III, p. 151.

31. Luxemburg, "Zum kommenden Parteitag," *Leipziger Volkszeitung* (September 1899), *Gesammelte Werke*, III, p. 172.

32. Ibid., pp. 172–73.

33. Rosa Luxemburg was not unaware, particularly in the early years of her activity in the German party, that opportunism was the ruling force in many comrades who refused to admit it and professed themselves radicals. "More than once during the debates on foreign policy she accused the foremost leaders of the German social democrats of saying one thing and doing another, noting when it came to voting resolutions the socialists were capable of showing first-class radicalism, but as soon as they found it necessary to fight against war or the government that had provoked it, they all seemed to disappear. At the time, these words were considered incredibly audacious. The German Social Democratic Party was at the height of its glory." Speech by Zinoviev to the St. Petersburg Soviet in *Karl Liebknecht et Rosa Luxemburg—Discours prononces par G. Zinoviev et L. Trotsky a la reunion du Soviet de Petrograd le 18 janvier 1919* (Petrograd: Editions de l'International Communiste, 1919), p. 19

34. Luxemburg, *Reform or Revolution* in *Rosa Luxemburg Speaks*, p. 87.

35. Luxemburg, "Zur Kommenden Parteitag," *Gesammelte Werke*, III, p. 178.

36. Ibid., p. 180. After the victory of the reformists at the Milan congress of the Italian Socialist Party and shortly before the Reggio Emilia congress, she wrote, with regard to the so-called practical policy: "After a few years of this *practical policy* it is clear that it is the least practical of all, because its aim is to saw off the limb on which it is sitting. By losing contact with the masses of the proletariat, it pulls the ground out from under its own feet and becomes a plaything of bourgeois politics, dragging syndicalism, that anarchist caricature of revolutionary socialism, behind it. But the experiment carried out with such pitiless logic by socialist opportunism can only have one consequence in Italy: the regeneration of the working class." Luxemburg, "Ristscenza Socialista," *La Soffita* (Rome, May 15, 1911).

37. "I think that Schweitzer and the others have honest intentions, but they are '*practical politicians*.' They want to take existing circumstances into considera-

tion and refuse to surrender this *privilege* of 'practical politics' to the exclusive use of Messrs. Miquel at Co. . . . They want to take things as they are, and not irritate the government, etc., just like our 'republican' practical politicians, who are willing to 'take along with them' a Hohenzollern emperor. But since I am not a 'practical politician' I together with Engels have found it necessary to give notice to the Social-Demokrat in a public statement . . . of our intention to quit." Letter to Kugelmann of February 23, 1865 in Karl Marx and Frederick Engels, *Selected Correspondence* (Moscow: Progress Publishers, 1965), p. 170.

3

LUXEMBURG AS THINKER
AND REVOLUTIONARY

Raya Dunayevskaya

Raya Dunayevskaya, once a secretary to Leon Trotsky and a former collab-
orator of C. L. R. James, had from the mid-1950s onward become the
internationally recognized leader of a small intellectual current known as
"Marxist-Humanists." As in the essay included here, Dunayevskaya was
aggressively internationalist and intent on interweaving philosophical con-
cerns with contemporary liberation struggles. This contribution is excerpted
from a talk she gave, "Women as Thinkers and as Revolutionaries," while
preparing her final major book, Rosa Luxemburg, Women's Liberation,
and Marx's Philosophy of Revolution.

L et's turn to the twentieth century and see, firstly, what can we learn
from women as masses in motion, initiating nothing short of the
overthrow of the reactionary Russian colossus, Tsarism—the dramatic,
creative, empire-shaking five days in February 1917; and, secondly, let's
turn to the 1919 German Revolution and its greatest theoretician, Rosa
Luxemburg.

First appeared in *Women's Liberation and the Dialectics of Revolution: Reaching for the Future* (Atlantic Highlands, N.J.: Humanities Press, 1985). Reprinted with permission from *News and Letters*.

That first day, February 23 [March 8 according to Western calendars
—Ed.], in Russia appeared simple enough as a celebration of International
Women's Day by the textile workers in Petrograd. But was it that simple,
when they insisted it become a strike, despite a raging world war in which
their country was doing very badly? Was it that simple when all revolutionary parties—Bolsheviks, Left Mensheviks, Social Revolutionaries,
Anarchists—were telling them that they were courting a massacre, and
they shouldn't go out on strike? Was that first day of the revolution, when
50,000 women marched despite all advice against it, a "male-defined" revolution? Was the letter they addressed to the metal workers, which the
metal workers honored by joining the strike—and the 50,000 grew to
90,000: men and women, housewives as well as factory workers—a proof
of the fact that they didn't really "know" what they were doing?

When the Bolsheviks did join the women textile workers and the
strike turned into political opposition to the imperialist war and the Cos-
sacks did open fire, it was too late to save the Russian empire. By then the
soldiers also joined the masses in revolt, and "spontaneously" the whole
rotten empire toppled.

It is true that those five historic days that crumbled the might of
Tsarism led, in turn, to the Revolution of October 25 [November 7
—Ed.], and that certainly was led by the Bolshevik Party. That, however,
can no more detract from what the women workers initiated on February
25, than the October Revolution can be blamed for its transformation into
opposite under Stalin a decade later.

What had happened in action, what had happened in thought, what
had happened in consciousness of the mass participants—all this is the
ground on which we build today. Or should be. But even if some still
insist on playing down women *both* as masses in motion and as leadership,
let them consider the German Revolution, January 1919, led by Rosa
Luxemburg. None questioned that she was the leader.

From 1898 when she fought the first appearance of reformism in the
Marxist movement, through the 1905 Revolution in which she was both a
participant and out of which she drew her famous theory of the Mass Strike;
from 1910–13 when she broke with Karl Kautsky—four years in advance of
Lenin's designation of Kautsky as not only opportunist but betrayer of the
proletariat—and when she first developed her anti-imperialist struggles and

writings, not only as political militant but carving out her greatest and most original theoretical work, *Accumulation of Capital,* to the 1919 Revolution; she made no division between her theory and he practice.

Take her Reform or Revolution against Bernstein, who demanded that "the dialectical scaffolding" be removed from Marx's "materialism." Talking of Bernstein, she wrote:

> When he directs his keenest arrows against our dialectic system, he is really attack the specific mode of thought employed by the conscious proletariat in its struggle for liberation. . . . It is an attempt to shatter the intellectual arm with the aid of which the proletariat, though materially under the yoke of the bourgeoisie, is yet enabled to triumph over the bourgeoisie. For it is our dialectical system that shows to the working class the transitory character of this yoke, proving to the workers the inevitability of their victory, and is already realizing a revolution in the domain of thought.

The next great historic event—the Russian Revolution of 1905—again reveals her as theorist and activist-participant who did not stop at oratory but, with gun in hand, made the proprietor-printer print a workers' leaflet. What she singled out, however, from the great experience, what she made ground for other revolutions, what she created as a theory also for the relationship of spontaneity to party, was *The Mass Strike, the Political Party, and the Trade Unions:*

> The revolution is not an open field of maneuver of the proletariat, even if the proletariat was social democracy at its head plays the leading role, but it is a struggle in the middle of incessant movement, the creaking, crumbling and displacement of all social foundations. In short, the element of spontaneity plays such a supreme role in the mass strikes in Russia, not because the Russian proletariat is "unschooled," but because revolutions are not subject to schoolmastering.

It is this concept and this activity and this perspective that led, in 1907, to Luxemburg's joining Lenin and Trotsky to amend the resolution at the Stuttgart meeting of the International that declared socialist opposition to war and the imperative need to transform it into a revolution.

At the time when Luxemburg recognized the nonrevolutionary character of Karl Kautsky, when all other Marxists, Lenin included, were still acknowledging him as the greatest theoretician of the Second International, she embarked on the most hectic point of activity outside of a revolution itself.

She felt very strongly that the German Social Democracy had been hardly more than a bystander instead of a militant fighter against Germany's imperialist adventures. It was this, and not mere "organizational" questions, which made her return to her original analysis of mass strike which had always meant to her that "the masses will be the active chorus, and the leaders only 'speaking parts,' the interpreter of the will of the masses."

Luxemburg was not only involved in lecturing and developing an anti-imperialist struggle over the Morocco crisis which would, in turn, lead to her greatest theoretical work, *Accumulation of Capital*, but she also turned to work on the "Woman Question," which heretofore she had left entirely to Clara Zetkin, who was editing the greatest German women's magazine, *Die Gleichheit*, from 1891 to 1917.

The magazine's circulation rose from 9,500 in 1903 to 112,000 in 1913. Indeed, by the outbreak of the war, the female membership of the German Social Democracy was no less than 170,000. It is clear that, as great a theoretician as Rosa Luxemburg was, and as great an organizer as Clara Zetkin was, they were not exceptions to the alleged apathy of German women. On the contrary, it would be more correct to say that there wouldn't have been as massive and important a revolution in Germany were there not that many women involved in the revolution. Naturally none could compare with Rosa Luxemburg as theoretician. That is certainly true of genius whether that be women or man. As one of the very few persons who has written on the subject put it, were it not for the proletarian women, "there might have been no revolution in Germany." [William A. Pelz, "The Role of Proletarian Women in the German Revolution, 1918–19," presented at the Conference on the History of Women, College of Ste. Catherine, St. Paul, Minn., October 24–25, 1975—Ed.]

Despite all of the misrepresentation of her position on the Russian Revolution, Luxemburg had hailed it as the greatest proletarian revolution ever, insisting that the Russian Bolsheviks alone had dared and dared again. It was exactly such a daring act that she was preparing herself from her jail cell, from which she was not freed until November 9, 1918, when the German masses in revolt had driven the Kaiser from the throne. Anyone who tried to use her criticism of the Russian Revolution as the German Revolution unfolded got from her the following: Where did you learn the ABCs of revolution? Is it not from the Russians? Who taught you the slogan "all power to the soldiers, workers, and peasants"? Isn't it the Russians? This is the dialectics of revolution: that is what Spartakus wants; this is the road we are taking now.

Rosa Luxemburg lived only two and a half months after being let out of jail. Two and a half months in which the upsurge of the masses led to the establishment first of the Spartakus League and then the independent Communist Party in Germany. Two and a half months in which to call for all power to the soldiers' and workers' councils. And then the counterrevolution caught up with her, shot her, bashed in her head, and threw her body into the Landwehr Canal.

Does the beheading of the German Revolution—Liebknecht and Jogiches were murdered along with Luxemburg—mean that we're not to learn from a revolution because it was "unsuccessful"?

Has the Women's Liberation Movement nothing to learn from Rosa Luxemburg just because she hasn't written "directly" on the "Woman Question"? Outside the fact that the latter doesn't happen to be true, should not the corpus of her works become the real test of woman as revolutionary and as thinker and as someone who has a great deal to tell us as Women's Liberationists today? Are we to throw all that into the dustbin of history because she has not written on the "Woman Question"?

4

LUXEMBURG AND LENIN ON REVOLUTIONARY ORGANIZATION

Paul Le Blanc

Paul Le Blanc's article is related to work he did in his study Lenin and the Revolutionary Party. *He argues that the perspectives of Luxemburg and Lenin were closer than is often acknowledged, and that the thinking of the two revolutionaries on the question of how revolutionary organizations should function can be fruitfully integrated, adding up to a more balanced approach to the question than would otherwise be achieved.*

Among the greatest representatives of the revolutionary Marxist movement in the twentieth century are Rosa Luxemburg and Vladimir Ilyich Lenin. The foremost leader of Russian socialism's left wing, Lenin forged a Bolshevik (majority) Faction of the Russian Social Democratic Labor Party (RSDLP) in 1903 which, by 1912, separated to form a distinctly revolutionary workers' party that—five years later—proved itself by leading the world's first socialist revolution. Luxemburg was in the same period a central leader in the left wing of both the Polish and German socialist movements. Associated throughout her revolutionary

First appeared in *International Marxist Review* 2, no. 3 (summer 1987).

career with the Social Democracy of the Kingdom of Poland and
Lithuania (SDKPiL) and, in exile from her native Poland, a brilliant light
in the massive German Social Democratic Party (SPD), she was the most
prominent critic of the theoretical revisionism and practical reformism
which were eating away at the integrity of the German workers' movement. Like Lenin, she was a perceptive analyst of imperialism and an
uncompromising opponent of the First World War. Shortly before she and
Karl Liebknecht were murdered during the abortive uprising of 1919,
Luxemburg was a founder of the German Communist Party.[1]

Yet much of the attention on Luxemburg in later years has been
focused on her 1904 critique of Lenin's ideas on the question of revolutionary organization. Standard interpretations of Luxemburg's critique have
her "demonstrate the bureaucratic tendencies inherent in Lenin's conception, speaking of the inevitable strangling of individual initiative in such an
organization." This is the interpretation of the former German Communist
Franz Borkenau in his anti-Communist classic *World Communism* (1938).
"Where Lenin, instead of the belief in the proletarian revolution, had put
his hopes in a centralized group under his leadership," Borkenau explained,
"Rosa Luxemburg almost alone continued to believe in the proletariat. . . .
The masses must not be ordered about by an 'infallible' central committee.
They must learn from their own experience, their own mistakes. Revolu-
tion must be the result of their increasing political understanding. She
believed, in short, in the spontaneity of the proletarian masses."[2]

This interpretation has found an echo across the political spectrum—
among Cold War anti-Communist crusaders, among moderate reformist
socialists, and even among many who consider themselves revolutionary
opponents of capitalism. But it's a myth which obscures not only the realities of Lenin's politics but also of Luxemburg's. It even blurs the genuine
insights which can be found in her critique of Lenin's ideas. Only if we
clear away the deadwood of distortion and romanticization can we hope
to understand these two revolutionaries, particularly their ideas on the vital
question of how revolutionaries should organize themselves in order to be
effective in advancing the socialist cause.

Luxemburg and the Polish Movement

The standard generalizations about Luxemburg's opposition to organizational centralism are at once thrown into question if—unlike most commentators—we focus our attention on the the the role she played in the Polish revolutionary movement, particularly from 1903 to 1913. In Poland, unlike Germany (but like Russia), revolutionaries were compelled to operate in underground conditions. The Polish organization in which she was involved was hardly "Luxemburgist" in the libertarian way that the term is commonly understood. "The Social Democracy of Poland and Lithuania, which she led, was, if anything, far more highly centralized and far more merciless toward those in its ranks who deviated from the party's line, than was the Bolshevik party under Lenin," wrote Max Shachtman in 1938. The knowledgeable ex-anarchist Max Nomad put it more strongly: "And she was also hated by some prominent members of her own Polish Marxist Party whom she mercilessly expelled from the ranks of the organization when they dared to dissent from her views—even though it was known that the dissenters had behind them the majority of the underground membership." More recently, the prominent Belgian Trotskyist Ernest Mandel commented: "In fact, while criticizing Lenin, Rosa was busy building a centralized (one could say: overcentralized) illegal party in Poland, and conducting faction fights against minorities at least in the same (if not more) 'harsh' manner as Lenin. This is often forgotten in the analysis of the Lenin-Luxemburg controversy on organization, and merits closer attention."[3]

One account of the events alluded to in these judgements has been offered in Peter Nettl's biography *Rosa Luxemburg*. Nettl argued that "Rosa Luxemburg was herself not directly involved," in fact "had nothing to do with" and "disapproved of" the harsh organizational measures for which, according to Nettl, her close comrade Leo Jogiches was primarily responsible.[4]

A more recent study, however, makes it difficult to accept Nettl's interpretation. Although Jogiches (whose party name was Tyszka) was certainly a central leader in the SDKPiL, Robert Blobaum has documented that "while Tyszka's claims to political hegemony in the SDKPiL are both undeniable and well-documented, one must be able to distinguish between pretense and fact. The truth of the matter is that Tyszka lacked the political base among the party rank and file necessary to the realization of his ambitions." The central organizational figure was Feliks Dzierzhinski, a sincere and dedicated revolutionist whose talents were ultimately to result in his becoming, after the Bolshevik Revolution, the first head of the Soviet republic's secret police, the Cheka. But in the years before that he played a role aptly described in this manner: "As the inspiration behind a constantly evolving organizational apparatus, and as the dominant figure in the executive institutions of the SDKPiL, Dzierzhinski translated the ideas of Luxemburg—edited as they were by Tyszka—into more easily digestible forms of political action." A member of the oppositional faction bitterly commented in 1904 that 'the triumvirate of Tyszka, Luxemburg, and Dzierzhinski does what it wants without coming to an agreement with the rest of the members.'[5]

Dzierzhinski was determined to forge, in his words, "a new type of organization with no rights but to work, to carry out the instructions of the Foreign Committee (in which Luxemburg's perspectives predominated), to educate itself, to distribute literature, etc. This section shall have no voice at all or any right of representation in the party; its aim is simply to become Social Democratic and to be at the beck and call of the Foreign Committee." This organizational perspective, justified as a necessary expedient due to Poland's repressive environment, was utilized to ensure the triumph of the political orientation of "the Luxemburg group" in the SDKPiL. "In assuring the victory of Luxemburg and Tyszka over their emigre opponents," notes Blobaum, "Dzierzhinski had introduced fundamental organizational innovations that were to transform the appearance of the party. By placing himself at the head of party institutions—in the Foreign Committee, in the Main Directorate, and on the editorial board of *Czerwony sztander*—Dzierzhinski concentrated considerable power in his own hands which served to centralize the organization as a whole." Blobaum indicates that all of this had "Luxemburg's blessing" and that she "realized her faction's debt to Dzierzhinski and heaped praise upon his work in a congratulatory letter."[6]

Blobaum argues persuasively that Dzierzhinski was not interested in power for its own sake and was, in fact, committed to a collective leadership with Luxemburg and Jogiches. Channeling his creative energy into tireless organizational work, his goal was to translate the political *Weltan-*

schauung of "Luxemburgism"—identified by Blobaum as "the emphasis on maximalist demands, exclusiveness in relation to non-proletarian segments of the population, inflexible opposition to the goal of Polish independence under any circumstances, the territorial as opposed to the national character of party work"—into action, bringing it to life through cohesive organization. Blobaum stresses that he was "a Polish revolutionary of the 'internationalist' wing, a true believer of the ideology of Marxism as interpreted by Rosa Luxemburg; significantly, it was her portrait that years later stared at him from a wall of his office at the Lubianka (Cheka headquarters) in Moscow."[7]

Nor can we simply assume that Luxemburg was so immersed in other matters that she was completely ignorant of Dzierzhinski's mode of operation. In 1905 she had an opportunity to get into Poland and Russia where the two revolutionary leaders worked closely and harmoniously. In the period after the defeat of the 1905 revolution, Dzierzhinski "would not suffer any attempts at organized opposition to the authority of the ZG (Zarzad Glowny—Main Directorate of the SDKPiL) and, moreover . . . he was prepared to employ all means at his disposal to eliminate such opposition." This resulted in 1911–12, in a split in which Luxemburg played a significant role. One aspect of it was "the Radek case," which involved an effort to expel the dissident Karl Radek not only from the Polish socialist movement but also from the German movement. Luxemburg became deeply involved in this sad and dubious effort.[8]

It is worth noting that Lenin, although an "outsider," himself sympathized with the politics and organizational rights of the dissidents during this affair.

The Immediate Context of Luxemburg's Critique

The fact remains, however, that Luxemburg's primary field of operation was within the German Social Democracy. And her 1904 polemic "Organizational Questions of Russian Social Democracy" is more than simply a critique of Lenin's *One Step Forward, Two Steps Back*. Appearing in the German Marxist theoretical magazine *Neue Zeit*, it was introduced with the following editorial comment:

The present work deals with Russian conditions, but the organizational questions with which it deals are also important for the German Social Democracy. This is true not only because of the great international significance which our Russian brother party has achieved, but also because similar questions of organization presently occupy our own party.[9]

If we fail to recognize the significance of Luxemburg's critique for the *German* context, we will not be able to understand what she was saying. The profound difference between German and Russian realities has been cogently described by Max Shachtman:

> The "professional revolutionists" whom Luxemburg encountered in Germany were not, as in Russia, the radical instruments, for gathering together loose and scattered local organizations, uniting them into one national party imbued with a firm Marxist ideology and freed from the opportunistic conceptions of pure-and-simple trade unionism. Quite the contrary. In Germany, the "professionals" were careerists, the conservative trade-union bureaucrats, the lords of the ossifying party machine, the reformist parliamentarians, the whole crew who finally succeeded in disemboweling the movement. . . . The "centralism" of Lenin forged a party that proved able to lead the Russian masses to victorious revolution, the "centralism" that Luxemburg saw growing in the German social democracy became a conservative force and ended in a series of catastrophes for the proletariat.[10]

It is also worth noting that while, in this period, Lenin tended to idealize the German Social Democratic model (even as he unconsciously diverged from it) because from afar it still seemed a bulwark of Marxist orthodoxy, Luxemburg was already poignantly aware of its deficiencies (even as she was unable fully to transcend them).

Of course, Luxemburg's article has a relevance transcending the German context. The very way in which she frames the problem has had a universal resonance down to our own times:

> On the one hand, we have the mass; on the other, its historic goal, located outside of existing society. On the one hand we have the day-to-day struggle; on the other, the social revolution. Such are the terms

of the dialectical contradiction through which the socialist movement makes its way.

It follows that this movement can best advance by tacking betwixt and between the two dangers by which it is constantly being threatened. One is the loss of its mass character, the other, the abandonment of its goal. One is the danger of sinking back into the condition of a sect; the other, the danger of becoming a movement of bourgeois social reform.[11]

Luxemburg goes on to criticize Lenin for an "overanxious desire to establish the guardianship of an omniscient and omnipotent Central Committee" in order to protect the Russian workers' movement from opportunism. She argues that "opportunism appears to be a product of an inevitable phase of the historic development of the labor movement," and that it "can be overcome only by the movement itself—certainly with the aid of Marxist theory, but only after the dangers in question have taken tangible form in practice."[12] Compressed into this point is a complex argument which is far richer than such interpreters as Franz Borkenau imply.

The fact remains that the entire argument is advanced as a polemic against Lenin's views. In 1904 Luxemburg did not fully grasp what those views were. In part this was because she, like most well-read Marxists outside of Russia, was influenced by what Lenin's Menshevik opponents (who included most of the best-known Russian Marxists: Plekhanov, Axelrod, Zasulich, Deutsch, Martov, Potresov, Trotsky, etc.) were asserting. In order to better evaluate Luxemburg's critique, we need to examine the circumstances under which the split in the Russian movement took place.

The Russian Realities

At the Second Congress of the RSDLP in 1903, which resulted in the Bolshevik/Menshevik split, Lenin did not intend to enunciate some "Leninist" doctrine about "a party of a new type." The term *Leninism* at this time was nothing more than a factional epithet hurled at Lenin and his co-thinkers, who saw themselves, simply, as being the most consistent defenders of the traditional party perspective held in common by Marxists throughout Russia and the world. Even Pavel Axelrod, a veteran socialist on the Menshevik side of the split, believed that there were "no clear, defined differences concerning either principles or tactics," and that on the organizational questions there were no principled differences regarding "centralism, or democracy, autonomy, etc." Rather there were differing opinions regarding the "application or execution of organizational principles . . . (which) we have all accepted."[13]

With the passage of time, far-reaching political differences between the Bolsheviks and Mensheviks *did* become evident, but Lenin perceived this only after he wrote his 1904 discussion of the split, *One Step Forward, Two Steps Back*. The sources of the split were tangled and complex.

Political ideas are held by, and political organizations are composed of, human beings. We cannot afford to lose sight of the interplay between political principles and human dynamics as we attempt to grasp the vibrant reality of an organization's life and development. The 1903 congress of the RSDLP is a classic illustration.

"We all knew each other," wrote Lenin's companion Nadezhda Krupskaya, "not only as Party workers, but in intimate personal life. It was all a tangle of personal sympathies and antipathies. The atmosphere grew tenser as the time for voting approached." In spite of this dynamic, Lenin viewed the upcoming congress from the standpoint of a "professional revolutionary" determined to place political principle and organizational coherence above purely personal factors; he wanted this to be the case not only within the RSDLP as a whole, but also within the influential current of which he was a part, associated with the newspaper *Iskra*. Particularly among the leadership of the *Iskra* current—including Plekhanov, Axelrod, Zasulich, Martov, Potresov, and himself, i.e., the paper's editorial board—relations had a "family character" marked by "painful, long-drawn-out, hopeless quarrels . . . which were often repeated, making it impossible for us work for *months* on end." The idea that personal quarrels would dominate over political considerations and that policies affecting the entire organization would be settled by "arrangements among ourselves" within "the old family editorial board" was intolerable to him. He wanted to ensure that "in the Party, on its formal basis, with subordination of *everything* to the Rules," such a situation would be "absolutely impossible, both judicially and morally."[14]

To advance this development, Lenin made it clear that he would call for the *election* at the 1903 party congress of *Iskra*'s editorial board, and also that he would propose the reduction of the board from six to three— Plekhanov, Martov, and himself. These three had done the bulk of the writing and editorial work, and each represented a distinctive element within the RSDLP leadership; the fact that there would be three instead of six also ensured that decision-making deadlocks could be overcome by a majority vote. As he explained later to Potresov: "I consider this trio the *only* businesslike arrangement, the *only* one capable of being an official institution, instead of a body based on indulgence and slackness, the *only* one to be a real center, each member of which, I repeat, would always state and defend his party view, *not one grain more*, and irrespective of all personal motives, *all* considerations concerning grievances, resignations, and so on."[15] We can see here that Lenin had no objection to *political* disagreements arising in the Party and among its leaders, that in fact he expected that all comrades would "always state and defend" their particular party viewpoint. But he wanted to see commonly accepted organizational rules which would ensure "business-like" functioning, filtering out "personal motives" as a major factor in party life.

Another aspect of this outlook can be seen in Lenin's attitude toward the Party congress, vividly described by Krupskaya: "He always, as long as he lived, attached tremendous importance to party congresses. He held the party congress to the the highest authority, where all things personal had to be cast aside, where nothing was to be concealed, and everything was to be open and above board. He always took great pains in preparing for Party congresses, and was particularly careful in thinking out his speeches."[16] While everyone at the Second Congress of the RSDLP subscribed in general to these organizational principles, however, many were shocked by the thoroughgoing application which Lenin proposed. Historian Neil Harding has noted:

> What Lenin failed to take into account was the immense emotional and psychological hurt that this entailed for Axelrod and Zasulich in particular. Earlier in the debate over Article I (defining membership), Plekhanov had openly ridiculed Axelrod's objections to Lenin's formulations, pouring public scorn on the man who had, for so long, been his friend and who had been so utterly dependent upon him. Now the final blow

was to deprive him of that one mark of prestige which might have given
him sorely needed esteem in the eyes of the movement and recognition
of a lifetime devoted to it. Much the same would have applied to
Zasulich and Potresov . . . Martov rallied to their defense, as they had
earlier supported him, and categorically refused to serve on the editorial
board which was, nonetheless, ratified by the majority.[17]

Krupskaya later recalled:

Many were inclined to blame Plekhanov's tactlessness, Lenin's "vehe-
mence" and "ambition," Pavlovich's pinpricks, and the unfair treatment
of Zasulich and Axelrod—and they sided with those who had a grievance. They missed the substance through looking at personalities. . . .
And the substance was this—that the comrades grouped around Lenin
were far more seriously committed to principles, which they wanted to
see applied at all cost and pervading all the practical work. The other
group had more of the man-in-the-street mentality, were given to compromise and concessions in principle, and had more regard for persons.[18]

After the congress, Lenin wrote to a concerned comrade:

The story goes that the "praetorians" ousted people because of a slan-
derous accusation of opportunism, that they cast slurs on and removed
people, etc. That is mere idle talk, the fruit of an imaginary grievance,
rien de plus (nothing more). No one, absolutely no one had "slurs" cast
upon him or was removed, prevented from taking part in the work.
Some one or other was merely removed from the *central body*—is that a
matter for offense? Should the Party be torn apart for that? Should a
theory of (Lenin's) hypercentralism be constructed on that account?
Should there be talk of rule by rod of iron, etc., on that account?[19]

Despite Lenin's pained objections, this is exactly what was said and
repeated far and wide by his Menshevik adversaries, who organized a
fierce campaign to disrupt RSDLP activities until the decisions of the congress were overturned, Plekhanov abandoned the Bolsheviks and Lenin
himself was forced off the editorial board of *Iskra*.[20] Lenin went on to
organize a Bolshevik faction around the organizational perspectives to

which he had won the 1903 congress, and he wrote *One Step Forward, Two Steps Back* in order to explain what had happened and to clarify the disputed organizational questions.

It was at this point that Rosa Luxemburg took the field against Lenin, in an essay more influenced by the accounts of prestigious Mensheviks than by the actual policies of Lenin.

Luxemburg's Critique and Lenin's Reply

Much of Luxemburg's polemic against Lenin consists of interpretations which simply cannot hold up under the weight of the facts. This becomes clear if we go through it point-by-point while referring to Lenin's generally ignored point-by-point reply to her.

Luxemburg writes that *One Step Forward, Two Steps Back* "is a methodical exposition of the ideas of the ultracentralist tendency in the Russian movement. The viewpoint is that of pitiless centralism." Lenin complains that Luxemburg's article "does not acquaint the reader with my book, but with something else. . . . Comrade Luxemburg says, for example, that my book is a clear and detailed expression of the point of view of "intransigent centralism." Comrade Luxemburg thus supposes that I defend one system of organization against another. But actually that is not so. From the first to the last page of my book, I defend the elementary principles of any conceivable system of party organization. My book is not concerned with the difference between one system of organization and another, but with how any system is to be maintained, criticized, and rectified in a manner consistent with the party idea."[21]

Luxemburg writes: "Lenin's thesis is that the party Central Committee should have the privilege of naming all the local committees of the party. . . . It should have the right to impose on all of them its own ready-made rules of conduct." Lenin replies: "Actually that is not so. What my views on this subject are can be documentarily proved by the draft Rules of Party Organization which I proposed. In that draft there is nothing about any right to organize the local committees. That right was introduced into the Party Rules by the commission elected by the (1903) Party Congress to frame them, and the Congress adopted the commission's text. . . . In

this commission which gave the Central Committee the right to organize
the local committees, it was my opponents who had the upper hand."[22]

Luxemburg writes: "the two principles on which Lenin's centralism
rests are precisely these: (1) The blind subordination, in the smallest detail,
of all party organs, to the party center, which alone thinks, guides, and
decides for all. (2) The rigorous separation of the organized nucleus of
revolutionaries from its social revolutionary surroundings. Such centralism
is the mechanical transposition of the organizational principles of Blanquism into the mass movement of the socialist working class." Blanquism,
named after the nineteenth-century revolutionary Auguste Blanqui, was a
non-Marxist conception of revolution, to be made by conspiracies of a
small revolutionary elite instead of by the self-conscious working class.
Lenin responds: "She has confused the defense of a specific point relating
to a specific clause of the Rules (in that defense I was by no means intransigent, for I did not object at the plenary session to the amendment made
by the commission) with the defense of the thesis (truly 'ultra-centralist,'
is it not?) that Rules adopted by a Party congress must be adhered to until
amended by a subsequent congress. This thesis (a 'purely Blanquist' one, as
the reader may readily observe) I did indeed defend in my book quite
'intransigently.' Comrade Luxemburg says that in my view 'the Central
Committee is the only active nucleus of the Party.' Actually that is not so.
I have never advocated any such view."[23] He went on to offer a succinct
summary of what he believed the 1903 split had been about:

> Our controversy has principally been over whether the Central Com-
> mittee and Central Organ should represent the trend of the majority of
> the Party Congress, or whether they should not. About this "ultra-cen-
> tralist" and "purely Blanquist" demand the worthy comrade says not a
> word, she prefers to declaim against mechanical subordination of the part
> to the whole, against slavish submission, blind obedience, and other such
> bogeys. I am very grateful to Comrade Luxemburg for explaining the
> profound idea that slavish submission is very harmful to the Party, but I
> should like to know: does the comrade consider it normal for supposed
> party central institutions to be dominated by the minority of the Party
> Congress?[24]

According to Luxemburg, Lenin "is convinced that all the conditions necessary for the formation of a powerful and centralized party already exist in Russia." Lenin replies: "The thesis I advanced and advance expresses something else: I insisted, namely, that all the conditions already exist for expecting Party Congress decisions to be observed, and that the time was passed when a Party institution could be supplanted by a private circle."[25]

Lenin also responded ably to Luxemburg's charges that he wanted to impose "the regulated docility" of factory discipline inside the Party and that he was a self-proclaimed Jacobin who confused this with Marxism. The factory and Jacobin analogies, he pointed out, were introduced into the debate by Mensheviks, and his direct responses to them were being distorted by Luxemburg.[26]

Luxemburg as "Vanguardist"

Having cleared away various false arguments, we are almost ready to confront the substantive challenge to Lenin's outlook which Luxemburg raises. First, however, we should take note of the common ground shared by the two revolutionaries, which is far more considerable than is generally acknowledged. In fact, much of what Luxemburg has written seems like an elaboration of the Leninist conception of the party. Even in her 1904 polemic, she stresses the need for "a proletarian vanguard, conscious of its class interests and capable of self-direction in political activity." This "self-direction" she also calls "social-democratic centralism," which she defines as the "self-centralism" of the advanced sectors of the proletariat. It is the rule of the majority within its own party." Far from denigrating organization on behalf of "spontaneity," she insists on the need for a party which "possesses the gift of political mobility, complemented by unflinching loyalty to principles and concern for unity."[27]

Two years later, in her classic *The Mass Strike, the Political Party, and the Trade Unions*—often interpreted (mistakenly) as a "spontaneist" document —she was to write:

> The social democrats are the most enlightened, most class-conscious vanguard of the proletariat. They cannot and dare not wait, in a fatalist

fashion, with folded arms for the advent of the "revolutionary situation," to wait for that which in every spontaneous people's movement, falls from the clouds. On the contrary, they must now, as always, hasten the development of things and endeavor to accelerate events. . . . If the widest proletarian layer should be won for a political mass action of the social democrats, and if, vice versa, the social democrats should seize and maintain the real leadership of a mass movement—should they become, in a *political sense*, the rulers of the whole movement, then we must, with the utmost clearness, consistency and resoluteness, inform the German proletariat of their tactics and aims in the general period of the coming struggle.[28]

After the Russian Revolution of 1917, in her sympathetic critique of Bolshevik policy, Luxemburg was to repeat these eminently "vanguardist" assertions in 1918, though perhaps even more forcefully: "Thus it is clear that in every revolution, only that party is capable of seizing the leadership and power which has the courage to issue the appropriate watchwords for driving the revolution ahead, and the courage to draw all the necessary conclusions from the situation." Particularly scornful of the Mensheviks, Luxemburg noted that only the Bolsheviks were able to grasp "the true dialectic of revolutions" and to stand the "wisdom of parliamentary moles on its head: not through a majority to revolutionary tactics, but through revolutionary tactics to a majority—that is the way the road runs. Only a party which knows how to lead, that is, to advance things, wins support in stormy times. . . . Whatever a party could offer of courage, revolutionary farsightedness and consistency in a historic hour, Lenin, Trotsky and the other comrades have given in good measure."[29]

Luxemburg's Challenge

We are now in a position to examine the substantive disagreement between Lenin and Luxemburg.

Despite the underlying similarity in outlooks, there is an element in Luxemburg's 1904 critique of Lenin which is inconsistent with one of his fundamental premises.

The leading Menshevik Julius Martov, calling for a "broad Social Democratic working-class party," had argued: "The more widespread the title of Party member the better. We could only rejoice if every striker, every demonstrator, answering for his actions, could proclaim himself a Party member." Lenin disagreed with this conception because "the borderline of the Party remains absolutely vague. . . . Its harm is that it introduces a *disorganizing* idea, the confusing of class and party." In *One Step Forward, Two Steps Back* he elaborated: "The stronger our Party organizations, consisting of *real* Social Democrats, the less wavering there is *within* the Party, the more varied, richer, and more fruitful will be the Party's influence on the elements of the *masses* surrounding it and guided by it. The Party, at the vanguard of the working class, must not be confused, after all, with the entire class."[30]

At one point in her polemic, Luxemburg says precisely the opposite: The fact is that the social democracy is not *joined* to the organization of the proletariat. It is itself the proletariat." This appears to be inconsistent, as well, with the thrust of her own "vanguardist" inclination which we've documented. But it is an assertion related to another key point to which she gives particular stress: "The social-democratic movement cannot allow the erection of an air-tight partition between the class-conscious nucleus of the proletariat already in the party and its immediate popular environment, the nonparty sections of the proletariat." The attempt to safeguard revolutionary principles by stressing the distinction between the vanguard and the class as a whole, and efforts to establish an organizational structure reinforcing that distinction, can make the party not a living expression of the working class, but a sterile sect. "Stop that natural pulsation of a living organism, and you weaken it, and you diminish its resistance and combative spirit—in this instance, not only against opportunism but also (and that is certainly of great importance) against the existing social order. The proposed means turn against the end they are supposed to serve."[31]

The essence of Luxemburg's 1904 critique, as we can see, is the opposite of the point put forward by many latter-day anti-Leninists who appeal to her authority. She is *not* saying that the kind of party Lenin is building will establish a bureaucratic dictatorship once it makes a revolution. Rather, she is saying that it is in danger of degenerating into a sect which will be *incapable of making a revolution*! Lenin sees the party not as *embracing* the working class, but as *interacting* with it for the purpose of influencing it to go in a revolutionary direction. For Luxemburg, in the passage we're looking at, the point is to blend into the working class as it exists, the better to contribute to its organic development as a revolutionary force.

A problem with the organizational perspective which Luxemburg appears to be proposing here is that she offers no clear alternatives to Lenin's orientation except for the organizational form of the German Social Democracy, with its growing bureaucratic conservatism and opportunism which she was more keenly aware of than Lenin. But she concluded that such a development arises "out of unavoidable social conditions" and "appears to be a product and an inevitable phase of the historic development of the labor movement." The problem would be corrected, she seemed to feel, by the crises of capitalist society and by the working-class radicalism and upsurges generated by those crises. "Marxist theory offers us a reliable instrument enabling us to recognize and combat typical manifestations of opportunism," she wrote. At the same time, "the working class demands the right to make its mistakes and learn in the dialectic of history."[32]

The Test of History

The sectarian potential in Lenin's conception which Luxemburg identified soon became evident in 1905. The network of Bolshevik committees, "professional revolutionaries" distinct from the Russian working class, proved to be ill-prepared for the tumultuous, unplanned revolutionary upsurge which pushed tsarism to the brink of the abyss. The stalwart Bolshevik "committeemen" were blind to the revolutionary potential of the mass workers movement led by Father Gapon, were resistant to the workers' struggles for immediate demands and to the upsurge of trade unionism, were skeptical about the value of democratic nonparty committees (soviets) of the workers, and were resistant to allowing too many radicalizing but "untempered" workers into the Bolshevik organizations. The pressure of events—combined with Lenin's own unrelenting attacks on his comrades' sectarian inclinations—gradually forced the Bolsheviks to shift on all of these questions and, by the end of 1905, to become an effective revolutionary force. But it became clear that Luxemburg's warning was not entirely unwarranted.[33]

When the Bolsheviks embraced *democratic centralism* in 1906, special emphasis was put on the democratic component which, as Lenin saw it, would result in "a less rigid, more 'free,' more 'loose' organization," involving "a decisive step towards the full application of the democratic principle in Party organization." Favoring the dramatic influx of working-class militants (Bolshevik membership swelled from perhaps 4,000 in 1905 to about 46,000 in 1907), Lenin explained: "We are profoundly convinced that the workers' Social Democratic organizations must be united, but in these united organizations there must be wide and free discussion of Party questions, free comradely criticism and assessments of events in Party life." In short, there must be "the principles of democratic centralism, guarantees for the rights of all minorities and for all loyal opposition, the autonomy of every Party organization, . . . recognizing that all Party functionaries must be elected, accountable to the Party and subject to recall."[34]

None of this contradicted the points which Lenin made in 1903–04 regarding the subordination of personal considerations to party rules and to majority decisions of the party congress; if anything, the policy of strengthening party democracy contributed to the realization of these points, while also contributing to the overcoming of the sectarian tendencies which had cropped up.

Even with this, however, the sectarian impulse surfaced again in 1907–11, under the leadership of such prominent Bolsheviks as Alexander Bogdanov, Leonid Krassin, Anatoly Lunacharsky, and others concerned to defend Bolshevik "purity" against a Lenin who was inclined to "entangle" the party in trade union, reform, and electoral activities. Krupskaya later recalled: "A Bolshevik, they declared, should be hard and unyielding. Lenin considered this view fallacious. It would mean giving up all practical work, standing aside from the masses instead of organizing them on real-life issues."[35] As Gregory Zinoviev put it:

> Comrade Lenin's main idea was that we had to remain with the working class and be a mass party and not to coop ourselves up exclusively in the underground and turn into a narrow circle. If the workers are in the trade unions then we must be there too; if we can send just one man into

the Tsar's Duma then we shall: let him tell the workers the truth and we can publish his speeches as leaflets. If something can be done for the workers in the workers' clubs then we shall be there. We have to use every legal opportunity, so as not to divorce ourselves from the masses. . . .[36]

Rejecting such "semi-Menshevik" perspectives, the ultralefts led by Bogdanov maintained their commitment to a "true Bolshevism" which was in many ways similar to what Luxemburg had criticized. An organizational split with Lenin was followed by their evolution into a sect which soon disintegrated.

The Leninist Bolsheviks, on the other hand, became the most cohesive revolutionary force in the Russian working class from 1912 to 1914. Despite fierce repression with the onset of the First World War, they made an impressive comeback with the overthrow of tsarism. By the middle of 1917 they were able to begin winning a working-class majority to the goal of socialist revolution, which was accomplished in October/November.[37]

The trajectory of Rosa Luxemburg's own SDKPiL was less fortunate. The high degree of centralization helped it to remain intact and become an effective force during the 1905 upsurge. From 1904 to 1906 its membership grew from 1,500 to 40,000. Yet it made no programmatic or organizational shifts. Robert Blobaum recounts how the SDKPiL failed to evolve in the manner that was to bring success to the Bolsheviks:

> Always the realist, Lenin was to argue that a revolutionary party had to take into consideration the existing social conditions in the empire if it wished to broaden its political base. It should therefore appeal to the nonurban masses who made up a substantial majority of the population; it should reject the sectarian approach to nonparty workers, leaving a door open to them primarily through trade union activity; and it should identify itself, however vaguely, with the national aspirations of the non-Russian sections of the population. On all of these issues, the SDKPiL was much less flexible, opting for the continuation of strict conspiratorial tactics, rigid organizational discipline, and "proletarian internationalist" positions that had characterized its recent past.[38]

Over the next several years it succumbed to sectarian isolation and debilitating splits. As it turned out, Luxemburg's polemical diagnosis of 1904 was even more apt in regard to her own organization than it was in regard to Lenin's.

No less instructive was Luxemburg's fate inside the German Social Democratic Party, where she followed an orientation more consistent with her 1904 polemic. Luxemburg and her revolutionary comrades found themselves trapped in the left wing of a bureaucratized mass party which, when World War I erupted in 1914, supported the imperialist war effort instead of organizing working-class resistance. In the aftermath of the war, as the working-class radicalization foreseen by Luxemburg gathered momentum, the Social Democratic bureaucracy was able to divert much of the proletarian militancy into "safe" channels; Luxemburg and the most determined revolutionaries were first blocked and finally ejected, left without an adequate revolutionary instrument of their own. In the midst of a rising proletarian ferment and counterrevolutionary violence, they were forced to begin rebuilding an organization.[39]

That this experience, combined with the 1917 achievement of the Bolsheviks, had an impact on her thinking should be clear from the 1918 comments of hers already quoted. There is also the testimony of those who knew her. For example, Karl Kautsky—her erstwhile comrade turned bitter opponent—noted in 1921 (two years after her death) that "in the course of the war Rosa drew steadily closer to the communist world of thought, so that it is quite correct when Radek says that "with Rosa Luxemburg there died the greatest and most profound theoretical head of communism."[40] Indeed, as early as 1916 one of her closest coworkers, Karl Liebknecht, complained that her organizational orientation had become "too mechanically centralist," with "too much 'discipline,' too little spontaneity"—which sounded, as Michael Löwy has commented, like "a distant and paradoxical echo of the criticisms that Rosa herself had made in another context, addressed to Lenin."[41]

Conclusions

The purpose of this article is by no means to shrug off the insights in Luxemburg's essay "Organizational Questions of Russian Social Democracy."

The bureaucratic-sectarian tendency to which she directs our attention, while not an iron law, was very real among Lenin's Bolsheviks, and Lenin himself was forced to confront and combat it time after time. It also cropped up in Luxemburg's own Polish Marxist organization, and it has been an ever stronger tendency among many self-styled "Leninist" organizations and grouplets that have proliferated like mushrooms over the past seven decades.[42] The truth which Luxemburg insists on has, therefore, a great resonance even in our own time.

What is being suggested, however, is that it makes little historical sense to counterpose "Luxemburgism" to "Leninism" in regard to the question of revolutionary organization. More fruitful both for Marxist historians and activists would be a critical-minded integration of "Luxemburgist" into Leninist insight and experience.

Notes

1. For a full political biography of Lenin, the following three volumes read in sequence are recommended: Leon Trotsky, *The Young Lenin* (Garden City: Doubleday & Co., 1972); N. K. Krupskaya, *Reminiscences of Lenin* (New York International Publishers, 1970); Moshe Lewin, *Lenin's Last Struggle* (New York: Vintage Books, 1970). The best political biography of Rosa Luxemburg remains that of her comrade Paul Frölich, *Rosa Luxemburg: Her Life and Work* (New York: Monthly Review Press, 1972), but also see Norman Geras, *The Legacy of Rosa Luxemburg* (London: Verso, 1983).

2. Franz Borkenau, *World Communism* (Ann Arbor: University of Michigan Press, 1962), pp. 45, 141.

3. Max Shachtman, "Lenin and Luxemburg," in *New International* (May 1938): 144; Max Nomad, *Aspects of Revolt* (New York: Noonday Press, 1961), p. 264; Ernest Mandel, letter to author, May 14, 1986.

4. Peter Nettl, *Rosa Luxemburg* (London: Oxford University Press, 1969), pp. 344, 353.

5. Robert Blobaum, *Feliks Dzierzynski and the SDKPil: A Study of the Origins of Polish Communism* (New York: Columbia University Press, 1994), pp. 4, 5, 103.

6. Nettl, p. 181; Blobaum, pp. 89, 104, 85, 254.

7. Blobaum, pp. 112–13, 146, 201, 226, 231.

8. Ibid., pp. 150–51, 164, 203, 205–208.

9. Rosa Luxemburg, *Selected Political Writings*, ed. Dick Howard (New York: Monthly Review Press, 1971), p. 283.

10. Shachtman, p. 143.

11. *Rosa Luxemburg Speaks*, ed. Mary-Alice Waters (New York: Pathfinder Press, 1970), pp. 128–29.

12. Ibid.

13. Neil Harding, *Lenin's Political Thought*, vol. 1 (New York: St. Martin's Press, 1975), p. 195.

14. Krupskaya, p. 94; V. I. Lenin, *Collected Works*, vol. 34 (Moscow: Progress Publishers, 1960–1970), pp. 161, 165, 162.

15. Lenin, *Collected Works*, vol. 34, p. 166.

16. Krupskaya, p. 89.

17. Harding, pp. 193–94.

18. Krupskaya, p. 96.

19. Lenin, *Collected Works*, vol. 34, p. 161.

20. This comes through even in the pro-Menshevik account by Israel Getzler, *Marrov: A Political Biography of a Russian Social Democrat* (Cambridge: Cambridge University Press, 1967)—see pp. 83, 88–89.

21. *Rosa Luxemburg Speaks*, p. 116; Lenin, *Collected Works*, vol. 7, p. 472.

22. *Rosa Luxemburg Speaks*, p. 116; Lenin, *Collected Works*, vol. 7, pp. 472–73.

23. *Rosa Luxemburg Speaks*, p. 118; Lenin, *Collected Works*, vol. 7, pp. 473–74.

24. Lenin, *Collected Works*, vol. 7. p. 474.

25. *Rosa Luxemburg Speaks*, p. 119; Lenin, *Collected Works*, vol. 7, p. 474.

26. *Rosa Luxemburg Speaks* , pp. 119, 117; Lenin, *Collected Works*, vol. 7, pp. 474, 475.

27. *Rosa Luxemburg Speaks*, pp. 119, 122.

28. Ibid., p. 200.

29. Ibid., pp. 374, 375.

30. Brian Pearce, ed., *1903, Second Congress of the Russian Social Democratic Labour Parry, Complete Text of the Minutes* (London: New Park, 1978), pp. 312, 328; V. I. Lenin, *Selected Works*, vol. 1 (New York: International Publishers, 1967), pp. 312, 306.

31. *Rosa Luxemburg Speaks*, pp. 119, 118, 129.

32. Ibid., pp. 129, 130.

33. See Solomon Schwarz, *The Russian Revolution of 1905: The Workers' Movement and the Formation of Bolshevism and Menshevism* (Chicago: University of Chicago Press, 1967); and Marcel Liebman, "Lenin in 1905: A Revolution That Shook a Doctrine," *Monthly Review* (April 1970).

34. Lenin, *Collected Works*, vol. 10, pp. 34, 33, 314.

35. Krupskaya, p. 167.

36. Gregory Zinoviev, *History of the Bolshevik Party* (London: New Park, 1973), pp. 153–54.

37. See Leopold H. Haimson, "The Problem of Social Stability in Urban Russia, 1905–1917," in *Slavic Review*, December 1964 and March 1965, and Ronald Grigor Suny, "Toward a Social History of the October Revolution," in *American Historical Review* (February 1983).

38. Blobaum, pp. 145–46, 148, 217–19, 228–29.

39. See Carl Schorske, *German Social Democracy, 1905–1917* (Cambridge, Mass.: Harvard University Press, 1955), and Paul Frölich, *Rosa Luxemburg: Her Life and Work.*

40. Shachtman, p. 144.

41. Michael Löwy, "Rosa Luxemburg's Conception of Socialism or Barbarism," *Bulletin in Defense of Marxism*, January 1986, p. 15. For details see Helmut Trotnow, *Karl Liebknecht: A Political Biography* (Hamden, Conn.: Archon Books, 1984), pp. 165–168, 174.

42. On the U.S. scene, see: Paul Le Blanc, "The Tragedy of American Communism," in *Michigan Quarterly Review* (summer 1982); James O'Brien, "American Leninism in the 1970s," in *Radical America* (November 1977–February 1978); John Trinkl, "Where Have All the Party Builders Gone?" in *Guardian* (August 21, September 4, September 11, 1985); Cliff Connor, *Crisis in the Socialist Workers Party* (New York: F. I. T., 1984).

5

LUXEMBURG AND SOCIALIST FEMINISM

Andrea Nye

Andrea Nye, a capable feminist philosopher, has written a fascinating work entitled Philosophia: The Thought of Rosa Luxemburg, Simone Weil, and Hannah Arendt, *from which this selection has been excerpted. Unlike the two other thinkers in the study, Luxemburg was an uncompromising revolutionary socialist activist and penetrating Marxist theorist for all of her adult life. Weil's intellectual trajectory in the early 1930s, however, engages classical philosophy, revolutionary Marxism, and anarchism; this was "transcended" as she turned to Roman Catholicism, remaining faithful until her early death during World War II. Arendt is well known for the development—from the late 1940s to the early 1970s—of her own distinctive "radical conservative" political philosophy that also seriously engages with, yet fundamentally challenges, Marxist thought. It is Nye's virtue that she seeks to do justice to the thought of each of these people, although it is possible that none of them would feel entirely comfortable with her ambitious synthesis. In the following excerpt she identifies what she sees as essential elements of Luxemburg's perspective that have relevance for contemporary feminist thought.*

Internationalist Feminism

Luxemburg did not pretend to speak for colonized people. Her concern was European workers. They had been co-opted and duped. They had let racism and ethnocentricity blind them to the fact of slave labor and brutal military rule in colonies and spheres of interest. They had been bought off by an illusion of Western supremacy that hides the crude violence that establishes and maintains that rule. They had accepted the pretext of just wars to release their frustrations. Her indictment illuminates some of the painful debate that has gone on recently between white feminists and women of color.

The issue has been understood in much academic discussion as a conflict between an essentialism that takes femininity as a constant and a postmodern refusal of universals. Meanwhile, white feminists continue to pay little attention to the material fact of racial and economic oppression. If race riots break out in the slums of Los Angeles or New York, it is seldom a feminist matter. If government policy supports dictators in developing countries, it is men's politics. In practice in Western democracies, feminist leaders, often from privileged groups, direct and ordain the course of a reformist feminist politics that helps women like themselves win elections and employment battles. International capitalism funds a comfortable existence for many of these women, siphoning wealth from capitalist spheres of influence into Western economies, and maintaining a racially segregated domestic work force, including exploited illegal aliens, which provides cheap, menial labor in support of middle-class lifestyles.

Even when feminists proclaim a "radical" separatism or activism, the aim is not revolution in Luxemburg's sense. If there is no revolution when a few women manage to be elected to Congress; there is no revolution when a small group of radicals manage to take over an organization. Revolution, for Luxemburg, is in spontaneous movements of masses of people as occurred in the Russian Revolution and may even now be occurring in race riots in large cities, inchoate protests of welfare mothers, migrant or illegal labor movements, popular liberation movements in developing countries. In a feminism aspiring to revolutionary social transformation, feminist leaders would study such movements, encourage their self-organization, isolate the aspirations that motivate them. They would work to close gaps between feminist leaderships and masses of women in poorly paid service jobs, welfare mothers racially defined, women suffering debilitating, unpaid labor in non-Western countries.

Many feminists have called for contact and solidarity with non-Western women. A Luxemburgian socialism could give that sentiment a theoretical grounding which is lacking in both liberal tolerance of diversity and postmodern politics of difference. Neither the granting of minimal rights nor transgressive textual studies is likely to lead to a viable mass feminist politics. Luxemburg offers instead the committed stance with oppressed groups from which it is possible to get the coherent grasp of reality which can inform intelligent action. Because that commitment is to others in a common material world, it is necessarily shared. There are not different realities projected by different symbolic constructions, but one reality, the material world in which people live together in different but always interrelated ways. If the view is better from some positions than from others, this is consistent with the restraints of physical existence. Conflicting claims of truth can be weighed in discussion and critical analysis.

The theory of a shared material world and the basis for a Luxemburgian socialist feminism would be an economic analysis no longer veiled in mathematized mystery. It is not surprising that few feminists have wanted to take on such a formidable enemy as economic rationalism, barricaded as it is behind masculine privilege and academic discipline. Researchers whose theories promote the interests of those in power, fortified by research grants and fellowships, have strong vested interests in maintaining the authority of classical economics. At stake is the coherent view of the whole, which Luxemburg believed was necessary for revolutionary politics. No feminist peace movement, claim to abortion rights, reform of the family, or protest against male aggression taps the "Plutonian" depths of economic relations between militarism, war, capital, international monetary systems, and working lives that Luxemburg examined. No theory of women's rights, masculine aggression, or family justice can be adequate to women's knowledge of their global situation without an economic analysis of working experience.

The theory of a shared material world that might inform a mass feminist movement is a global economics that does not take as the object of

interest increased production swelling capitalist profits, or the realization of
the species-being of Marxist man making his mark on nature, but the satisfaction of human needs. To that end, Luxemburgian economics could
address systems of distribution as well as the organization of production,
could develop indexes for production that are qualitative as well as quantitative, could critically assess the covert assumptions of value that define the
objects of quantitative analyses. Such an economics would *use* mathematical models in the service of an economic thought the aims and motives of
which are continually critically and democratically assessed. Instead of the
fiction of an abstract economic functioning divorced from family and social
life, Luxemburgian economics could plot intersections between relations of
production and familial, cultural, and community relations. It could
develop categories and concepts necessary to represent the neglected economic function of women in both Western and non-Western countries.

Writing in support of women's right to the vote, Luxemburg identified the failure to count women's work in the home as productive with the
"brutality and insanity of the present capitalist economy" (PW [*Selected
Political Writings of Rosa Luxemburg*, ed. Dick Howard—Ed.], 221). Even
more striking, she noted, is the untapped potential power of masses of
working women in industrial, clerical, and service work. A feminist economic analysis would take account of structural relations between housework, part-time work, service work and mainstream industrial labor, both
in the West and in developing countries, to develop new strategies for feminist action. Such analyses are impossible without knowledge of and concern for the situation of working women in industrial and nonindustrial-
ized countries. Luxemburgian economics requires independent researchers, not in the pay of any government or corporation, directly conversant
with women's work experience and postcolonial cultures, knowledgeable
in global economic history, and, most important, in communication with
material reality.

Luxemburg was sometimes accused of catastrophism, the view that
capitalism is doomed and, therefore, no revolutionary action is necessary.
In fact, she argued that, well before the point when capitalism succeeds in
exhausting all external markets, economic dislocations would make life
unlivable in many parts of the world. The antidote, as she saw it, was neither passive reliance on the workings of history nor desperate vanguard

action, but a committed and integrated economic thought moving toward a coherent view of global reality. The stimulant that might motivate such thought is no longer likely to be the oppression of male industrial workers or the suffering of middleclass women in industrial countries, real as that suffering may be, but the global effects of capitalist expansion: violent conflict in developing countries between indigent rural populations and wealthy elites in alliance with foreign capitalists, disputes over essential resources such as oil, environmental collapse, the unrestrained marketing of drugs and arms, the almost universal unwillingness to tolerate women in positions of power. International movements, action groups, federations that form around these issues might be the source and the training ground for a new, mass, global, feminist politics.

A Mass Movement of Women

If there are obvious differences between socialist party organizations and the contemporary feminist movement, there are also commonalities. In feminism, as in Marxism, there has been an explosion of theory. Marxism and feminism both have become alternative academic establishments in some universities and departments, with vested interests and standards of political correctness. As in Marxism, much feminist theorizing is now internally generated, as feminist scholars respond to other scholars, establishing reputations and publication records. In addition, like the split between Bernstein's reformism and radical Leninism, feminists are often divided between liberals who look to the defense of rights in capitalist democracies and radicals who urge more extreme measures of exclusion, separatism, and militant action.

Most important, corresponding to the distance between well-educated, theoretically sophisticated leaders of Communist parties and their constituencies, is a distance between highly visible and publicized feminist leaders and poor, working, radically oppressed, unemployed and underemployed women. For the latter, many of the issues which occupy liberal feminist politics, such as pornography and abortion, are peripheral to a crushing burden of poverty, crime, and drug addiction. Issues which define radical feminism such as lesbian separatism and the refusal of motherhood may be equally tangential to women whose family responsibilities are not white or middle class. If legal remedies phrased in terms of civil rights, on which so much current liberal feminist politics focuses are often beside the point for women struggling for bare survival, even more remote from their needs may be the sophisticated textual studies which now occupy the energies of many academic feminists. From the perspective of nonwhite women, official feminism can seem mired in intellectualism, tokenism, and marginalization, stalled in defensive tactics, as conservative forces in Western democracies become more self-confident with the proclaimed demise of socialism and the resurgence of religious fundamentalism.

Luxemburg's conception of the relation between political leadership and political constituency, her insistence that mass action is the only means to revolution, might inspire another kind of relationship between feminist leaderships and masses of women. Although national feminist leaderships have on occasion sent out successful calls for demonstrations on issues such as abortion rights, the failure of mainstream feminism to fully engage the interest of poor women and women of color in feminist politics has been a source of general frustration. The resultant soul-searching has generally focused on feminist theorists and leaders themselves: How have we been inadvertently racist? How have *we* failed to make our organization attractive to diverse women?

Luxemburg suggests another tack. The solution, as she saw it, is not to find out why feminism or socialism or any liberatory theory fails to appeal to workers or poor women, or to try to refashion white feminist goals in terms they might accept. It is to study the embryonic political activism of working people themselves, their initiatives, strikes, alliances, peaceful and violent demonstrations in ghettoes, slums, factories, depressed neighborhoods. Like reformist Social Democrats, many activist feminists have allied themselves with liberal political parties against conservativism. They have endorsed, at least in practice, the liberal political agenda of free markets tempered by government-provided welfare services. They have urged retrenchment as rights come under attack from conservatives. They have cited the gains of liberal feminism. The wisdom gained in a Luxemburgian mass movement of the disadvantaged clients of welfare systems and their allies might inform new feminist agendas independent of the establishment poles of liberal welfare state versus conservative free market. The locus for such a socialist feminist politics would be more local than national, revitalizing community democracy and citizens' initiatives in which the sensitive relation between Luxemburg's leaders and their constituencies can come into play. Luxemburgian leaders would not dictate, but would encourage, guide, inform, according to the "compass" of women's own developing and forming aspirations to a better life. Women participating in mass action would develop their initiatives expressing a deepening knowledge of their and other women's situations.

In recent feminist philosophy, a feminine ethical voice has been a topic of considerable discussion. Like Luxemburg, feminist philosophers have pointed out the moral deficiencies in philosophical systems of ethics such as Kantian idealism and utilitarianism. Emergent in feminist philosophy is an alternate view of ethics as contextual, affective, perspectival. The tendency however, in reaction to philosophical ethics, has been to defend such an alternative ethics as feminine, based either on feminine psychology, women's different perspective, or women's maternal instincts. Luxemburg suggests a feminist "moral compass," grounded in the aspirations and active knowledge of working women and men. Values for Luxemburg are never independent of fact, but are framed in engagement with material reality. The substance of a feminist socialist ethics, would be goals and aims that evolve in the course of feminist struggle.

In 1912, Luxemburg insisted that women's suffrage could not be a job for women alone, but was a "common class concern for women and men of the proletariat" (PW 218). Similarly, a Luxemburgian mass feminist movement would find those points of solidarity with oppressed men that could undo the "links in the chain of the reaction that shackles people's lives" (PW 218). In such an ethics of solidarity, the aspirations of women, whose poorly paid labor is vitally necessary in the work force but who also continue to be responsible for most of the work of maintaining human life in childcare, housework, and nursing of the sick, might be a source of values for both men and women. In the past few decades, feminist standpoint theories of knowledge have pointed to the necessity for knowledge from the perspective of women's lives. At issue has been not so much political action as it has been philosophical theories of knowledge which claim rational grounding independent of context or interest. Luxemburg's socialist knowledge requires more than empathetic imagination, more than a theorist putting herself in the position of women of poorer classes or racial minorities and attempting to see things from their perspective. It requires a standing with and acting with poor, racially oppressed women and a resulting coproduction of values and knowledge.

Luxemburg's support for spontaneous revolutionary action and her insistence on working-class experience as the basis for socialist knowledge suggest an approach to standpoint ethics and theories of knowledge which circumvents the relativism and political stasis that often infects perspectival theories. From the mass action of working women, as it is conceived, understood, and carried out by them and their allies, might come objective and coherent feminist understandings of the ensemble of national and international economic and political relationships that hold oppressive relations in place. Much of recent feminist politics has concentrated on single issues such as the Equal Right's Amendment, peace, abortion, pornography, welfare services. When a victory is won on one of these issues—a constitutional amendment passes, laws are blocked banning abortion—power structures that can rescind these measures and reinterpret laws and amendments are left intact. In contrast, a Luxemburgian socialist politics, informed by a coherent grasp of the system gained in the political action of masses of poor and disadvantaged women, engages the economic and cultural matrix of capitalist society. An issue like abortion can bog down in idealist debate between a right to life and a right to choose. A revived socialist feminism would relate abortion to the economics of poverty and the propagation of a marginally employed labor force that generates repressive reproductive policies. Luxemburg's socialist grasp of the whole allows evaluation of feminist action not as a means to rescindable short-term gains but as part of a far-reaching revolutionary agenda.

Essential in any recovery of a Luxemburgian socialist feminism would be the reworking of the vexed concept of democracy. Marxists, like Lenin, were quick to point out the lack of real democracy in the legislative maneuvering of interest groups and the corporate financing of elections in capitalist countries. Concentrated as they were on winning state power, democracy was hardly a priority for the Bolsheviks either. If the slogan, "socialist democracy" had concrete meaning at all, it was a euphemism for a coercive rallying of public opinion behind the decisions of the supreme Communist party. While European Social Democrats continued to participate in parliaments and legislatures as if winning elections was an end in itself, in Russia the Soviets that were to have been the basis of socialist democracy became an instrument of party control. Democracy in both cases was deferred to a distant, utopian future when workers would be mature and true Communism possible.

Like other Marxists, Luxemburg did not describe in detail what democratic institutions and practices might be like in socialism. Her Marxist materialism ruled out in principle ideals that are not generated in actual economic and historical processes; a workers' democracy would have to emerge in the course of revolution. But she grappled with problems inherent in any attempt to install a true "rule of the people." How can the unity necessary in political or social movements be achieved in a way that does not do violence to the diversity and freedom of individuals? An answer to this question, passionately and sometimes angrily discussed between feminists, is crucial for any revolutionary movement. For feminists, the question has often taken the form of the essentialist/relativist dilemma. Either some sufficiently general definition of "woman" or "femininity" must provide unity, a definition which inevitably is exclusive of some groups and perspectives, or diversity and pluralism are claimed as the basis of a unfocused politics of difference.

Luxemburg suggests an alternative. A coherence of aims that might provide a nonoppressive unity to replace doctrinal fidelity or party policy can be generated, as were Luxemburg's own theoretical positions, out of close observation and involvement in actual women's movements. Study of, participation in, and hard thought about the actions of oppressed people in times of crisis and discontent isolates directions, meanings, tendencies, common aspirations, and goals to unify policy. The politics that results is not the autonomous creation of any theorist, the intuition of any idealist essence or the application of any theory, but reflects the "sensuous activity" of social agents themselves. As she guides, facilitates, and directs, stands with a social movement, a Luxemburgian leader speaks for others without dictating, makes clear what their actions mean in the aggregate and how they might be organized, coordinated, and carried forward. Such a politics requires open channels of communication, constant reciprocity between leaders and masses, healthy grass-roots activist groups, and institutions that make each accountable to the other.

Luxemburg could not have predicted the extent to which the very possibility of action would be co-opted in capitalist production by marketing techniques and mass psychology. Citizens in capitalist countries, persuaded to limit their freedom of action to the choice of preselected candidates for office and preselected commodities for consumption, engage in little of the kind of spontaneous political activity in which a Luxemburgian socialist ethics might be developed. Crucial for a renewed socialist feminism, therefore, would be identification of occasions and spaces for mass political struggle. These spaces, in which political action may still be possible, are no longer in the traditionally male industrial workplace, where strikes and wage disputes can be settled at the expense of foreign workers. Elsewhere in the family, citizens' groups, welfare institutions, women's groups, environmental and peace movements, in personal relations between the sexes—women, men of ethnic minorities, and other oppressed groups in affiliation with international organizations, might find occasions for action that has reference not only to national conflicts, but also to their global setting.

6

REFLECTIONS ON ROSA LUXEMBURG BY A COMMUNITY ACTIVIST

Claire Cohen

Claire Cohen approaches Luxemburg in the manner that she sought to be understood—as someone whose thinking is relevant to practical work in the here-and-now. This means, in a sense, having a serious, comradely discussion with Luxemburg on the ideas she advances, and not being afraid to engage with those ideas critically on the basis of one's own political experience. An African American psychiatrist and political activist, Cohen prepared her contribution, published here for the first time, as part of a 1994 series of discussions by study group in Pittsburgh dealing with Marxist theory.

It is still impressive to me that many of the writings of Rosa Luxemburg are not outdated. Someone could have written these things— with only a few changes—today, so very pertinent are they for our own time. I think the way we need to read her is not simply to accept everything she has to say uncritically, but to treat her with respect by considering the ways her thinking fits or doesn't fit the realities we encounter in our own political work today. In these remarks I would like to highlight salient points in some of her writings and at the same time raise a few questions on what she has to say, coming to all of this as someone who has

113

been involved in struggles within the African American community for a number of years.

In these brief remarks, I will focus on several texts—one in which she discusses the nature of Marxism, another in which she discusses the superiority of the revolutionary as opposed to the reformist orientation, another in which she discusses the meaning of imperialism, and yet another in which she deals with the struggle for women's rights. And I want to raise questions—sometimes questioning Luxemburg, sometimes joining her in questioning others—questions having to do with political consciousness and political strategy, and also having to do with the role of culture, class consciousness, class alliances, and also having to do with the role of revolutionary activists.

In her early essay "Stagnation and Progress in Marxism," Luxemburg responds to the accusation that Marxism is a dogmatic, rigid, sectarian type of theory. She argues that Marxism itself is not really such a rigid and dogmatic thing, but that this is often the impression given because of the way it is interpreted and used by some people who consider themselves to be Marxists. Marxism is not a set of unchanging dogmas. It is an approach that develops an understanding of history, economics, and society in order to help advance liberation struggles of workers and oppressed people. Because reality is so complicated, it has to be used in a flexible way.

Luxemburg then goes beyond this, arguing that a lot of how Marxism gets interpreted, used, and looked at is a function of the culture, the times, the conditions we are in. She also says that basically workers (in fact, all of us) in a society tend to see things and function within the context of the bourgeois culture, the ruling-class culture, that the workers cannot develop their own culture, and that the only way for them—for us—to do that is through the struggle. A new culture will emerge, apparently, after winning the fight for liberation.

If I read Luxemburg correctly, I agree and disagree with some of what she is saying. I agree with her that a lot of people's feeling that Marxism is rigid is not based on Marxism itself but on the way it has been interpreted and used by many different people, which is in a very dogmatic and rigid way—not with careful study and understanding of what Marx is really about and what he is trying to say. But I disagree—if I understand her—that the working class, the nonruling class, doesn't or can't develop its own culture. I think that oppressed peoples do struggle constantly for a culture of their own, separate from the culture of the ruling class. It is true that what pervades throughout the culture of society is the dominant ruling-class culture, and that certainly has a major influence on everybody, and how everybody thinks and looks at things. But at least from my experience among black people, I think people—groups of oppressed people—are always struggling, and there is always at least some bit of some opposition to that culture of the upper class, and at least some beginning of the formation of an opposition culture. I would be willing to agree that maybe you couldn't fully develop the culture of an oppressed people, or realize that culture, or have your culture influence or be pervasive throughout society without winning victory and taking power. But I think that definitely there is that cultural undercurrent of opposition.

Of course, it depends on how one defines the term *culture*. But the question arises for me, in trying to tie this to my experiences as a political activist, of how we help people to begin to have a different perspective on, a different way of looking at, a variety of issues. It comes up in efforts to affect people's understanding, and to mobilize them around an alternative understanding, of what's going on in the world and why. To some extent, people have a different set of values than those of the capitalists, and that is something we appeal to and build on, so that people are persuaded to not just buy in to what we're told in the mainstream the news-and-opinion media around questions of poverty, welfare, and so on. We have to grapple more seriously with the question of how much of an alternative culture and perspective, how much of an oppositional way of looking at the world, can be developed among the general population. It seems to me that an oppositional culture is important in helping to build a revolutionary movement. We can't expect it simply to happen the other way around—to emerge after a revolutionary movement is victorious.

I think this more activist orientation to culture is consistent with other aspects of Luxemburg's outlook. In her polemic *Reform or Revolution*, she basically argues against the moderate and reformist perspectives—similar to those of modern-day Social Democrats (such as those in the U.S. group Democratic Socialists of America) and some of the well-intentioned progressives in the Democratic Party. I also saw her remarks as presenting a transitional approach to revolutionary politics. Luxemburg was responding to the views of Eduard Bernstein, who postulated that you don't need really a revolution, that the reforms that one can successfully demand under capitalism, and also some of the developments within capitalism itself, will mitigate the negative effects of capitalism. Through legislation and other gradualist means capitalism could therefore be fundamentally reformed. Bernstein was calling himself a socialist, but he believed that capitalism could be reformed out of existence somehow, or reformed to the point that it would look just like socialism.

Luxemburg argued that if capitalism is so transformable, if it was possible to create so friendly a form of capitalism, then there would be no point to fighting for socialism. At the same time, she was dealing with another problem: that people get disillusioned because they think revolutionary changes have to happen tomorrow. She talked about the fact that the struggle for socialism was going to be a more protracted process. It wasn't going to go in a straight line, but in more of a zigzag like a lightening bolt. It would go backward and forward, with losses and gains. It was a more complex thing than just saying "oh we've got to win this particular fight or it means that socialism can't be won." She also came out against the idea that the fight for democracy was in opposition to, or qualitatively different from, the fight for socialism. In fact, she saw the proletarian fight, the workers' fight, the regular people's fight for democracy under bourgeois culture and government as actually something that would give people more of a class consciousness. As they carried on such a fight, they would come to see what their real class interests were. The fight for reforms to secure and expand people's rights, if carried out in a consistent manner, necessarily leads in a revolutionary direction.

Luxemburg also focused attention on the difference between legislative and electoralist reform efforts on the one hand and revolutionary reform efforts on the other. She believed that you cannot win a revolution through legislative efforts and electoralism. It's going to have to be a mass struggle. She wasn't opposed to electoral and legislative activity that would be beneficial to the workers and oppressed people, but she believed you can't legislate your way to socialism. The question is how to balance struggles for present-day reforms with the goal of revolution. How do we successfully do that, and how does electoral work fit in with that? How is electoral work supportive of bringing about the fundamental political change that will result in the realization of socialism? One could also ask how a labor movement which necessarily focuses on reform struggles in the here and now—which Luxemburg supported and was part of—leads to the socialist revolution which she believed was necessary.

In her essay on *The Mass Strike, the Political Party, and the Trade Unions*, Luxemburg addresses the question of how today's working-class movement is related to the socialist goal. Here, basically, her argument is against "the mechanical bureaucratic" conception of unions, and a big argument against the elitist view that some unions have of only struggling for their own organized members and not making it a people's movement. Her point is that the movement and the struggles of the organized workers have the the task of building a broad people's movement, including organized and unorganized workers, as well as those who are unemployed. She was not talking about going to the opposite extreme of saying that everybody has to be organized before you move. She did a nice little thing of comparing the Russian workers with the German workers. The German workers were "more advanced" organizationally and in their consciousness, but it was the Russian workers who pulled off the Russian Revolution of 1905. She pointed out how there was a contradictory situation. Sometimes the people who can be the most revolutionary are those who are not the most organized, or not the "most advanced" in terms of their consciousness.

For me that raises an issue that goes back to the first question we looked at. Many people that we've sought to reach out to in our own organizing tend not to have a "conscious" consciousness. Rather than having a complete lack of political consciousness, rather than being unconscious, or completely without a class consciousness, people tend to have a contradictory consciousness. How do you help people develop that consciousness so that it's less contradictory and more of a consistent working-class consciousness?

Part of the answer is that socialists must find a way to reach out to such people, to patiently explain our own ideas, and to involve people in positive struggles through which they can learn. Another part of the answer is that objective reality—capitalism itself—teaches important lessons. This brings us to another issue that Luxemburg focuses on.

Modern imperialism is a form of economic expansionism that en-

riches big capitalist corporations but is detrimental to the majority of
people throughout the world. In her discussions on imperialism, Luxemburg is saying that imperialism and militarism at this stage (in the early
twentieth century) are necessities of capitalism. You can't get rid of them
without getting rid of capitalism. This seems to be fully confirmed
throughout the twentieth century, right down to our own time. Today's
"peaceniks" who don't confront the class issue, or the issue of capitalism
versus socialism, are really utopian. If you have capitalism, ipso facto you
have an economy that needs to expand—which means you're going to
have imperialism and militarism.

So this obviously raises questions about, for example, those of us who
were involved in such things as the fight against the Gulf War. If we agree
that imperialism and militarism are an integral part of capitalism and can't
be separated from it, what then should be the goal of the antiwar movement in its struggles against militarism? Of course, our ultimate goal is to
overthrow capitalism and bring about socialism—but more immediately,
how do we focus on what we're really trying to do, to keep people from
having the illusion that somehow what the antiwar movement can
accomplish is that we're going to have this peaceful nice world? It seems
to me that under capitalism the peace that can be achieved is an *oppressive
peace*, a peace without justice, in which much of the world continues to
be oppressed by imperialists who continue to defend their interests
through military might and the threat of violence. This obviously ties in
with Luxemburg's view on the need for a revolutionary instead of a
reformist approach.

In her discussions of the struggle for women's rights and its relation to
the class struggle, one thing Luxemburg raised seemed very provocative to
me. In struggling for women's rights, she seemed to be saying, working-
class women should really view bourgeois women, upper-class women,
more or less as the enemy, and that such women couldn't really be allies of
working-class and poor women in the struggle for women's rights. She
doesn't quite say this so explicitly as that, but the whole tone of her discussion seems to go in that direction. This raises the question of to what
extent it is advisable or permissible—in Luxemburg's opinion, and also for
us today—for there to be alliances across class lines in a united effort in
certain democratic and human rights struggles. For example, what do we

think of struggles of the black liberation struggle in which those in the black bourgeoisie join with those in the black working class to fight against racism? What are the pitfalls as well as the positives of such an alliance?

One of the things that makes Luxemburg's work interesting but also makes it something that we need to study is that her method is not dogmatic or rigid, not cut and dried and finished. It doesn't reduce itself to simple formulas and simple answers. What she had to say about the women's struggle needs to be understood by understanding the actual meanings of the terms she used, and the underlying dynamic of what she was reaching for. Often leftists have denounced as "bourgeois feminists" not women from the capitalist class, not simply rich women who want to buy control of the women's movement, but instead simply well-meaning women who may not see themselves as working class, and women who may not be sensitive to the needs and consciousness of poor women or black women. But in this case it may not mean that those feminists are "bourgeois," but that they have not adequately developed their own consciousness. We find this problem in a different way also among black people. But there is also a question—what about that tiny percentage of wealthy blacks, powerful and successful black business people, who want to involve themselves and their money in the struggle against racism? How do we deal with that? It seems to me that the appropriate way to proceed is to say: "This is the way that *we*, working class and poor blacks, have decided to conduct our struggle. These are our issues and goals and methods. If you feel comfortable with that, if you want to give money to that, fine." The important question that arises from Luxemburg is *whose agenda* will be followed.

What I find when talking to people who are not of my persuasion politically, is that there is a mixed consciousness. Although there are some notions that show a right-wing influence, there are others—generally deeper notions—that are quite different and that have a progressive content. One of the most fundamental things is the desire of people to gain power over their own lives, and to gain control over government policies affecting their lives. People are angry about the way things are going, and these things can be traced to the way capitalism works. You can tap into that disgruntlement and discuss with people the nature and roots of the problems. Certain things resonate with them. After all, socialism means the majority of people taking control of our economic resources to guarantee a decent life for all, giving the people—not an elite of businessmen or politicians—control over their own lives. In order to be effective in talking with people, and in the organization and mobilization of people for progressive change, it is important to have a clear, realistic, practical orientation for one's self, and such an orientation needs to be radical, in the sense of going to the root of things. It seems to me that Rosa Luxemburg's ideas contribute to developing such an orientation.

PART TWO.

WRITINGS

7

MARTINIQUE

(1902)

> *Shortly after a terrible volcanic eruption killed 40,000 people at the port of St. Pierre on the island of Martinique, Luxemburg wrote this brief article for the May 15, 1902, socialist daily* Leipziger Volkszeitung. *Major newspapers expressed horror and deep human sympathy—thereby displaying a double standard. Luxemburg movingly compared this natural calamity to the murderous impact of imperialism and of the many instances of repression against working-class insurgencies (for example, the mass executions of men and women after the defeat of the Paris Commune of 1871). This selection later appeared in the U.S. socialist paper* News and Letters.

Mountains of smoking ruins, heaps of mangled corpses, a steaming, smoking sea of fire wherever you turn, mud and ashes—that is all that remains of the flourishing little city which perched on the rocky slope of the volcano like a fluttering swallow. For some time the angry giant had been heard to rumble and rage against this human presumption, the blind self-conceit of the two-legged dwarfs. Greathearted

From *News and Letters*, January–February 1983. Translated by David Wolff. Reprinted with permission from *News and Letters*.

even in his wrath, a true giant, he warned the reckless creatures that crawled at his feet. He smoked, spewed out fiery clouds, in his bosom there was seething and boiling and explosions like rifle volleys and cannon thunder. But the lords of the earth, those who ordain human destiny, remained with faith unshaken—in their own wisdom.

On the 7th, the commission dispatched by the government announced to the anxious people of St. Pierre that all was in order in heaven and on earth. All is in order, no cause for alarm!—as they said on the eve of the Oath of the Tennis Court in the dance-intoxicated halls of Louis XVI, while in the crater of the revolutionary volcano fiery lava was gathering for the fearful eruption. All is in order, peace and quiet everywhere!—as they said in Vienna and Berlin on the eve of the March eruption fifty years ago. The old, long-suffering titan of Martinique paid no heed to the reports of the honorable commission; after the people had been reassured by the governor on the 7th, he erupted in the early hours of the 8th and buried in a few minutes the governor, the commission, the people, houses, streets, and ships under the fiery exhalation of his indignant heart.

The work was radically thorough. Forty thousand human lives mowed down, a handful of trembling refugees rescued—the old giant can rumble and bubble in peace, he has shown his might, he has fearfully avenged the slight to his primordial power.

And now in the ruins of the annihilated city on Martinique a new guest arrives, unknown, never seen before—*the human being*. Not lords and bondsmen, not Blacks and whites, not rich and poor, not plantation owners and wage slaves—*human beings* have appeared on the tiny shattered island, human beings who feel only the pain and see only the disaster, who only want to help and succor. Old Mt. Pelee has worked a miracle! Forgotten are the days of Fashoda, forgotten the conflict over Cuba, forgotten "la Revanche"—the French and the English, the Tsar and the Senate of Washington, Germany, and Holland donate money, send telegrams, extend the helping hand. A brotherhood of peoples against nature's burning hatred, a resurrection of humanism on the ruins of human culture. The price of recalling their humanity was high, but thundering Mt. Pelee had a voice to catch their ear.

France weeps over the tiny island's 40,000 corpses, and the whole world hastens to dry the tears of the mourning Mother Republic. But how was it then, centuries ago, when France spilled blood in torrents for the Lesser and Greater Antilles? In the sea off the east coast of Africa lies a volcanic island—*Madagascar*: Fifty years ago there we saw the disconsolate Republic who weeps for her lost children today, how she bowed the obstinate native people to her yoke with chains and the sword. No volcano opened its crater there: the mouths of French cannons spewed out death and annihilation; French artillery fire swept thousands of flowering human lives from the face of the earth until a free people lay prostrate on the ground, until the brown queen of the "savages" was dragged off as a trophy to the "City of Light."

On the Asiatic coast, washed by the waves of the ocean, lie the smiling *Philippines*. Six years ago we saw the benevolent Yankees, we saw the Washington Senate at work there. Not fire-spewing mountains—there, American rifles mowed down human lives in heaps; the sugar cartel Senate which today sends golden dollars to Martinique, thousands upon thousands, to coax life back from the ruins, sent cannon upon cannon, warship upon warship, golden dollars millions upon millions to Cuba, to sow death and devastation.

Yesterday, today—far off in the African south, where only a few years ago a tranquil little people lived by their labor and in peace, there we saw how the English wreak havoc, these same Englishmen who in Martinique save the mother her children and the children their parents: there we saw them stamp on human bodies, on children's corpses with brutal soldiers' boots, wading in pools of blood, death and misery before them and behind.

Ah, and the Russians, the rescuing, helping, weeping Tsar of All the Russians—an old acquaintance! We have seen you on the ramparts of Praga, where warm Polish blood flowed in streams and turned the sky red with its steam. But those were the old days. No! Now, only a few weeks ago, we have seen you benevolent Russians on your dusty highways, in ruined Russian villages eye to eye with the ragged, wildly agitated, grumbling mob; gunfire rattled, gasping muzhiks fell to the earth, red peasant blood mingled with the dust of the highway. They must die, they must fall because their bodies doubled up with hunger, because they cried out for bread, for bread!

And we have seen you, too, oh Mother Republic, you tear-distiller. It

was on May 23 of 1871: the glorious spring sun shone down on Paris;
thousands of pale human beings in working clothes stood packed together
on the streets, in prison courtyards, body to body and head to head;
through loopholes in the walls, mitrailleuses thrust their bloodthirsty muzzles. No volcano erupted, no lava stream poured down. Your cannons,
Mother Republic, were turned on the tight-packed human crowd, screams
of pain rent the air—over 20,000 corpses covered the pavements of Paris!

And all of you—whether French and English, Russians and Germans,
Italians and Americans—we have seen you all together once before in
brotherly accord, united in a great league of nations, helping and guiding
one another: it was *in China*. There, too, you forgot all quarrels among
yourselves, there too you made a peace of peoples—for mutual murder
and the torch. Ha, how the pigtails fell in rows under your bullets, like a
ripe grainfield lashed by the hail! Ha, how the wailing women plunged
into the water, their dead in their cold arms, fleeing the torture of your
ardent embraces!

And now they have all turned to Martinique, all one heart and one
mind again; they help, rescue, dry the tears and curse the havoc-wreaking
volcano. Mt. Pelee, greathearted giant, you can laugh; you can look down
in loathing at these benevolent murderers, at these weeping carnivores, at
these beasts in Samaritan's clothing. But a day will come when another
volcano lifts its voice of thunder: a volcano that is seething and boiling,
whether you heed it or not, and will sweep the whole sanctimonious,
blood-spattered culture from the face of the earth. And only on its ruins
will the nations come together in true humanity, which will know but one
deadly foe—blind, dead nature.

8

THE NATIONAL QUESTION
AND AUTONOMY

(1909; EXCERPTS)

One of the most controversial aspects of Luxemburg's thought involves her approach to the question of national self-determination, which she often dismissed and always subordinated to what she perceived as the needs of the working-class struggle. Critical of the approach by the majority of the Russian Social Democratic Labor Party, Luxemburg clashed with the Bolshevik orientation of V. I. Lenin, who would develop the view that a distinction must be made between the nationalism of oppressor nations (whose imperialist policies must be opposed) and the nationalism of oppressed nations and peoples (whose struggles for self-determination must be supported). Even many who have disagreed with Luxemburg's conclusions find something of value in much of her analysis here, which was first serialized in the Polish theoretical journal Przeglad Sozialdemokratyczny *in 1908 and 1909.*

In point of fact, the political programs of the modern workers' parties do not aim at stating abstract principles of a social ideal, but only at the

From *The National Question: Selected Writings by Rosa Luxemburg*, ed. Horace B. Davis (New York: Monthly Review Press, 1976). Copyright © 1976 by Horace B. Davis. Reprinted by permission of Monthly Review Foundtation.

formulation of those practical social and political reforms which the class-conscious proletariat needs and demands in the framework of bourgeois society to facilitate the class struggle and their ultimate victory. The elements of a political program are formulated with definite aims in mind: to provide a direct, practical, and feasible solution to the crucial problems of political and social life, which are in the area of the class struggle of the proletariat; to serve as a guideline for everyday politics and its needs; to initiate the political action of the workers' party and to lead it in the right direction; and finally, to separate the revolutionary politics of the proletariat from the politics of the bourgeois and petit bourgeois parties.

The formula, "the right of nations to self-determination," of course doesn't have such a character at all. It gives no practical guidelines for the day to day politics of the proletariat, nor any practical solution of nationality problems. For example, this formula does not indicate to the Russian proletariat in what way it should demand a solution of the Polish national problem, the Finnish question, the Caucasian question, the Jewish, etc. It offers instead only an unlimited authorization to all interested "nations" to settle their national problems in any way they like. The only practical conclusion for the day to day politics of the working class which can be drawn from the above formula is the guideline that it is the duty of that class to struggle against all manifestations of national oppression. If we recognize the right of each nation to self-determination, it is obviously a logical conclusion that we must condemn every attempt to place one nation over another, or for one nation to force upon another any form of national existence. However, the duty of the class party of the proletariat to protest and resist national oppression arises not from any special "right of nations," just as, for example, its striving for the social and political equality of sexes does not at all result from any special "rights of women" which the movement of bourgeois emancipationists refers to. This duty arises solely from the general opposition to the class regime and to every form of social inequality and social domination, in a word, from the basic position of socialism. But leaving this point aside, the only guideline given for practical politics is of a purely negative character. The duty to resist all forms of national oppression does not include any explanation of what conditions and political forms the class-conscious proletariat in Russia at the present time should recommend as a solution for the nationality problems of Poland, Latvia, the Jews, etc., or what program it should present to match the various programs of the bourgeois, nationalist, and pseudosocialist parties in the present class struggle. In a word, the formula, "the right of nations to self-determination," is essentially not a political and problematic guideline in the nationality question, but only a means of *avoiding that question.* . . .

The general and cliché-like character of the ninth point in the program of the Social Democratic Labor Party of Russia shows that this way of solving the question is foreign to the position of Marxian socialism. A "right of nations" which is valid for all countries and all times is nothing more than a metaphysical cliché of the type of "rights of man" and "rights of the citizen." Dialectic materialism, which is the basis of scientific socialism, has broken once and for all with this type of "eternal" formula. For the historical dialectic has shown that there are no "eternal" truths and that there are no "rights." . . . In the words of Engels, "What is good in the here and now, is an evil somewhere else, and vice versa"—or, what is right and reasonable under some circumstances becomes nonsense and absurdity under others. Historical materialism has taught us that the real content of these "eternal" truths, rights, and formulae is determined only by the *material* social conditions of the environment in a given historical epoch.

On this basis, scientific socialism has revised the entire store of democratic clichés and ideological metaphysics inherited from the bourgeoisie. Present-day Social Democracy long since stopped regarding such phrases as "democracy," "national freedom," "equality," and other such beautiful things as eternal truths and laws transcending particular nations and times. On the contrary, Marxism regards and treats them only as expressions of certain definite historical conditions, as categories which, in terms of their material content and therefore their political value, are subject to constant change, which is the *only* "eternal" truth.

When Napoleon or any other despot of his ilk uses a plebiscite, the extreme form of political democracy, for the goals of Caesarism, taking advantage of the political ignorance and economic subjection of the masses, we do not hesitate for a moment to come out wholeheartedly against that "democracy," and are not put off for a moment by the majesty or the omnipotence of the people, which, for the metaphysicians of bourgeois democracy, is something like a sacrosanct idol.

When a German like Tassendorf or a tsarist gendarme, or a "truly Polish" National Democrat defends the "personal freedom" of strike-breakers, protecting them against the moral and material pressure of organized labor, we don't hesitate a minute to support the latter, granting them the fullest moral and historical right to *force* the unenlightened rivals into solidarity, although from the point of view of formal liberalism, those "willing to work" have on their side the right of "a free individual" to do what reason, or unreason, tells them.

When, filially, liberals of the Manchester School demand that the wage worker be left completely to his fate in the struggle with capital in the name of "the equality of citizens," we unmask that metaphysical cliché which conceals the most glaring economic inequality, and we demand, point-blank, the legal protection of the class of wage workers, thereby clearly breaking with formal "equality before the law."

The nationality question cannot be all exception among all the political, social, and moral questions examined in this way by modern socialism. It cannot be settled by the use of some vague cliché, even such a fine-sounding formula as "the right of all nations to self-determination." For such a formula expresses either absolutely nothing, so that it is an empty, noncommittal phrase, or else it expresses the unconditional duty of socialists to support all national aspirations, in which case it is simply false.

On the basis of the general assumptions of historical materialism, the position of socialists with respect to nationality problems depends primarily on the concrete circumstances of each case, which differ significantly among countries, and also change in the course of time in each country. Even a superficial knowledge of the facts enables one to see that the question of the nationality struggles under the Ottoman Porte in the Balkans has a completely different aspect, a different economic and historical basis, a different degree of international importance, and different prospects for the future, from the question of the struggle of the Irish against the domination of England. Similarly, the complications in the relations among the nationalities which make up Austria are completely different from the conditions which influence the Polish question. Moreover, the nationality question in each country changes its character with time, and this means that new and different evaluations must be made about it. Even our three national movements beginning from the time of the Kościuszko Insurrection [of 1794—Ed.] could be seen as a triple, stereotyped repetition of the same historical play (that is, "the struggle of a subjugated nationality for independence") only in the eyes of either a metaphysician of the upper-class Catholic ideology such as Szujski, who believed that Poland had a historical mission to be the "Christ of nations," or in the eyes of an ignoramus of the present-day social-patriotic "school." Whoever cuts deeper with the scalpel of the researcher—more precisely, of the historical-materialist researcher—will see beneath the surface of our three national uprisings three completely different sociopolitical movements, which took on an identical form of struggle with the invader in each case only because of external circumstances. To measure the Kościuszko Insurrection and the November and January [1863–64—Ed.] insurrections by one and the same yardstick—by the sacred laws of the "subjugated nation"—actually reveals a lack of all judgment and the complete absence of any historical and political discrimination. . . .

It is true that it sounds much more generous, and is more flattering to the overactive imagination of the young "intellectual," when the socialists announce a general and universal introduction of freedom for all existing suppressed nations. But the tendency to grant all peoples, countries, groups, and all human creatures the right to freedom, equality, and other such joys by one sweeping stroke of the pen, is characteristic only of the youthful period of the socialist movement, and most of all of the phraseological bravado of anarchism.

The socialism of the modern working class, that is, scientific socialism, takes no delight in the radical and wonderful sounding solutions of social and national questions, but examines primarily the real issues involved in these problems.

The solutions of the problems of Social Democracy are not in general characterized by "magnanimity," and in this respect they are always outdone by socialist parties which are not hampered by scientific "doctrines," and which therefore always have their pockets full of the most beautiful gifts for everyone. Thus, for example, in Russia, the Social Revolutionary Party leaves Social Democracy far behind in the agricultural question; it has for the peasants a recipe for the immediate partial introduction of socialism in the village, without the need of a boring period of waiting for the conditions of such a transformation in the sphere of industrial development. In comparison with such parties, Social Democracy is and always will be a poor party, just as Marx in his time was poor in comparison with the expansive and magnanimous Bakunin, just as Marx and Engels were both poor in comparison with the representatives of "real" or rather "philosophical" socialism. But the secret of the magnanimity of all socialists with an anarchist coloration and of the poverty of Social Democracy, is that anarchistic revolutionism measures "strength by intentions, not intentions according to strength"; that is, it measures its aspirations only by what its speculative reason, fumbling with an empty utopia, regards as "good" and "necessary" for the salvation of humanity. Social Democracy, on the other hand, stands firmly on historical ground in its aspirations, and therefore reckons with historical possibilities. Marxian socialism differs from all the other brands of socialism because, among other things, it has no pretensions to keeping patches in its pocket to mend all the holes made by historical development.

Actually, even if as socialists we recognized the immediate right of all nations to independence, the fates of nations would not change an iota because of this. The "right" of a nation to freedom as well as the "right" of the worker to economic independence are, under existing social conditions, only worth as much as the "right" of each man to eat off gold plates, which, as Nicolaus Chernyshevski wrote, he would be ready to sell at any moment for a ruble. In the 1840s the "right to work" was a favorite postulate of the Utopian Socialists in France, and appeared as an immediate and radical way of solving the social question. However, in the Revolution of 1848 that "right" ended, after a very short attempt to put it into effect, in a terrible fiasco, which could not have been avoided even if the famous "national workshops" had been organized differently. An analysis of the real conditions of the contemporary economy, as given by Marx in his *Capital*, must lead to the conviction that even if present-day governments were forced to declare a universal "right to work," it would remain only a fine-sounding phrase, and not one member of the rank and file of the reserve army of labor waiting on the sidewalk would be able to make a bowl of soup for his hungry children from that right.

Today, Social Democracy understands that the "right to work" will stop being an empty sound only when the capitalist regime is abolished, for in that regime the chronic unemployment of a certain part of the industrial proletariat is a necessary condition of production. Thus, Social Democracy does not demand a declaration of that imaginary "right" on the basis of the existing system, but rather strives for the abolition of the system itself by the class struggle, regarding labor organizations, unemployment insurance, etc., only as temporary means of help.

In the same way, hopes of solving all nationality questions within the capitalist framework by insuring to all nations, races, and ethnic groups the possibility of "self-determination" is a complete utopia. And it is a utopia from the point of view that the objective system of political and class forces condemns many a demand in the political program of Social Democracy to be unfeasible in practice. For example, important voices in the ranks of the international workers' movement have expressed the conviction that a demand for the universal introduction of the eight-hour day by legal enactment has no chance of being realized in bourgeois society because of the growing social reaction of the ruling classes, the general stagnation of social reforms, the rise of powerful organizations of businessmen, etc. Nonetheless, no one would dare call the demand for the eight-hour day a utopia, because it is in complete accordance with the progressive development of bourgeois society.

However, to resume: the actual possibility of "self-determination" for all ethnic groups or otherwise defined nationalities is a utopia precisely because of the trend of historical development of contemporary societies. Without examining those distant times at the dawn of history when the nationalities of modern states were constantly moving about geographically, when they were joining, merging, fragmenting, and trampling one another, the fact is that all the ancient states without exception are, as a result of that long history of political and ethnic upheavals, extremely mixed with respect to nationalities. Today, in each state, ethnic relics bear witness to the upheavals and intermixtures which characterized the march of historical development in the past. Even in his time, Marx maintained that these national survivals had no other function but to serve as bastions of the counterrevolution, until they should be completely swept from the face of the earth by the great hurricane of revolution or world war. . . .

The development of *world powers*, a characteristic feature of our times growing in importance along with the progress of capitalism, from the very outset condemns all small nations to political impotence. Apart from a few of the most powerful nations, the leaders in capitalist development, which possess the spiritual and material resources necessary to maintain their political and economic independence, "self-determination," the independent existence of smaller and petty nations, is an illusion, and will become even more so. The return of all, or even the majority of the nations which are today oppressed, to independence would only be possible if the existence of small states in the era of capitalism had any chances or hopes for the future. Besides, the big-power economy and politics—a condition of survival for the capitalist states—turn the politically independent, formally equal, small European states into mutes on the European stage and more often into scapegoats. Can one speak with any seriousness of the "self-determination" of peoples which are formally independent, such as Montenegrins, Bulgarians, Rumanians, the Serbs, the Greeks, and, as far as that goes, even the Swiss, whose very independence is the product of the political struggles and diplomatic game of the "Concert of Europe"? From this point of view, the idea of insuring all "nations" the possibility of self-determination is equivalent to reverting from Great-Capitalist development to the small medieval states, far earlier than the fifteenth and sixteenth centuries.

The other principal feature of modern development, which stamps such an idea as utopian, is capitalist *imperialism*. The example of England and Holland indicates that under certain conditions a capitalist country can even completely skip the transition phase of "national state" and create at once, in its manufacturing phase, a colony-holding state. The example of England and Holland, which, at the beginning of the seventeenth century, had begun to acquire colonies, was followed in the eighteenth and nineteenth centuries by all the great capitalist states. The fruit of that trend is the continuous destruction of the independence of more and more new countries and peoples, of entire continents.

The very development of international trade in the capitalist period brings with it the inevitable, though at times slow ruin of all the more primitive societies, destroys their historically existing means of "self-determination," and makes them dependent on the crushing wheel of capitalist development and world politics. Only complete formalist blindness could lead one to maintain that, for example, the Chinese nation (whether we regard the people of that state as one or several nations) is today really "determining itself." The destructive action of world trade is followed by outright partition or by the political dependence of colonial countries in various degrees and forms. And if Social Democracy struggles with all its strength against colonial policy in all its manifestations, trying to hinder its progress, then it will at the same time realize that this development, as well as the roots of colonial politics, lies at the very foundations of capitalist production, that colonialism will inevitably accompany the future progress of capitalism, and that only the innocuous bourgeois apostles of "peace" can believe in the possibility of today's states avoiding that path. The struggle to stay in the world market, to play international politics, and to have overseas territories is both a necessity and a condition of development for capitalist world powers. The form that best serves the interests of exploitation in the contemporary world is not the "national" state, as Kautsky thinks, but a state bent on conquest. When we compare the different states from the point of view of the degree to which they approach this ideal, we see that it is not the French state which best fits the model, at least not in its European part which is homogeneous with respect to nationality. Still less does the Spanish state fit the model; since it lost its colonies, it has shed its imperialist character and is purely "national" in composition. Rather do we look to the British and German states as models, for they are based on national oppression in Europe and the world at large—and to the United States of America, a state which keeps in its bosom like a gaping wound the oppression of the Negro people, and seeks to conquer the Asiatic peoples. . . .

The formula of the "right of nations" is inadequate to justify the position of socialists on the nationality question, not only because it fails to take into account the wide range of historical conditions (place and time) existing in each given case and does not reckon with the general current of the development of global conditions, but also because it ignores completely the fundamental theory of modern socialism—the theory of social classes.

When we speak of the "right of nations to self-determination," we are using the concept of the "nation" as a homogeneous social and political entity. But actually, such a concept of the "nation" is one of those categories of bourgeois ideology which Marxist theory submitted to a radical

revision, showing how that misty veil, like the concepts of the "freedom
of citizens," "equality before the law," etc., conceals in every case a definite
historical content.

In a class society, "the nation" as a homogeneous sociopolitical entity
does not exist. Rather, there exist within each nation, classes with antag-
onistic interests and "rights." There literally is not one social area, from
the coarsest material relationships to the most subtle moral ones, in which
the possessing class and the class-conscious proletariat hold the same attitude, and in which they appear as a consolidated "national" entity. In the
sphere of economic relations, the bourgeois classes represent the interests
of exploitation—the proletariat the interests of work. In the sphere of
legal relations, the cornerstone of bourgeois society is private property; the
interest of the proletariat demands the emancipation of the propertyless
man from the domination of property. In the area of the judiciary, bourgeois society represents class "justice," the justice of the well fed and the
rulers; the proletariat defends the principle of taking into account social
influences on the individual, of humaneness. In international relations, the
bourgeoisie represent the politics of war and partition, and at the present
stage, a system of trade war; the proletariat demands a politics of universal
peace and free trade. In the sphere of the social sciences and philosophy,
bourgeois schools of thought and the school representing the proletariat
stand in diametric opposition to each other. The possessing classes have
their world view; it is represented by idealism, metaphysics, mysticism,
eclecticism; the modern proletariat has its theory—dialectic materialism.
Even in the sphere of so-called universal conditions—in ethics, views on
art, on behavior—the interests, world view, and ideals of the bourgeoisie
and those of the enlightened proletariat represent two camps, separated
from each other by an abyss. And whenever the formal strivings and the
interests of the proletariat and those of the bourgeoisie (as a whole or in
its most progressive part) seem identical—for example, in the field of
democratic aspirations—there, under the identity of forms and slogans, is
hidden the most complete divergence of contents and essential politics.

There can be no talk of a collective and uniform will, of the self-
determination of the "nation" in a society formed in such a manner. If we
find in the history of modern societies "national" movements, and struggles for "national interests," these are usually class movements of the ruling

strata of the bourgeoisie, which can in any given case represent the interest of the other strata of the population only insofar as under the form of "national interests" it defends progressive forms of historical development, and insofar as the working class has not yet distinguished itself from the mass of the "nation" (led by the bourgeoisie) into an independent, enlightened political class. . . .

Social Democracy is the class party of the proletariat. Its historical task is to express the class interests of the proletariat and also the revolutionary interests of the development of capitalist society toward realizing socialism. Thus, Social Democracy is called upon to realize not the right of nations to self-determination but only the right of the working class, which is exploited and oppressed, of the proletariat, to self-determination. From that position Social Democracy examines all social and political questions without exception, and from that standpoint it formulates its programmatic demands. Neither in the question of the political forms which we demand in the state, nor in the question of the state's internal or external policies, nor in the questions of law or education, of taxes or the military, does Social Democracy allow the "nation" to decide its fate according to its own vision of self-determination. All of these questions affect the class interests of the proletariat in a way that questions of national-political and national-cultural existence do not. But between those questions and the national-political and national-cultural questions, exist usually the closest ties of mutual dependence and causality. As a result, Social Democracy cannot here escape the necessity of formulating these demands individually, and demanding actively the forms of national-political and national-cultural existence which best correspond to the interests of the proletariat and its class struggle at a given time and place, as well as to the interests of the revolutionary development of society. Social Democracy cannot leave these questions to be solved by "nations."

9

THEORY AND PRACTICE

(1910; EXCERPT)

In 1906, after the 1905 revolutionary upsurge in Russia and Eastern Europe, Rosa Luxemburg wrote her classic The Mass Strike, the Political Party, and the Trade Unions, *which has been widely reprinted and is available in English in various sources. Soon it became clear that the revisionist theoreticians whom she had targeted in earlier years were a reflection of a deep-rooted reformist practice in the German workers movement. While criticizing Bernstein, "orthodox Marxist" intellectuals such as Luxemburg's own friend Karl Kautsky defended the reformist policies of the German party and trade union leadership. With increasing urgency, Luxemburg argued that a practical implementation of the revolutionary orientation associated with the "mass strike" concept was essential if the movement's day-to-day practice was to be consistent with its Marxist theory—and with the needs and interests of the working class as a whole. She elaborates on these and related points in this 1910 polemic with Kautsky in the Marxist theoretical journal* Neue Zeit.

From *Theory and Practice*, trans. David Wolff (Chicago: News and Letters, 1980). Reprinted with permission from *News and Letters*.

II

And now to the mass strike. To explain his unexpected stand against the slogan of the mass strike in the latest Prussian voting rights campaign, Comrade Kautsky created a whole theory of two strategies: the "strategy of overthrow" and the "strategy of attrition." Now Comrade Kautsky goes a step farther, and constructs ad hoc yet another whole new theory of the conditions for political mass strikes in Russia and in Germany.

He begins with general reflections on the deceptiveness of historical examples, and how plausibly one can, with insufficient caution, find appropriate justification in history for all strategies, methods, aims, institutions, and earthly things in general. These observations, of a harmless nature in their initial breadth and generality, soon show their less than harmless tendency and purpose in this formulation: that it is "especially dangerous to appeal to revolutionary examples." These warnings, in spirit somewhat reminiscent of Comrade Frohme's fatherly admonitions, are directed specifically against the Russian Revolution [of 1905—Trans.]. Thereupon follows a theory intended to show and prove the total antithesis of Russia and Germany; Russia, where conditions for the mass strike exist and Germany, where they do not.

In Russia we have the weakest government in the world, in Germany the strongest; in Russia an unsuccessful war with a small Asian land, in Germany the "glory of almost a century of continuous victories over the strongest great powers in the world." In Russia we have economic backwardness and a peasantry which, until 1905, believed in the Tsar like a god; in Germany we have the highest economic development, and with it the concentrated might of the cartels which suppresses the working masses through the most ruthless terrorism. In Russia we have the total absence of political freedom; in Germany we have political freedom which provides the workers various "safe" forms for their protest and struggle, and hence they "are totally preoccupied with organizations, meetings, the press, and elections of all sorts." And the result of these contrasts is this: in Russia the strike was the only possible form of proletarian struggle, and therefore the strike was in itself a victory, even though it was planless and ineffectual—and further, because strikes were forbidden, every strike was in itself a political act. On the other hand, in Western Europe—here the German schema is extended to all of Western Europe—such "amorphous, primitive strikes" have long been outmoded: here one only strikes when a positive result can be expected.

The moral of all this is that the long revolutionary period of mass strikes, in which economic and political action, demonstration, and fighting strikes continuously alternate and are transformed one into the other, is a specific product of Russian backwardness. In Western Europe, and especially in Germany, even a demonstration mass strike like the Russian ones would be extremely difficult, almost impossible, "not in spite, but because of the half-century-old socialist movement." As a means of struggle, the political mass strike could only be employed here in a single, final battle "to the death"—and therefore only when the question, for the proletariat, was to conquer or die.

In passing only, I wish to point out that Comrade Kautsky's depiction of the Russian situation is, in the most important points, an almost total reversal of the truth. For example, the Russian peasantry did not suddenly begin to rebel in 1905. From the so-called emancipation of the serfs in 1861, with a single pause between 1885 and 1895, peasant uprisings run like a red thread through the internal history of Russia: uprisings against the landowners as well as violent resistance to the organs of government. It is this which occasioned the Minister of Interior's well-known circular letter of 1898 which placed the entire Russian peasantry under martial law. The new and exceptional in 1905 was simply that, for the first time, the peasant masses' chronic rebellion took on political and revolutionary meaning as concomitant and totalization of the urban proletariat's goal-conscious, revolutionary class action.

Even more turned around, if this is possible, is Comrade Kautsky's conception of the question's main point—the strike and mass strike actions of the Russian proletariat. The picture of chaotic, "amorphous, primitive strikes" by the Russian workers—who strike out of bewilderment, simply to strike, without goal or plan, without demands and "definite successes"—is a blooming fantasy. The Russian strikes of the revolutionary period effected a very respectable raise in wages, but above all they succeeded in almost universally shortening the working day to ten hours, and in many cases to nine. With the most tenacious struggle, they were able to uphold the eight-hour day for many weeks in St. Petersburg. They won the right to organize not only for the workers, but for the state's postal and railroad employees as well: and until the counterrevolution gained the upper hand, they defended this right from all attacks. They broke the over-lordship of the employers, and in many of the larger enterprises they cre-ated workers' committees to regulate working conditions. They undertook the task of abolishing piecework, household work, night work, factory penalties, and of forcing strict observance of Sundays off.

These strikes, from which promising union organizations rapidly sprouted in almost all industries with vigorous life, and with solid leader-ship, treasuries, constitutions, and an imposing union press—these strikes, from which as bold a creation as the famous St. Petersburg Council of Workers' Delegates was born for unified leadership of the entire move-ment in the giant empire—these Russian strikes and mass strikes were so far from being "amorphous and primitive" that in boldness, strength, class solidarity, tenacity, material gains, progressive aims, and organizational results, they could safely be set alongside any "West European" union movement. Granted, since the revolution's defeat most of the economic gains, together with the political ones, have little by little been lost. But this plainly does not alter the character which the strikes had as long as the revolution lasted.

Not "organized" and hence "planless," these economic, partial, and local conflicts continuously, "spontaneously" grew into general political and revo-lutionary mass strikes—from which, in turn, further local actions sprouted up thanks to the revolutionary situation and the potential energy of the masses' class solidarity. The course and immediate outcome of such a general polit-ical-revolutionary action was also not "organized" and elemental—as will always be the case in mass movements and stormy times. But if, like Com-rade Kautsky, one wishes to measure the progressive character of strikes and "rational strike leadership" by their immediate successes, the great period of strikes in Russia achieved relatively greater economic and social-political suc-cesses in a few years of revolution than the German union movement has in the four decades of its existence. And all this is due to neither a special heroism, nor a special genius of the Russian proletariat: it is simply the mea-sure of a revolutionary period's quickstep, against the leisurely gait of peaceful development within the framework of bourgeois parliamentarianism.

As Comrade Kautsky said in his *Social Revolution*, 2nd edition, p. 63:

> There remains only one objection which can be, and hence all the more frequently will be raised to this "revolutionary romanticism": that the situation in Russia proves nothing for us in Western Europe because our circumstances are fundamentally different.
>
> Naturally, I am not unaware of the differences in circumstances: but they should not, on the other hand, be exaggerated. Our Comrade Luxemburg's latest pamphlet clearly demonstrates that the Russian working class has not fallen as low and achieved as little as is generally accepted. Just as the English workers must break themselves of looking down on the German proletariat as a backward class, so we in Germany must give up viewing the Russians in the same way.

And further on:

> As a political factor, the English workers today stand even lower than the workers of the economically most backward and politically least free of European states: Russia. It is their living revolutionary Reason that gives the Russians their great practical strength; and it was their renunciation of revolution and self-limitation to immediate interests, their so-called "political realism," that made the English a zero in real politics.

But for the present, let us set aside the Russian situation and turn to Comrade Kautsky's depiction of the Prusso-German situation. Strange to say, here, too, we learn of marvels. For example, it has been until now the prerogative of East Elbian Junkerdom to live by the ennobling conviction that Prussia possesses "the strongest contemporary government." How Social Democracy, on the other hand, should in all seriousness come to acknowledge a government to be "the strongest" which "is nothing but a military despotism embellished with parliamentary forms, alloyed with a feudal admixture, obviously influenced by the bourgeoisie, shored up with a bureaucracy, and watched over by the police"—I find that somewhat hard to grasp. That foolish picture of misery, the Bethmann-Hollweg "cabinet": a government reactionary to the bone and therefore without a plan or political direction, with lackeys and bureaucrats instead of statesmen, with a whimsical zigzag course; internally the football of a vulgar Junker clique and the insolent intrigues of a courtly rabble; in its foreign policy, the football of a personal authority accountable to none; only a few years ago the contemptible shoeshine boy of the "weakest government in the world," Russian Tsarism; propped up by an army which to an enormous extent consists of Social Democrats, with the stupidest drill, the most infamous mistreatment of soldiers in the world—this is the "strongest contemporary government"! In any case, a unique contribution to the materialist conception of history, which until now has not deduced the "strength" of a government from its backwardness, hatred of culture, "slavish obedience," and police spirit.

Besides, Comrade Kautsky has done yet more for this "strongest government": he has even wooed her with the "glory of almost a century of continuous victories over the strongest great powers in the world." In the veterans' associations they have lived, until now, solely on the "glorious campaign" of 1870. To construe his "century" of Prussian glory, Comrade Kautsky has apparently added in the Battle of Jena—as well as the Hunn Campaign in China led by our Count Waldersee,★ and Trotha's victory over the Hottentot women and children in the Kalahari.†

But as it says in Comrade Kautsky's beautiful article of December 1906, "The State of the Reich," at the end of a long and detailed description:

★[In 1899 the anti-imperialist popular uprising of I Ho Ch'uan broke out in north China; it was bloodily suppressed by the allied armies of eight imperialist powers under supreme command of the German army's chief of staff, Albert Graf von Waldersee. German participation became known as the "Hunn Campaign" through a speech by Kaiser Wilhelm II to the departing troops of the China expedition, which Luxemburg recalled in her speech of May 27, 1913, "The World Political Situation": "Then came the Hunn Campaign in China, to which Wilhelm II sent the soldiers with the slogan: Quarter will not be given, prisoners will not be taken. The soldiers were to wreak havoc like the Hunns so that for a thousand years no Chinese would dare cast squinting, envious eyes on a German." *Gesammelte Werke*, Vol. 3, p. 214.—Trans.]

†[From 1904 to 1907 the Nama, a Khoikhoi people ("Hottentot" was the derogatory Afrikander name for all Khoikhoi) and the Hereros fought a guerrilla war against German colonial rule in Namibia, then known as German Southwest Africa. The uprising ended with the devastating defeat of these peoples, after which German colonial troops were employed against them with the utmost cruelty. Luxemburg analyzed it in her speech of June 14, 1911, "Our Struggle for Power." (See chapter 2 of Raya Dunayevskaya's work-in-progress, *Ross Luxemburg, Women's Liberation, and Marx's Philosophy of Revolution*, published in *News and Letters*, April 1980.)—Trans.]

Comparing the Reich's shining outward state at its beginning with the present situation, one must confess that never has a more splendid inheritance of might and prestige been more rashly squandered . . . , never in its history has the German Reich's position in the world been weaker, and never has a German government more thoughtlessly and willfully played with fire than at the present time.[1]

Of course, at that time the main thing was to paint the shining electoral victory that awaited us in the 1907 elections★ and the overwhelming catastrophes which, according to Comrade Kautsky, would inevitably follow it—with the same inevitability with which he now has them follow the next Reichstag election.

On the other hand, from his depiction of economic and political conditions in Germany and Western Europe, Comrade Kautsky constructs a strike policy which—measured against reality—is a downright astonishing fantasy. "The worker," Comrade Kautsky assures us, "in Germany—and throughout Western Europe as a whole—takes up the strike as a means of struggle only when he has the prospect of attaining *definite successes* with it. If these successes fail to appear, the strike has failed its purpose." With this discovery, Comrade Kautsky has pronounced a harsh judgment on the practice of German and "West European" unions. For what do the strike statistics in Germany show us? Of the 19,766 strikes and lockouts we have had, in all, from 1890 to 1908, an entire quarter (25.2 percent) were wholly unsuccessful; almost another quarter (22.5 percent) were only partly successful; and less than half (49.5 percent) were totally successful.[2]

These statistics just as crassly contradict the theory of Comrade Kautsky that because of the effective development of the workers' organizations as well as the cartels, "the struggles between these organizations likewise grow ever more centralized and concentrated" and on this account "ever more *infrequent*." In the decade 1890 through 1899, we had a total of 3,722 strikes and lockouts in Germany; in the nine years 1900

★[Reichstag elections of 1907 became known as the "Hottentot elections" because the Chancellor, von Bülow, campaigned on an imperialist platform intended to brand Social Democrats as traitors. Although Social Democracy raised its total vote count by almost 300,000, it lost 38 seats due to the apportionment of electoral districts and a second ballot alliance of the bourgeois parties.—Trans.]

through 1908, the time of greatest growth for both cartels and unions, we
had 15,994. So little are strikes growing "ever more infrequent" that they
have rather grown four times as numerous in the last decade. And while in
the previous decade 425,142 workers took part in strikes, in the last nine
years 1,709,415 did; once again four times as many, and thus on the
average approximately the same number per strike.

According to the schema of Comrade Kautsky, one quarter to one half of
all these union struggles in Germany have "failed their purpose." But every
union agitator knows very well that "definite successes" in the form of material gains absolutely are not and cannot be the sole purpose, the sole determining aspect in economic struggles. Instead, union organizations "in Western
Europe" are forced step by step into a position which compels them to take
up the struggle with limited prospects of "definite successes": as specifically
shown by the statistics of purely defensive strikes, of which a whole 32.5 percent turned out completely unsuccessful. That such "unsuccessful" strikes
have, nevertheless, not "failed their purpose"; that on the contrary they are a
direct condition of life for the defense of the workers' standard of living, for
sustaining the workers' fighting spirit, for impeding future onslaughts by the
employers: these are the elementary ground rules of German union practice.

And further, it is generally known that besides a "definite success" in
material gains, and indeed *without* this success, strikes "in Western Europe"
have perhaps their most important effect as beginning points of union *organization*: and it is specifically in backward places and hard-to-organize
branches of labor that such "unsuccessful" and "ill-advised" strikes are
most common, from which over and over arise the foundations of union
organization. The history of the Vogtland textile workers' struggles and
sufferings, whose most famous chapter is the great Crimmitschau strike,★
is but a single testimony to this. The "strategy" which Comrade Kautsky
has now set forth is not merely incapable of directing a great political mass
action, but even a normal union movement.

★[In August 1903, 8,000 textile workers in Crimmitschau struck for pay raises and a
ten-hour day. In spite of state intervention and the decree of limited martial law in Crimmitschau, all attempts to break the strike were frustrated by the determination of the
workers, which was strengthened by the solidarity of the German and international
working class: but the intervention of reformist union leaders forced them to return to
work without any gains in January 1904.—Trans.]

But the above-mentioned schema for "West European" strikes has yet another gaping hole—just at the point, in fact, where the economic struggle brings the question of the mass strike, and thus our own proper theme, into consideration. That is, this schema entirely excludes the fact that it is just "in Western Europe" where ever longer, more violent strikes without much "plan" break like an elemental storm over those regions where a great exploited mass of proletarians stands opposed to the concentrated ruling power of capital or the capitalistic state; strikes which grow not "ever more infrequent" but ever more frequent; which mostly end without any "definite successes" at all—but in spite, or rather just because of this are of greater significance as explosions of a deep inner contradiction which spills over into the realm of politics. These are the periodic giant strikes of the *miners* in Germany, in England, in France, in America; these are the spontaneous mass strikes of the *farm workers*, as they have occurred in Italy and in Galicia; and further, the mass strikes of the *railroad workers* which break out now in this state, now in that one.

As it says in Comrade Kautsky's excellent article on "The Lessons of the Miners' Strike" of 1905 in the Ruhr district:

In this way alone can substantial advances be realized for the miners. The strike against the mine owners has become hopeless: from now on the strike must step forward as *political*; its demands, its tactics must be calculated to set legislation in motion. . . .

And Comrade Kautsky continues:

This new union tactic of the *political strike*, of uniting union and political action, is in fact the only one which remains possible for the miners; and it is the only one certain to reanimate union as well as parliamentary action, and to give heightened aggressive strength to both.

It could appear, perhaps, that here under "political action" we are to understand parliamentary action and not political mass strikes. Comrade Kautsky destroys every doubt, declaring point-blank:

But the great decisive actions of the struggling proletariat will be fought out more and more through various sorts of political strikes. And here

practice strides forward faster than theory. For while we discuss the political strike and search for its theoretical formulation and confirmation,
one mighty political mass strike after another flames up through the
spontaneous combustion of the masses—or rather every mass strike
becomes a political action, every great political test of strength climaxes
in a mass strike, whether among the miners, the proletariat of Russia, the
Italian farm workers and railroad workers, etc.[3]

So wrote Comrade Kautsky on March 11, 1905.

Here we have "the spontaneous combustion of the masses" and the
union leadership, economic struggle and political struggle, mass strikes and
revolution, Russia and Western Europe in the most beautiful confusion, all
rubrics of the schema fused together in the living interconnection of a
great period of fierce social storms.

It seems that "theory" does not merely "stride forward" more slowly
than practice: alas, from time to time it also goes tumbling backwards.

III

We have briefly examined the factual basis of Comrade Kautsky's newest
theory on Russia and Western Europe. But the most important thing
about this latest creation is its general tendency, which runs on to construct
an absolute contradiction between revolutionary Russia and parliamentary
"Western Europe," and sets down the prominent role played by the political mass strike in the Russian Revolution as a product of Russia's economic and political *backwardness*.

But here Comrade Kautsky finds himself in the disagreeable position
of having proved much too much. In this case, somewhat less would have
been decidedly more.

Above all, Comrade Kautsky has not noticed that his current theory
destroys his earlier theory of the "strategy of attrition." At the center of the
"strategy of attrition" stands an allusion to the coming Reichstag elections.
My inexcusable error lay in this: I held that the mass strike was already
called for in the present struggle for Prussian voting rights, while Comrade
Kautsky declared that our overwhelming victory-to-come in next year's

Reichstag elections would create the "entirely new situation" which might make the mass strike necessary and appropriate. But now Comrade Kautsky has demonstrated with all desirable clarity that conditions for a period of political mass strikes in Germany—indeed, in all of Western Europe—are lacking after all. "Because of the half-century old socialist movement, Social Democratic organization and political freedom," even simple demonstration mass strikes of the extent and momentum of the Russian ones have become almost impossible in Western Europe.

Yet if this is so, then prospects for the mass strike after Reichstag elections seem fairly problematic. It is clear that all the conditions which make the mass strike absolutely impossible in Germany—the strongest contemporary government and its glittering prestige, the slavish obedience of the state employees, the unshakable opposing might of the cartels, the political isolation of the proletariat—that all this will not suddenly disappear after next year. If the reasons which speak against the political mass strike no longer lie in the situation of the moment, as the "strategy of attrition" would have it, but in the direct results of "half a century of socialist enlightenment and political freedom," in the highly developed level of "Western Europe's" economic and political life—then postponement of expectations for a mass strike until the year after the Reichstag elections turns out to be no more than a modest fig leaf covering the "strategy of attrition's" only real content: the commendation of Reichstag elections. In my first reply★ I tried to show that in reality the "strategy of attrition" amounted to "Nothing-But-Parliamentarianism." Now Comrade Kautsky himself confirms this in elaborating his theories.

Yet more. Comrade Kautsky has, to be sure, postponed the great mass action until after the Reichstag elections: but at the same time he must admit that in the present situation, the political mass strike could become necessary "at any moment"—for "never in the history of the German Reich were the social, political, and international contradictions under such tension as now."† But if in general the social conditions and historic ripeness of "Western Europe," and specifically of Germany, make a mass strike action impossible now, how can such an action suddenly "at any moment" be set

---

★[Rosa Luxemburg, "Attrition or Collision?"—Trans.]
†[K. Kautsky, "What Now?" *Neue Zeit* XXVIII, 2 (15 April 1910): 80—Trans.]

in motion? A brutal provocation by the police, a massacre at a demonstration could greatly heighten the masses' agitation and sharpen the situation: yet it obviously could not be that "great occasion" which would abruptly overturn the entire economic and political structure of Germany.

But Comrade Kautsky has proved yet another superfluous thing. If the general economic and political conditions in Germany are such as to make a mass strike action like the Russian one impossible, and if the extension which the mass strike underwent in the Russian Revolution is the specific product of Russian *backwardness*, then not only is the use of the mass strike in the Prussian voting rights struggle called into question, but the Jena resolution as well. Until now, the resolution of the Jena party convention [of 1905—Trans.] was regarded both here and abroad as such a highly significant announcement because it officially borrowed the mass strike from the arsenal of the Russian Revolution, and incorporated it among the tactics of German Social Democracy as a means of political struggle. Admittedly this resolution was formally so composed, and by many exclusively interpreted so that Social Democracy seemed to declare it would only turn to the mass strike in case of an attack on Reichstag voting rights. But once, in any case, Comrade Kautsky did not belong to those formalists; indeed, in 1904 he emphatically wrote:

> If we learn one thing from the Belgian example, it is that it would be a fatal error for us in Germany to commit ourselves to a specific time for proclaiming the political strike—*for example, in the event of an attack on the present Reichstag voting rights.*[4]

The chief significance, the essential content of the Jena resolution lay not in this formalistic "commitment," but in the fact of German Social Democracy's principled acceptance of the lessons and example of the Russian Revolution. It was the spirit of the Russian Revolution which ruled the convention of our party in Jena. And now when Comrade Kautsky directly derives the role of the mass strike in the Russian Revolution from Russian *backwardness*, thereby constructing a contradiction between revolutionary Russia and parliamentary "Western Europe"; when he emphatically warns against the examples and methods of revolution—yes, when by implication even the proletariat's defeat in the Russian Revolution is debited in his account to the grandiose mass strike action, through which the proletariat "must eventually be exhausted"—in short, when Comrade Kautsky declares point-blank "but be that as it may, the schema of the Russian mass strike before and during the revolution does not fit German conditions": then from *this* standpoint it seems an incredible blunder, that German Social Democracy officially borrowed the mass strike directly from the Russian Revolution as a new means of struggle. At bottom, Comrade Kautsky's current theory is a frightfully fundamental revision of the Jena resolution.

To justify his individual, cockeyed stand in the last Prussian voting rights campaign, Comrade Kautsky step-by-step sells out the lessons of the Russian Revolution—the most significant extension and enrichment of proletarian tactics in the last decade.

IV

In light of the conclusions which follow from Comrade Kautsky's newest theory, it now becomes clear how very false, from the ground up, this theory is. To derive the mass strike action of the Russian proletariat, unparalleled in the history of modern class struggle, from Russia's social backwardness—in other words, to explain the outstanding importance and leading role of the urban industrial proletariat in the Russian Revolution as Russian "backwardness"—is to stand things right on their heads.

It was not economic retardation, but precisely the high development of capitalism, modern industry, and commerce in Russia which made that grandiose mass strike action possible, and which caused it. It was just because the urban industrial proletariat was already so numerous, concentrated in the great centers, and so strongly moved by class consciousness, just because the genuine modern capitalist contradiction had progressed so far, that the struggle for political freedom could be decisively led by this proletariat alone. But because of this it could be no purely constitutional struggle after the liberal formula, but a genuine modern class struggle in all its breadth and depth, fighting for the economic as well as the political interests of the workers—against capital as well as Tsarism, for the eight-hour day as well as a democratic constitution. And only because capitalist industry and the modern means of commerce bound to it had become a condition of existence for the state's economic life, could the mass strikes of the proletariat in Russia realize such a staggering, decisive-effect; that the revolution celebrated its victories with them, and with them went down in defeat and grew silent.

At this moment I can think of no more exact formulation of the factors in question here, than that which I gave in my pamphlet on the mass strike in 1906:

> We have seen that the mass strike in Russia represents not the synthetic product of a deliberate Social Democratic tactic, but a natural historic figure on the ground of the present revolution. What are the forces in Russia now which have brought forth this new manifestation of revolution?
>
> The immediate task of the Russian Revolution is putting an end to absolutism and establishing a modern bourgeois-parliamentary constitutional state. Formally, this is exactly the same task faced by the March Revolution in Germany and by the Great Revolution in France at the end of the eighteenth century. But the circumstances, the historic milieu in which these formally analogous revolutions took place, are fundamentally different from those of today's Russia. The difference in circumstances is the entire cycle of capitalist development which has run between those bourgeois revolutions in the West and the present bourgeois revolution in the East. That is, this development has not seized the Western European lands alone, but absolutist Russia as well. Large scale industry with all its consequences—the modern class division, the glaring social contrasts, modern metropolitan life and the modern proletariat—has become the leading form of production in Russia (i.e., the decisive one for its social development).
>
> But from this has resulted a strange, contradictory historical situation: that a revolution whose formal objectives are bourgeois will be carried out under the leadership of a modern, class-conscious proletariat, and in an international milieu which stands under the sign of bourgeois democracy's downfall. Now the bourgeoisie is not the leading revolutionary element it was in the earlier revolutions of the West, when the proletarian mass, dissolved in the petty bourgeoisie, served as its military levies. All is reversed: the class-conscious proletariat is the leading, driving element; the big bourgeois strata are in part directly counterrevolutionary, in part weakly liberal; only the rural petty bourgeoisie, along

with the urban petty bourgeois intelligentsia, are decidedly oppositional, indeed revolutionary minded. But the Russian proletariat, so clearly destined for the leading role in the bourgeois revolution, is itself free from all illusions about bourgeois democracy—and therefore it enters the struggle with a strongly developed consciousness of its own specific class interests in the acutely sharpened opposition of capital and labor.

This contradictory state of affairs is expressed in the fact that in this formally bourgeois revolution, bourgeois society's opposition to absolutism will be commanded by the proletariat's opposition to bourgeois society; that the proletariat's struggle will be simultaneously directed, with equal force, against absolutism and capitalist exploitation; that the program of revolutionary struggle is directed, with equal emphasis, toward political freedom and the eight-hour day, as well as a material existence for the proletariat worthy of humanity. *This two-fold character of the Russian Revolution manifests itself in that inner unity and reciprocal action of economic and political struggle in which we have been instructed by the events in Russia, and which finds its natural expression in the mass strike.* . . .

So the mass strike shows itself to be no specifically Russian product, arising from absolutism, but a universal form of proletarian class struggle resulting from the present stage of capitalist development and class relations. From this standpoint, the three bourgeois revolutions—the Great French Revolution, the German March Revolution, and the present Russian one—form an on-running chain of development in which the prosperity and the end of the capitalist century are reflected. . . .

The present revolution realizes, in the special circumstances of absolutist Russia, the universal results of international capitalist development: and in this *it seems less a final descendant of the old bourgeois revolutions than a forerunner of a new series of proletarian revolutions in the West.* Just because it has so inexcusably delayed its bourgeois revolution, the most backward land shows *ways and methods of extended class struggle for the proletariat of Germany and the most advanced capitalist lands.*★

Earlier, Comrade Kautsky also viewed the Russian Revolution in the same historical perspective. In December 1906, in complete agreement with my interpretation, he wrote:

★[Rosa Luxemburg, *The Mass Strike, the Political Party, and the Trade Unions*—Trans.]

We may most speedily master the lessons of the Russian Revolution and the tasks which it sets us, if we regard it as neither a bourgeois revolution in the traditional sense nor a socialist one, but as a wholly unique process taking place on the border line between bourgeois and socialist society; it demands dissolution of the one, prepares for the formation of the other, and in either case brings all of humanity under capitalist civilization a mighty step forward in its march of development.[5]

If thus one grasps the real social and historical conditions which lie at the root of the Russian Revolution's specific new form of struggle, the mass strike action—and another interpretation is not very well possible without phantasizing the *actual* course of this action out of thin air, as Comrade Kautsky now does with his "amorphous, primitive strikes"— then it is clear that mass strikes as the form of the proletariat's revolutionary struggle come into consideration even more for Western Europe than in Russia, to the extent which capitalism (in Germany, for example) is much more highly developed.

In fact, all the conditions which Comrade Kautsky mobilizes against the political mass strike are just so many forces which must make the mass strike action in Germany even more inevitable, extensive, and powerful.

The opposing might of the cartels which Comrade Kautsky invokes, "searching" in vain "for its like," the slavish obedience in which the enormous category of German state employees is sunken—these are the very things which make a peaceful, profitable union action ever more difficult for the bulk of the German proletariat. They feed ever mightier trials of strength and explosions in the economic sphere, whose elemental character and mass extension take on more and more political meaning the longer they continue.

It is just the political isolation of the proletariat in Germany to which Comrade Kautsky refers, just the fact that the united bourgeoisie down to the last petty bourgeois stands behind the government like a wall, that shapes every great political struggle against the government into a struggle against the bourgeoisie, against exploitation. And the same circumstances guarantee that every energetic revolutionary mass action in Germany will not take parliamentary forms of liberalism or the previous form of the revolutionary petty bourgeoisie's struggle, the brief barricade battle, but the classic proletarian form of the mass strike.

And finally: it is just because we in Germany have "a half century of socialist enlightenment and political freedom" behind us, that as soon as the situation has so ripened that the masses take to the field, the action of the proletariat set in motion by every political struggle will roll together all ancient reckonings against private and state exploitation, and unite the political with an economic mass struggle. For, as Comrade Kautsky wrote in 1907:

> We have not the slightest ground to assume that the degree of exploitation of the German proletariat is less than that in Russia. On the contrary, we have seen that with the advance of capitalism the exploitation of the proletariat increases. If the German worker is in a somewhat better position than the Russian, the productivity of his labor is also much greater, and his needs in relation to the general national standard of living are much higher: so that the German worker finds the capitalist yoke perhaps even more galling than the Russian does.[6]

Comrade Kautsky, who paints in such splendid colors how the German worker is "totally preoccupied with organizations, meetings, and elections of all sorts," has for the moment forgotten the quite enormous slave herds of Prusso-German state employees, railroad workers and postal workers, as well as the farm workers, who unfortunately enjoy very limited measure of that contented preoccupation with "organizations, meetings, and options of all sorts" as long as the right to organize is legally or practically denied them. He has forgotten that in the midst of royal Prussian freedom these enormous categories live politically as well as economically in genuine "Russian" conditions, and that therefore these very categories—not to mention the miners—will find it impossible, in the midst of a political convulsion, to maintain their slavish obedience or to refrain from presenting their special bill of reckoning in the form of giant mass strikes.

But let us look at "Western Europe." In disputing all this, Comrade Kautsky has yet another opponent besides myself to deal with: reality. Specifically, what do we see here when we only direct our attention to the most important mass strikes of the last ten years?

The great Belgian mass strikes which won universal suffrage stand by themselves in the '90s as a bold experiment. Nevertheless, what depth and multidimensionality!

In 1900 the mass strike by the miners in Pennsylvania which, according to the testimony of American comrades, did more to spread socialist ideas than ten years of agitation; also in 1900, mass strike by the miners in Austria; 1902, mass strike by the miners in France; 1902, general strike by all production workers in Barcelona in support of the struggling metal workers; 1902, demonstration mass strike in Sweden for universal, equal suffrage; 1902, mass strike in Belgium for universal, equal suffrage; 1902, mass strike by the farm workers in all east Galicia (over 200,000 taking part) in defense of the right to organize; 1903, in January and April, two mass strikes by the railroad workers in Holland; 1904, mass strike by the railroad workers in Hungary; 1904, demonstration mass strike in Italy protesting the massacres in Sardinia; in January 1905, mass strike by the miners in the Ruhr district; in October 1905, demonstration mass strike in and around Prague (by 100,000 workers) for universal, equal suffrage in Bohemian Landtag elections; in October 1905, demonstration mass strike in Lemburg for universal, equal suffrage in Galician Landtag elections; in November 1905, demonstration mass strike in all of Austria for universal, equal suffrage in Reichsrat elections; 1905, mass strike by the Italian farm workers; 1905, mass strike by the Italian railroad workers; 1906, demonstration mass strike in Triest for universal, equal suffrage in landtag elections *which victoriously forced the reform through*; 1906, mass strike by the foundry workers in Witkowitz (Mähren) in support of 400 shop stewards fired because of the May Day celebration—victoriously concluded; 1909, mass strike in Sweden in defense of the right to organize; 1909, mass strike by the postal workers in France; in October 1909, demonstration mass strike by all workers in Trient and Rovereto protesting the political persecution of Social Democracy; 1910, mass strike in Philadelphia in support of the streetcar workers' struggle for the right to organize; and at this moment, preparations for a mass strike by the railroad workers in France.

This is the "impossibility" of "West European" mass strikes, especially demonstration mass strikes, which Comrade Kautsky has so beautifully demonstrated in black and white. Comrade Kautsky has theoretically proved the obvious impossibility of mixing political and economic strikes, the impossibility of impressive, general demonstration mass strikes, the impossibility of mass strikes being a *period* of repeated hand-to-hand combat. He has forgotten that for the last ten years we have lived in a period of economic, political, fighting, and demonstration strikes; a period which has extended, with striking unity, over almost all "West European lands" as well as the United States; over the capitalistically most backward like Spain, and the most advanced like North America; over lands with the weakest union movements like France, and those with strapping Social Democratic unions like Austria; over agrarian Galicia and highly industrialized Bohemia; over half-feudal states like the Hapsburg monarchy, republics like France, and absolutist states like Russia. And of course, in addition to the above enumerated stands Russia's grandiose mass strike action from 1902 to 1906, which has shown how the significance and extent of the mass strike initially grow together with the revolutionary situation and the political action of the proletariat.

> For while we discuss the political strike and search for its theoretical formulation and confirmation, one mighty political mass strike after another flames up through the spontaneous combustion of the masses—or rather every mass strike becomes a political action, every great political test of strength climaxes in a mass strike, whether among the miners, the proletariat of Russia, the Italian farm workers and railroad workers, etc.[7]

From this it almost seems as if Comrade Kautsky, through his newest theory of the impossibility of a period of political mass strikes in Germany, has demonstrated not so much a contradiction between Russia and Western Europe as a contradiction between Germany and the rest of the world—Western Europe and Russia thrown in together. Prussia must in fact be the exception among all capitalist lands, if what Comrade Kautsky has worked out on the impossibility of even short general demonstration mass strikes in Prussia is true. It would be "entirely unthinkable that in a demonstration strike against the government here, commuter railways, streetcars, and gas works come to a standstill," that we in Germany experience a demonstration strike which "alters the entire landscape, and in so doing makes the deepest impression on the entire bourgeois world as well as the most indifferent strata of the proletariat." But then what is "unthinkable" in Germany must be what has already proved itself possible in

Galicia, in Bohemia, in Italy, in Trieste and Trento, in Spain, and in
Sweden. In all these lands and cities, splendid demonstration strikes have
taken place which completely altered "the landscape." In Bohemia on
November 20, 1905, an absolute, general work stoppage reigned which
extended even to *agriculture*—a thing they have not yet experienced in
Russia. In Italy in September 1904 the farm workers, streetcars, electric
and gas works took a holiday, and even the daily press had to stop publication. "It has indeed become the most total general strike," wrote the
Neue Zeit, "that history knows of: for three whole days the city of Genoa
was left without light and bread and meat; all economic life was paralyzed."[8] In Sweden's capital Stockholm, in 1902 as well as 1909, all means
of communication and commerce—streetcars, cabs, wagons, municipal
services—were shut down in the first week. In Barcelona in 1902, all economic life rested for many days.

And so in Prusso-Germany—with its "strongest contemporary government," and its special "German conditions" which supposedly show
proletarian methods of struggle, possible in all the rest of the world, to be
all sorts of impossibilities—we have finally acquired an unexpected counterpart to those special "Bavarian" and "south German" conditions which
Comrade Kautsky once so heartily derided with us. But in particular,
these German "impossibilities" plume themselves on the fact that precisely
in Germany we have the strongest party, the strongest unions, the best
organization, the greatest discipline, the most enlightened proletariat, and
the greatest influence of Marxism. By this method we would come, in
fact, to the singular conclusion that the stronger Social Democracy is, the
more powerless the proletariat. But I believe that to say mass strikes and
demonstration strikes which were possible in various other lands are
impossible today in Germany, is to fix a brand of incapacity on the
German proletariat which it has as yet done nothing to deserve.

V

What actually remains of Comrade Kautsky's mass strike theory, after he
has pointed out all the "impossibilities"? The one, "final," pure political
mass strike, disengaged from economic strikes: which once only, but with

absolute conclusiveness, smashes down like thunder out of the clear blue sky. Says Comrade Kautsky:

> Here, in this conception, lies the deepest ground of the differences between my friends and me over the mass strike. They anticipate a *period of mass strikes*. Under the existing conditions in Germany, I can imagine a political mass strike only as *a one-time event* into which the entire proletariat of the Reich enters with its entire strength; as a struggle to the death; as a struggle which either overthrows our enemies, or smashes—or at least cripples—the totality of our organizations and our entire strength for years on end.

As for this image of the "final mass strike" which swims before Comrade Kautsky, one must first of all say that it is, at any rate, a totally new creation: for it is not drawn from reality, but out of pure "imagination." For not only does it fit no Russian pattern: not *one* mass strike of the many which have taken place in "Western Europe" or the United States approximately resembles the exemplar which Comrade Kautsky has invented for Germany. None of the mass strikes known till now was a "final" struggle "to the death"; none led to the total victory of the workers, but none "smashed the totality of organizations and the entire strength" of the proletariat "for years on end." Success was mostly a partial and an indirect one. The miners' giant strikes usually ended in a direct defeat: but as a further consequence, they realized important social reforms through their pressure—in Austria the nine-hour day, in France the eight-hour day. The most important consequence of the Belgian mass strike in 1893 was the conquest of universal, unequal suffrage. Last year's Swedish mass strike, formally concluded with a compromise, actually warded off a general attack by the confederated business world on the Swedish unions. In Austria, demonstration strikes have mightily hastened electoral reform. The mass strikes of the farm workers, with their formal partial ineffectiveness, have greatly strengthened the *organization* among the farm workers of Italy and Galicia. *All* mass strikes, whether economic or political, demonstration or fighting strikes, have contained what Comrade Oda Olberg so compellingly described in her report of the Italian railroad workers' strike in the *Neue Zeit*:

The achievements of the political mass strike are incalculable: its worth continuously grows with the degree of proletarian class consciousness. A political strike carried out with energy and solidarity is never lost, because it *is* what it *aims at*—a developing exercise of the proletariat's power in which the fighters steel their strength and sense of responsibility, and the ruling classes become conscious of their adversary's might.[9]

But if until now every mass strike without exception, "West European" as well as Russian, in direct contradiction to Comrade Kautsky's newest schema has brought on neither the total victory nor the destruction of the proletariat, but on the contrary an almost invariable *strengthening* of the workers' organizations, class consciousness, and self-confidence, then on the other side the question arises: how can that great and "final," that apocalyptic mass strike in which the stoutest oaks crack, the earth bursts asunder and the graves open actually come to pass in Germany, if the mass of the proletariat has not previously been prepared, schooled, and aroused by an entire lengthy *period* of mass strikes, of economic or political mass struggles?

According to Comrade Kautsky, "the entire proletariat of the Reich" will plunge into this "final" mass strike, and what is more "with its entire strength." But how are the Prusso-German state employees, the railroad workers, postal workers, etc., who today are paralyzed in "slavish obedience," the farm workers who have no right to organize and no organization, the broad strata of workers still stuck in enemy organizations in Christian, Hirsch-Dunckerist,* yellow unions—in short, the great mass of the German proletariat whom we have not yet reached with our union organization or Social Democratic agitation—how are they suddenly, with one leap, to be ready for a "final" mass strike "to the death" unless a preceding period of tempestuous mass struggles, demonstration strikes, partial mass strikes, giant economic struggles, etc., loosens them little by little from their paralysis, their slavish obedience, their fragmentation, and incorporates them among the followers of Social Democracy?

---

*[The German Christian (Catholic) and Hirsch-Duncker unions were antisocialist—the latter were also opposed to strikes. In 1907, 14.9 percent of all German union members belonged to these unions; about another 4 percent belonged to various "independent" unions, some of which were openly controlled by the employers.—Trans.]

Even Comrade Kautsky had to see this. "Naturally," he says, "I do not imagine this one-time event as an isolated act 'shot from a pistol.' I, too, expect an era of embittered mass struggles and mass actions, but with the mass strike as the *final* weapon." But what "mass struggles and mass actions" does Comrade Kautsky have in mind which will lead to that "final" mass strike, which do not themselves consist of the mass strike? Could it be street demonstrations? But one cannot simply hold street demonstrations for decades on end. And Comrade Kautsky certainly rules out general, impressive demonstration strikes for Germany: indeed, it is "entirely unthinkable that in a demonstration strike against the government here, commuter railways, streetcars, and gas works come to a standstill." Likewise, economic mass strikes could not accomplish that preparation for the political mass strike; according to Comrade Kautsky they are to be kept at a strict distance from the political mass strike, to him they are not at all beneficial but even—almost harmful. Of what, finally, shall those "embittered" mass struggles and mass actions of the preparatory era consist? Perhaps of "embittered" Reichstag elections, or meetings with protest resolutions? But those enormous strata of the unorganized or oppositionally organized proletariat, upon whom the "final" mass strike depends, unfortunately stay away from our meetings. And so it is utterly impossible to conceive how we will actually win, arouse, and school the "entire proletariat of the Reich" for the final struggle "to the death."

Whether Comrade Kautsky wishes it or not, his final mass strike, just in ruling out a *period* of the mass strike's economic and political character, comes at us simply shot from a pistol.

But finally, one must ask: what kind of a "final" mass strike is this, that comes only *once* and in which the entire proletariat of the Reich will grapple to the death? Should we understand by this a *periodic* "final" mass strike which in every great political campaign—for example, for Prussian voting rights, to prevent the outbreak of war, etc.—will finally give the decision? But one cannot periodically struggle "to the death" again and again. Painted thus, a mass strike in which the "entire proletariat" grapples "with its entire strength" "to the death" can only be the struggle for total political power in the state: obviously the "final" struggle "to the death" can only be that in which the proletariat wrestles for its dictatorship and to finish off the bourgeois class-state. In this way, the political mass strike for Germany withdraws farther and farther. First, through the "strategy of attrition" it was expected the year after the Reichstag elections: now it vanishes from sight as the "final," the solitary mass strike and teases us, from beyond the blue horizon, with—the social revolution.

Let us now recall the stipulations which Comrade Kautsky, in his first article "What Now?" attaches to accomplishment of the political mass strike—strictest secrecy of preparations, decision-making by the supreme "war council" of the party, the greatest possible surprise of the enemy— and we unexpectedly receive a mental image which bears a strong resemblance to the "final Great Day" of the general strike after the anarchist formula. The idea of the mass strike is transformed from a historical process of the modern proletarian class struggles in their decades-long period of conclusion, into a free-for-all in which the "entire proletariat of the Reich," with one jolt, suddenly brings down the bourgeois social order.

But what did Comrade Kautsky write in 1907 in his *Social Revolution*, 2nd edition, p. 54?

> That is nonsensical. A general strike in which *all* workers in a country cease their labors at a given signal presupposes a unaminity and organization of the workers which can hardly be reached in the present society—and if it were reached, would be so irresistible as to dispense with the general strike. But such a strike, with one jolt, would suddenly render not merely the existing society, but every existence impossible— that of the proletarians even sooner than that of the capitalists. It would thus infallibly break at the very moment it began to unfold its revolutionary effect.
>
> As a means of political struggle, the strike could hardly (certainly not in the foreseeable future) assume the form of a strike by *all* workers in a country. . . . We face a period when the isolated, nonpolitical strike will be as hopeless against the superior strength of the cartels as the isolated parliamentary action of the workers' parties is against the force of the capitalist-controlled state power. It will become ever more urgent for each to supplement the other and draw new strength from their joint action.
>
> *Like the use of every new weapon, that of the political strike must first be learned.*

And so the more Comrade Kautsky turned to broad theoretical generalizations to justify his position in the Prussian voting rights struggle, the more he lost sight of the general perspective of the development of the class struggle in Western Europe and in Germany—which in previous years he never tired of pointing out. Indeed, he himself had an uncomfortable sense of his present viewpoint's incongruence with his earlier one, and was therefore good enough to completely reproduce his 1904 article series "Revolutionaries Everywhere" in the final, third part of his reply to me. The crass contradiction is not thereby done away with: it has only resulted in the chaotic, flickering character of that article's last part, which so remarkably lessens one's pleasure in reading it.

But not that article series alone is in shrill dissonance with what Comrade Kautsky now advances. In his *Social Revolution*, we read that we will enter a whole lengthy period of revolutionary struggles in which the political mass strike will "surely play a great role" (p. 54). The entire pamphlet *The Road to Power* is devoted to the depiction of the same perspective. Yes, here we have already entered into the revolutionary period. Here Comrade Kautsky reviews the "political testament" of Friedrich Engels and declares the time of the "strategy of attrition," which consists of legal exploitation of the given state groundwork, to be already past:

> At the beginning of the '90s, I acknowledged that a peaceful development of proletarian organizations and the proletarian class struggle on the given state groundwork would bring the proletariat farthest forward in the situation of that time. And so you cannot reproach me with a craving for the intoxication of revolution and radicalism when my observation of the present situation leads me to the view *that conditions have fundamentally changed since the beginning of the '90s, that we have every reason to assume we have entered into a period of struggles for the state institutions and state power*: struggles which under manifold changes of fortune *could be drawn out for decades*, whose forms and duration are unforeseeable at present, but which will most probably bring about a considerable increase in the proletariat's power in the foreseeable future, if not indeed its total power in Western Europe.

And farther on:

But in this universal instability, the immediate tasks of the proletariat are clearly given. We have already developed them. *There will be no further progress without altering the state groundwork on which we wage the struggle.* To most energetically strive for democracy in the Reich, but also in the individual states—specifically in Prussia and Saxony—that is its first task in Germany; its first international task is the struggle against geopolitics and militarism.

As clearly visible as these problems are the means at our command for their solution. To those previously employed is now added the mass strike, which we had already theoretically accepted at the beginning of the '90s, and whose applicability under favorable circumstances has since then been repeatedly demonstrated.[10]

In his *Social Revolution,* in *The Road to Power,* in the *Neue Zeit,* Comrade Kautsky preached the "political strike" to the German unions as the "new tactic" which would be compelled more and more as the cartels condemned the pure union strike to more and more ineffectiveness. Indeed it was this concept which led him, in bygone years, to an embittered feud with the *Correspondence Bulletin* of the General Commission of Unions.

Now Comrade Kautsky would strictly sever economic strikes from political action. Now he declares that all strikes in Western Europe must unconditionally achieve "definite successes" or they have "failed their purpose"; and as the means of "organizing the proletariat, heightening its insight and sense of strength, and increasing the masses' confidence in their organizations," he counts only "*successfully* fought campaigns for higher wages." After all, we need nothing so urgently now as "visible successes" to impress the masses. "But there are few successes which so visibly document our mounting strength to the masses as electoral victories, as the conquest of new mandates." Thus, Reichstag elections and mandates—that is Moses and the prophets!

Now we hear that the German worker is only ready for "safe" demonstrations, that "a mere demonstration strike is not even the most impressive" form of political protest, that "a victorious Reichstag election makes a far greater impact"! And finally "a real mass demonstration" worth anything at all, "which is not required for immediate defense, but which simply protests an injustice already existing for over half a century": such a demonstration strike "without a powerful motive" would hardly be possible in Germany. Comrade Kautsky has simply not noticed that with his argumentation he has, in passing, leaked out the finest theoretical ground for—*the abolition of May Day.*

Comrade Kautsky quite rightly reminds us that "even before the Russian Revolution" he gave an exact description of the working of a political mass strike in his article "Revolutionaries Everywhere." But it seems to me that what matters is not merely to sketch revolutionary struggles and their external course in theoretical abstraction—that is, in Never-Never Land—and to project their general schema: it is equally a matter of giving, at the same time, those slogans in practice which will release the maximum of the proletariat's revolutionary energy and drive the situation forward the farthest and fastest.

Granted, in his numerous articles and his pamphlets Comrade Kautsky has given us, with compelling clarity, a picture of the revolutionary struggles of the future. For example, in his 1904 description of the mass strike he already showed how "every mansion, every granary, every factory, every telegraph office, every stretch of railroad is militarily guarded"; how the soldiers are loosed upon the masses everywhere, and how in spite of this it never comes to a battle "for wherever they come the masses scatter, to reassemble wherever the soldiers have not yet arrived or have just left"; how first "gas and electric works shut down, streetcars stop running, finally even the mails and railroads are seized by the strike fever; first the state workers strike, then the junior civil servants as well"—in short, all is here with a three-dimensionality, life, and realism that are all the more remarkable, in that he deals with events coming at us out of the blue sky. But when from these aetherial heights, where theory calmly circles like an eagle, the question first plunged to the flat land of the Prussian voting rights campaign, then suddenly the brainless and planless Prussian government was transfigured into a *rocher de bronze* [rock of bronze—Trans.]; the German conditions depicted in *The Road to Power* as ready for social revolution (Hurrah! March on! March on!) turned into a frozen land where "it is absolutely unthinkable" that workers in state workshops and civil servants, be they junior or senior, take part in a demonstration; and the "revolutionary era which is arising" transformed itself into an industrious preparation for Reichstag elections, for "there are few successes which so visibly document our strength to the masses" as—Reichstag mandates.

Heaven-storming theory—and "attrition" in practice; most revolutionary perspectives in the clouds—and Reichstag mandates as sole perspective in reality. Comrade Kautsky declared his campaign against me with the urgent necessity of rescuing the idea of the mass strike from compromise. I fear it would have been better for the idea of the mass strike as well as Comrade Kautsky, if this rescue had been forborne.

VI

Let us return to Prussia.

At the beginning of March, in view of the voting rights campaign which had begun and the mounting demonstration movement, I declared that if the party wished to lead the movement farther forward it must make the slogan of the mass strike the order of the day, and that a demonstration mass strike would be the first step toward this in the present situation. I considered that the party faced a dilemma: it would either raise the voting rights movement to sharper forms or, as in 1908, the movement would go back to sleep after a short time. Indeed, this was what summoned Comrade Kautsky to the field of battle against me.

And what do we see? Comrade Kautsky points out that, me to the contrary, we have certainly not experienced a hint of a mass strike; he triumphs that the situation has struck my initiative "dead as a doornail." Now it seems that in his polemic zeal, Comrade Kautsky has completely overlooked something else that has unfortunately been struck "dead as a doornail"; namely the demonstrations, and with them the voting rights movement itself.

Comrade Kautsky argues against me that an intensification of the demonstrations is entirely unnecessary, that the party faces no dilemma, that the main thing is "to bring about the wider employment of street demonstrations—not to slacken in this, but on the contrary to make them ever mightier."[11] Well, since April the street demonstrations have totally ceased. And not, indeed, through some lack of enthusiasm and fighting spirit among the masses: their inner creativity has not gone to sleep. No, the street demonstrations were simply *called off* by the leading party authorities in the face of the struggles and endeavors of the provinces, as the 1st of May has shown, as the May demonstrations in Breslau and Braunschweig have further shown—deliberately called off. Just as I wrote in my first reply in the *Neue Zeit*, even at the end of March—without awaiting the further course of events and of the situation—under pressure of the mood of the provinces, they arranged the April 10 demonstration with the feeling: An end to this at last! And an end has been made. No demonstrations, not even meetings take up the voting rights question, the storm-breathing rubric of the voting rights struggle has disappeared from the party press. And this circumstance can serve as surest symptom that the thing, for the time being, is over and no longer actual: that our leading central organ *Vorwärts* began to concern itself with tactics in the voting rights struggle. "The popular movement in the grand style" is meanwhile sent back home.

What does Comrade Kautsky say to this? Does he who brought "Jest, Satire, Irony, and Deeper Meaning"★ to bear on me venture the slightest word of reproach to the "higher authorities" who, despite his warning "not to slacken in the street demonstrations," have plainly killed the demonstration movement? On the contrary: here Comrade Kautsky is all admiration, he can find only words of wonder for "the latest demonstration campaign" which "was the model of a successful strategy of attrition." Quite right. This is just how it looks in practice, this "strategy of attrition" which, "worn down" by two bold steps forward, rests on its laurels and lets the crashing overture of the "popular movement in the grand style" run down into the gentle purring of preparations for Reichstag elections.†

★[*Jest, Satire, Irony, and Deeper Meaning* is the title of a comedy by Christian Dietrich Grabbe.—Trans.]

†[Luxemburg is alluding to a passage from Section 3 of Marx's *The Eighteenth Brumaire of Louis Bonaparte.* "But the revolutionary threats of the petty bourgeoisie and their democratic representatives are merely attempts to intimidate the opponent. And when they have run themselves up a blind alley, when they have so compromised themselves that they are forced to act out their threats, then this is done in an ambiguous way that shuns nothing more than the means to the end and snatches at pretexts for defeat. The crashing overture which proclaimed the struggle dies down into a gentle purring as soon as the struggle is supposed to begin, the actors cease to take themselves *au sérieux,* and the performance falls as flat as an air-filled balloon pricked with a pin."—Trans.]

So the voting rights movement is again brought to a standstill for one, perhaps two years: and what is more, at such a well-chosen moment that we have rendered the government the greatest service anyone could have possibly done it.

The withdrawal of the suffrage bill by Bethmann-Hollweg was the decisive moment. The government was in a tight corner. The parliamentary patchwork of electoral reform and the parliamentary horse-trading were bankrupt. The enemy was at the end of his rope. If we really were serious about practicing the "voting rights storm," about the slogan "no peace in Prussia," about the great words of the Prussian party convention, then the collapse of the government bill was the given moment to immediately launch a general, grandiose attack out of this fiasco of parliamentary action with the cry "Give us a new bill!" with street demonstrations across the whole country which would then have led to a demonstration mass strike and mightily driven the struggle forward. Comrade Kautsky, who has most graciously proposed to acknowledge such brain storms as "armed" assembly in Treptower Park* application of my "strategy," has here a clear example of what "my strategy" really calls for. Not childish Don Quixoteries like those Comrade Kautsky demands of me, but political exploitation of the enemy's defeat as the only victory—which, moreover, is not so much the discovery of some "new strategy," but rather the ABC of every revolutionary, yes, of every serious battle tactic.

That was the party's task. And I am not here pronouncing the party's unqualified duty to open a "revolutionary period" every Monday and Thursday. But I feel that *if* the party begins an action, *if* it has summoned up the storm and called its men-at-arms the people to the field of battle, if it has spoken of a "popular movement in the grand style" and attack "by all forces"—then it dare not, after two advances, suddenly scratch its head, gape about, and declare: "Never mind . . . we didn't mean it seriously this

*[Berlin police chief Traugott Yon Jagow had banned street demonstrations with his "public notice" of February 13, 1910: "The 'right to the streets' is being proclaimed. The streets are exclusively for the purpose of commerce. Resistance to state authority will result in the use of weapons. I warn the curious." Berlin Social Democracy called a demonstration in Treptower Park on March 6, 1910, for democratic voting rights; as the police were waiting there in force it was redirected to the Berlin zoo, where 150,000 demonstrated for free, equal, and universal suffrage before the police arrived.—Trans.]

time . . . let's go home." In my opinion such storm-mongering on approval and at word of command is unworthy of the party's greatness and the seriousness of the situation, and inclined to discredit the party in the eyes of the masses. Further, the voting rights and demonstration movement which had begun was an excellent opportunity for arousing and enlightening the indifferent masses, and for winning unsympathetically minded circles of workers as our regular agitation is not in the least in a position to do. By deliberately stopping the movement short, the party has left this splendid opportunity unexploited after the most beautiful beginning.

But further, and above all, political points of view come into question. It is most shortsighted to mechanically divide the question of Prussian electoral reform from the question of Reichstag voting rights and to declare that our big guns won't go into action over the Prussian voting rights struggle, that we'll save them in case Reichstag voting rights are annulled after the Reichstag elections. Plainly, one must deliberately close one's eyes to the actual interconnections not to see that in the present situation, struggle for Prussian electoral reform is essentially nothing other than struggle for Reichstag voting rights. It is clear that an energetic and victorious campaign for Prussian voting rights is the surest way to parry, in advance, a blow against Reichstag voting rights. The resolute and persistent follow-through of the voting rights struggle would simultaneously have been a defensive action against the reaction's hankering for a coup d'état—an action which would have had all the advantages of an offense over a forced defense.

Now Comrade Kautsky objects—and this is his last trump—that since the mass strike has not, as we see, broken out, that is the best proof how little it flowed from the situation and how mistaken my standpoint was:

> But the very fact that it is still being debated shows that the situation is still not this ripe. As long as one can still dispute and investigate whether or not the mass strike is opportune, the proletariat as a collective mass is not filled with that mass exasperation and sense of strength which are necessary if the mass strike is to be accomplished. If the necessary mood for it had been present in March, then a dissuasive voice like mine would have been smothered under a protest of raging anger.

Here Comrade Kautsky shows an interesting oscillation between ex-
tremes: now the mass strike is a coup carefully hatched in the inner
sanctum of the war council, secretly prepared in whispers; now it is "an
elemental upheaval whose commencement cannot be brought about at
will, which one can await but not arrange." I feel that the task of the Social
Democratic Party and its leadership consists in neither the secretive
hatching of "great plans" nor the "awaiting" of elemental upheavals. Mass
strikes—as I clearly stated in my first article in the Dortmund *Arbeiter-
Zeitung*—cannot be "made" by an order from the "supreme command,"
they must arise from the masses and their advancing action. But *politically*,
in the sense of an energetic tactic, a powerful offensive, to so lead this
action forward that the masses are ever more conscious of their tasks—that
the party can do, and that is also its duty. Social Democracy cannot artificially create a revolutionary mass movement; but, circumstances permit-
ting, it can certainly cripple the finest mass action through its wavering,
feeble tactics. Proof is furnished by the aborted, or rather, the immediately
countermanded voting rights mass strike of 1902 in Belgium.★ How
effectively the party can prevent a mass strike, this "elemental upheaval,"
by putting on the brakes under certain circumstances, even when the
masses are battle-ready to the highest degree—Comrade Kautsky himself
has reported this with regard to Austria. "But even though," he tells us,

> Even though conditions in Austria favor a mass strike far more than they
> do here, and even though the Austrian masses were temporarily aroused
> to a level from which we in Germany remain far distant, to such an agi-
> tation that they could only be held back from launching into a mass
> strike by the utmost exertion of all forces; and finally, even though
> repeatedly and in the most positive way "threatened" with the mass
> strike, the comrades responsible for the tactics of the party have violently
> put on the brakes and prevented one up till now.[12]

★[On April 14, 1902, a mass strike began in Belgium in which over 300,000 workers
took part. It was broken off on April 20 by the General Council of the Belgian Workers'
Party, although the demands for changes in suffrage and the related constitutional amendment had been rejected on April 18 by the Belgian chamber.—Trans.]

It is self-explanatory that this obstructive role of the party leadership could appear most actively in Germany, in view of the extraordinarily developed organizational centralism and discipline in our party. As I earlier wrote in my article "What Next?":

> In a party where, as in Germany, the principle of organization and party discipline is so unprecedentedly cherished, and where in consequence the initiative of unorganized popular masses—their spontaneous, so to speak improvised capacity for action, such a significant, often decisive factor in all previous great political struggles—is nearly ignored, then it is the inescapable duty of the party to demonstrate the worth of this so highly developed organization and discipline even for great actions, and their worth even for other forms of struggle than parliamentary elections.

The past fate of the Prussian voting rights movement almost seems to demonstrate that our organizational apparatus and our party discipline prove themselves better, just now, at braking than at leading great mass actions. When even in advance the street demonstrations are timidly and reluctantly worked out; when every necessary opportunity to raise the demonstrations to a higher power—like March 18, like the 1st of May—is embarrassingly shunned; when our own victories like the conquest of our right to the streets on April 10, as well as the defeats of the enemy like the withdrawal of the government bill are left totally unexploited; when finally the demonstrations are put back on the shelf after all and the masses are sent home; in short, when everything is done to hold back, to cripple the mass action, to deaden the militancy: then obviously that tempestuous movement cannot arise from the masses, which must vent itself in a mass strike.

Naturally the obstructive effect of such leadership is most nearly decisive when the action is still in its initial stages—as is the case with us in Germany, where it is just taking its first steps. If once the revolutionary period is fully unfolded, if the clouds of battle are already rising high, then no brake-pulling by the party leaders will be able to accomplish much, for the masses will simply shove aside their leaders who set themselves against the storm of the movement. Thus could it also happen in Germany, one day. But in the interest of Social Democracy, I find it neither necessary nor desirable to steer that way. If we in Germany unquestioningly wait with the mass strike until the masses, with "raging anger," storm right over their brake-pulling leaders, this obviously can happen only at the expense of the influence and prestige of Social Democracy. And then it could easily appear that the complicated organizational apparatus and the strict party discipline of which we are justly proud are, unfortunately, only a first-rate makeshift for the parliamentary and union daily routine; and with the given disposition of our leading circles they are a *hinderance* to the mass action in the grand style, to what is demanded by the coming era of violent struggles.

And in the same connection, another especially weak point in our organizational relations could have a disastrous effect. If the union leaders had publicly come out on their own against the slogan of the mass strike in the latest voting rights campaign, it would only have clarified the situation and sharpened the critique of the masses. But that they didn't have to do this, that instead through the medium of the party and with the aid of the party apparatus they could throw the total authority of Social Democracy into the balance to put the brakes on the mass action—*that* has brought the voting rights movement to a standstill, and Comrade Kautsky has merely provided the theoretical music.

Yet in spite of all this our cause moves forward. The enemy works for us so unceasingly, it is through no merit of our own that we're in the clover both in and out of season. Yet in the end it is not the task of the class party of the proletariat simply to live on the sins and errors of its enemies despite its own errors, but to accelerate the course of events through its own energy and to release, not the minimum, but the maximum of action and class struggle in that impulse.

And when in the future the mass action again arises, then the party will face exactly the same problem it did two years ago and last spring. After these two trials, the broad circles of our party comrades must from now on clearly understand that a real mass action in the grand style can only be kindled and at length maintained when treated, not as a dry practice piece played to the time of the party leadership's baton, but as a great class struggle in which all significant economic conflicts must be utilized to the full and all forces which arouse the masses must be guided into the vortex of the movement, and in which one doesn't shun a mounting intensification of the situation and decisive struggles, but goes to meet them with resolute, consistent tactics. Perhaps the present discussion will contribute its part to this.

Notes

1. *Neue Zeit* xxv, 1, p. 427.

2. *Correspondence Bulletin of the General Commission of German Unions*, 1909, Nr. 7, Statistical Supplement.

3. *Neue Zeit*, XXIII, 1, pp. 780, 781.

4. "Revolutionaries Everywhere," *Neue Zeit* XXII, 1, p. 736. My emphasis.

5. "Driving Forces and Perspectives of the Russian Revolution," *Neue Zeit* XXV, 1, p. 333.

6. *The Social Revolution*, 2nd ed., p. 60.

7. K. Kautsky, "The Lessons of the Miners' Strikes," *Neue Zeit* XXIII [1], p. 781.

8. Oda Olberg, "The Italian General Strike," *Neue Zeit* XXIII, 1, p. 19.

9. *Neue Zeit* XXIII, 2, p. 385.

10. *The Road to Power*, pp. 53, 101. My emphasis.

11. "What Now?" *Neue Zeit*, 15 April 1910, p. 71.

12. *Neue Zeit* XXIV, 2, p. 856.

10

THE ACCUMULATION OF CAPITAL— AN ANTI-CRITIQUE

(1915; EXCERPTS)

While Luxemburg was a partisan of revolutionary Marxism, she rejected an inclination of many to treat all of the writings of Marx and Engels as holy dogma. She saw her major economic study, The Accumulation of Capital *(1913), partly as a correction of mistakes and limitations in Marx's masterwork* Capital, *and at the same time as an analysis of imperialist realities that had developed after Marx died—the dynamics of capitalist accumulation made economic expansion and exploitative aggression into less developed regions a necessity. In her view, this was a key element in explaining the eruption of World War I among those capitalist powers that were competing for access to the markets, raw materials and investment opportunities in the less developed areas. Many Marxists challenged her criticisms of Marx as well as her own economic analysis, one of the most formidable being Otto Bauer. While in prison for opposing the war, Luxemburg produced her response,* The Accumulation of Capital—An Anti-Critique *(1915), which she herself felt was a work of greater strength and clarity. The opening and closing of that work are offered here.*

From *The Accumulation of Capital—An Anti-Critique*, ed. Kenneth Tarbuck (New York: Monthly Review Press, 1972). Copyright © 1974 by Kenneth Tarbuck. Reprinted by permission of Monthly Review Foundation.

175

The Question at Issue

*H*abent sua fata libelli—books have their fates. When I wrote my *Accumulation* a thought depressed me from time to time: all followers of Marxist doctrine would declare that the things I was trying to show and carefully substantiate were self-evident. Nobody would voice a different opinion; my solution of the problem would be the only possible one imaginable. It turned out very differently: a number of critics in the Social Democratic press declared that the book was totally misguided to start with and that such a problem calling for solution did not exist at all. I had become the pitiful victim of a pure misunderstanding. There were events connected with the publication of my book which must be called rather unusual. The "review" of the *Accumulation* which appeared in *Vorwärts** of 16 February 1913 was striking in tone and content even to the less involved reader; and all the more astonishing since the criticized book is purely theoretical and strictly objective, and directed against no living Marxist. Not enough. Against those who had published a positive review of the book a high-handed action was taken by the central organ. A quite unique and somehow funny event—a purely theoretical study on an abstract scientific problem was censured by the entire staff of a political daily paper (of whom probably two at the most may have read the book). They did this by denying to men like Franz Mehring† and J. Karski‡ any expert knowledge of economics, but allowed only those who pulled my book to pieces to be "experts." Such a fate has happened to no other party

---

*[*Vorwärts* was the central daily newspaper of the Social Democratic Party of Germany, SPD, published in Berlin.—Trans.]

†[Franz Mehring (1846–1919). Biographer of Karl Marx and close collaborator of Rosa Luxemburg in her antiwar propaganda, 1914–18. Joined the SPD at the age of forty-six and was a brilliant contributor to its newspapers and journals. With Luxemburg and Liebknecht, he helped to found the Spartakus League in 1919 which was the immediate forerunner of the KPD (Communist Party of Germany).—Trans.]

‡[J. Karski, pseudonym for Julian Marchlewski. He was one of the leaders of the SDKP (Social Democracy of the Kingdom of Poland). Karski worked for many years in Germany as an SPD journalist. In 1919 he went to Russia and became an active member of the Bolshevik party. Died in 1925.—Trans.]

publication as far as I know and over the decades Social Democratic publishers have certainly not produced all gold and pearls. All these events
clearly indicate that there have been other passions touched on, one way
or another, than "pure science." But to judge that properly one has first to
know at least the main points of the material in question.

What is this so vehemently opposed book about?

To the reading public some external accessories like frequently used
mathematical formulae seem to be a great deterrent. In the criticism of my
book these formulae are especially the focus. Some of the esteemed critics
have undertaken to teach me a lesson by constructing new and even more
complicated formulae. The sheer sight of them brings quiet horror to the
ordinary mortal. We shall see that my critics' preference for the formulae
is not a matter of chance, but linked very closely to their points of view
on the subject. Yet the problem of accumulation is itself purely economic
and social; it does not have anything to do with mathematical formulae
and one can demonstrate and comprehend it without them. Marx uses
constructed mathematical models in the section on reproduction of the
gross social capital in his *Capital*, so did Quesnay, the founder of the phys-
iocratic school of economics★ as an exact science a hundred years before.
But that was simply to help in explaining and clarifying their theories. It
also assisted Marx as well as Quesnay to illustrate that the economic
processes of bourgeois society are as much determined by strict laws as the
processes of physical nature, in spite of superficial confusion and the
apparent rule of individual caprice. My writings are partly based on Marx,
partly critical of him—especially where he does not go any further into
the question of accumulation than to devise a few models and suggest an
analysis. This is where my critique begins, and so I must naturally use
Marx's formulae with Marx's models. I could not arbitrarily omit them
and I wanted especially to show the insufficiency of his line of argument.

Let us now try to understand the problem in its simplest form: the
capitalist form of production is governed by the profit motive. Production
only makes sense to the capitalist if it fills his pockets with "pure income,"

★[Physiocrats. Eighteenth-century school of economists. The main strand in their
theories was that only agricultural labour was productive. For elaboration and criticism see
Karl Marx, *Theories of Surplus Value*, pt. 1 (Moscow).—Trans.]

i.e., with profit that remains after all his investments; but the basic law of capitalist production is not only profit in the sense of glittering bullion, but constantly growing profit. This is where it differs from any other economic system based on exploitation. For this purpose the capitalist—again in contrast to other historical types of exploiters—uses the fruits of exploitation not exclusively, and not even primarily, for personal luxury, but more and more to increase exploitation itself. The largest part of the profits gained is put back into capital and used to expand production. The capital thus mounts up or, as Marx calls it, "accumulates."

As the precondition as well as the consequence of accumulation, capitalist production widens progressively. To do this, the goodwill of the capitalist is not sufficient. The process is tied to objective social conditions which can be summed up as follows. Primarily, there must be a sufficient labor force. Historically, once capitalist production is functioning and fairly consolidated, capital ensures this through its own mechanisms:

(a) by just enabling the worker to support himself for further exploitation and for reproduction;

(b) by forming a constantly available reserve army of the industrial proletariat by the proletarianization of the middle class as well as by facing the worker with the competition of machines.

After this condition is fulfilled, i.e., the proletariat is securely available for exploitation and the mechanisms of exploitation itself are governed by the wage system, a new basic condition of capital accumulation emerges— the possibility of selling the goods produced by the workers to recover, in money, the capitalist's original expenses as well as the surplus value stolen from the labor forces. "The first condition of accumulation is that the capitalist must have contrived to sell his commodities, and to reconvert into capital the greater part of the money so received."[1] A steadily increasing possibility of selling the commodities is indispensable in order to keep the accumulation a continuous process. Capital itself (as we see) creates the basic condition for exploitation. The first volume of Marx's *Capital* analyzed and described this process in detail. But what about the opportunities of realizing the fruits of this exploitation; what about the market? What do they depend on? Can capital itself, or its production mechanisms, expand its market according to its needs, in the same way that it adjusts the number of workers according to its demand? Not at all. Here capital depends on social conditions. Capitalist production has this in common with all other historical forms of production, in spite of fundamental differences between them. Objectively it has to fulfill the material needs of society, although subjectively only the profit motive matters. This subjective aim can only be reached so long as capital fulfills its objective task. The goods can be sold and the incoming profit turned into money only if these goods satisfy the requirements of society. So the continuous expansion of capitalist production, i.e., the continuous accumulation of capital, is linked to the equally continuous growth of social requirements. But what are the requirements of society? Can they somehow be more closely defined, measured, or must we depend only on this vague term? In fact, they seem intangible if one surveys the surface of day-to-day economic life from the standpoint of the individual capitalist. A capitalist produces and sells machines. His customers are other capitalists, who buy his machines to produce more goods. The one can sell more of his goods as the others expand their production. He can accumulate faster if others accumulate faster in their branches of production. This would be the "requirements of society" on which our capitalist is dependent: the need of other capitalists is the precondition for the expansion of production. Another capitalist produces and sells the means of subsistence to the workers. The more workers are employed by other capitalists (and by himself), the more goods he can sell and the more capital he can accumulate. But how can the "others" expand their plants? Obviously through the other capitalist; for example, the producers of machines, or means of subsistence, buying their goods in increasing measure.

So the social requirement, on which the accumulation of capital depends, seems at a closer look to be the accumulation of capital itself.

The more capital accumulates, the more it accumulates; it is all reduced to this blatant tautology, a dizzy circle. One cannot make out where it begins, or where the impelling force is. We are turning round in circles and the problem eludes our grasp. But it does so only for as long as we approach it from this superficial viewpoint, or examine it from the popular platform of vulgar economics, individual capital.

The pattern immediately takes shape if we approach it from the standpoint of total capital, once we see the process of capitalist production as a whole. This is the only relevant and right way. It is the standpoint Marx develops systematically for the first time in the second volume of *Capital*, and on which he bases his whole theory.

The self-sufficient existence of the individual capital is indeed only an external form, the surface of economic life, which only the vulgar economists use as their sole source of knowledge. Beneath that surface and through all contradiction of competition there remains the fact that all individual capitals in society form a whole. Then existence and movement are governed by common social laws which, with the unplanned nature and anarchy of the present system, only work behind the back of the individual capitalist. When one looks at capitalist production as a whole, then social requirements become a measurable quantity which can be divided into sections.

Let us imagine that all goods produced in capitalist society were stacked up in a big pile at some place, to be used by society as a whole. We will then see how this mass of goods is naturally divided into several big portions of different kinds and destinations.

Always, in any form of society, production has to provide two things. First it has to feed society, clothe it, and satisfy cultural needs through material goods, i.e., it must produce the means of subsistence in the widest sense of the word for all classes and ages. Secondly, each form of production must replace used up raw materials, tools, factories, and so on to allow the continued existence of society and the provision of work. Without the satisfaction of these two major requirements of any human society, cultural development and progress would be impossible. Even capitalist production with all its anarchy, and without injuring the profit motive, must meet these demands. Accordingly we will find in this aggregate of capitalist commodities produced, a large proportion for replacing the means of production used up in the year before. These are the raw materials, machinery, buildings, etc. (what Marx calls constant capital) which various capitalists must produce for each other and then exchange, so that production can be kept up in all branches. According to our assumption so far, it is capitalist business that provides all the necessary means for the work process. The exchange of commodities on the market is an internal or family matter between capitalists. The required money for this process, of course, comes out of the capitalists' pockets—as every employer must lay out the money capital in advance—and returns into the pockets of the capitalist class after the exchange on the market has taken place.

As we only assume the replacement of the means of production to its former extent, the same amount of money will suffice to keep this periodic process going and let the money return into the capitalists' pockets for a period of rest. A second large department of commodities must contain means of subsistence for the population, as in every society. But how is the population structured in capitalist society, and how does it get its means of subsistence?

Two basic structures are characteristic of the capitalist mode of production. Firstly, a general exchange of goods, i.e., nobody receives anything from the social stock of commodities without the means of purchase—money. Secondly, the capitalist wage system, i.e., the majority of the working population, must exchange its labor power with capital to acquire means of purchase, while the propertied class receives its means of subsistence only by exploiting this relationship. Thus capitalist production presupposes two great classes: capitalists and workers, who differ entirely in their acquisition of means of subsistence. The workers must be fed to maintain their labor power for further exploitation, however little their individual fates concern the capitalist. From the total quantity of commodities produced by the workers, a certain share is assigned to them by the capitalists, in direct proportion to their usefulness in production. The workers receive wages in money form to purchase these goods. By means of exchange the working class thus receives a certain sum of money every year. With this they buy their provisions from the social stock of commodities, which are, of course, the property of the capitalist; these provisions are allotted to them according to their cultural level and the stage of the class struggle. The money that initiates this second big exchange again comes out of the capitalists' pockets. Every capitalist must advance the necessary money capital to purchase his labor force—what Marx calls "variable capital"—in order to keep his enterprise going. But this money returns, down to the last penny, into the pockets of the capitalists as a class, after the worker has bought his means of subsistence (and every worker must do so to maintain himself and his family)—since it is the capitalists who sell means of subsistence to the workers as commodities. But what about their own consumption? The means of subsistence already belong to the capitalists in the form of the commodity stock before exchange, by virtue of capitalist relations, according to which all commodities—except for labor-power—come into this world as the property of the capitalist. Of course, precisely because they are commodities, the "better" class of provisions come into being as the property of many individual private capitalists. Therefore, as with constant capital, a general exchange must take place between capitalists before they can enjoy their own means of subsistence. This exchange, too, must be conducted with money, and the capitalist himself has brought the necessary amount into circulation. Once again, as with the renewal of constant capital, this is an internal, family arrangement of the employing class. Once more, this money returns whence it began—into the pockets of the capitalists as a class.

The same mechanism of capitalist exploitation which regulates the wage system ensures that the necessary amount of goods and luxuries is produced for the capitalists. If the workers only produced as much as they actually needed, then from the standpoint of capital it would be pointless to employ them. It begins to make sense when the worker provides enough to maintain his employer, over and above what he needs for himself—i.e., his wage: when he produces what Marx calls surplus value. And this surplus value has to provide, among other things, the provisions and luxuries required by the capitalists, as by any other exploiters in the course of history. All that is left for the capitalists to do is to go to the frightful bother of mutual exchange and to obtain the necessary money-means, in order to maintain the hard and spartan existence of their class and ensure its natural reproduction.

So far we have dealt with two big portions of the aggregate quantity of commodities in society: means of production to repeat the work process and means of subsistence to maintain the population, i.e., the working class and the capitalists.

Of course, what we have described could easily seem to be a creation of fancy. What living capitalist knows or cares what and how much is necessary to replace the used-up gross capital and to feed the entire population? Is it not the case that every capitalist goes blindly on producing, competing with others, and hardly sees what is happening in front of his nose? But there must obviously be invisible rules which somehow work in all this chaos of competition and anarchy, otherwise capitalist society would have been in ruins long ago. And it is the whole purpose of political economy as a science (and particularly of Marx's economic studies) to trace these hidden laws which organize the whole of society in the midst of the confusion of private enterprise. We have now to trace these objective invisible rules of capitalist accumulation—the amassing of capital through progressive extension of production. The laws which we expound here are not authoritative for the conscious actions of individual capitals; indeed, no general institution exists in society that would consciously construct and operate these laws. Consequently, production today is like a lurching drunkard, fulfilling its tasks through all these gluts and dearths, price instability and crises. But price instability and crises have only one function in society: to integrate chaotic private production into its broad general context, without which it would soon disintegrate. Let us here try to sketch, with Marx, the relation between total capitalist production and social needs. We will omit the specific capitalist *methods* of price fluctuation and crises, and concentrate on the basics.

There must be more than those two big portions of the social stock of commodities which we have dealt with so far. If the exploitation of the workers were only to permit a luxurious life for the exploiters, we would have a kind of modernized slave system of medieval feudalism, but not the modern rule of capital. Its aim and goal in life is profit in the form of money and accumulation of money capital. So the actual historical purpose of production only begins when exploitation aims beyond that. The surplus value must not only allow the capitalist class a living "befitting their rank," but must also contain a part destined for accumulation. This actual purpose is so important that workers are only employed if they produce this profit and if there is the expectation that it can be accumulated in money-form.

In our assumed total stock of commodities in capitalist society we must accordingly find a third portion, which is destined neither for the renewal of used means of production nor for the maintenance of workers and capitalists. It will be a portion of commodities which contains that invaluable part of the surplus value that forms capital's real purpose of existence: the profit destined for capitalization and accumulation. What sort of commodities are they, and who in society needs them?

Here we have come to the nucleus of the problem of accumulation, and we must investigate all attempts at solution. Could it really be the workers who consume the latter portion of the social stock of commodities? But the workers have no means beyond the wages covering bare necessities which they receive from their employers. Beyond that there is no possible chance of their being consumers of capitalist commodities, however many unsatisfied needs they may have. It is also in the interest of the capitalist class to make this portion of the gross social product and means of purchase as scarce as possible. According to the standpoint of the capitalists as a class—it is important to see this standpoint in opposition to the abstruse ideas of the individual capitalist—workers are not, like others, customers for their commodities, but simply the labor force, whose maintenance out of part of its own produce is an unfortunate necessity, reduced to the minimum society allows.

Could the capitalists themselves perhaps be the customers for that latter portion of commodities by extending their own private consumption? That might be possible, although there is enough for the ruling class in any case, even with its luxurious whims. But if the capitalists themselves were to spend the total surplus value like water there would be no accumulation. That would mean, from the standpoint of capital, a fantastic relapse into a sort of modernized slave economy, or feudalism. Of course, this is conceivable and even practiced occasionally in reverse: we could discern capitalist accumulation with forms of slavery and serfdom up until the sixties of the last century in the United States, still today in Rumania and various overseas colonies. But the other way, modern exploitation with a free wage system followed by ancient or feudal squandering of the surplus value, neglecting accumulation, this deadly sin against the *spiritus sanctus* of capital is unthinkable. Again, the standpoint of total capital differs basically from that of the individual employer. For the individual, the luxury of "high society" is a desirable expansion of sales, i.e., a splendid opportunity for accumulation. For all capitalists as a class, the total consumption of the surplus value as luxury is sheer lunacy, economic suicide, for it is the destruction of accumulation at its roots.

Who then could be the buyer and consumer of that portion of commodities whose sale is only the beginning of accumulation? So far as we have seen, it can be neither the workers nor the capitalists.

But are there not all sorts of strata in society like civil servants, military, clerics, academics, and artists which can neither be counted among the workers nor the employers? Must not all these categories of the population satisfy their needs, and could they not be the wanted purchasers of the surplus commodities? Once more: yes, they could for the individual capitalist! It is different again if we take the employers as a class, if we consider gross social capital. In capitalist society all those strata are economically only the hangers-on of the capitalist class. If we ask where the civil servants, clerics, officers, artists, etc., receive their means of purchase, we see that it is partly maintained out of the pockets of the capitalists, partly out of the wages of labor (via the indirect tax system). Economically these groups cannot be a special class of consumers, as they do not have any independent sources of purchasing power, but are included as parasites in the consumption of the two major classes, workers and capitalists.

So we still do not see any customers for the latter portion of commodities, who could initiate the process of accumulation.

In the end, the solution of the problem is quite simple. Perhaps we are acting like the rider who is desperately looking for the nag he is sitting on. Perhaps the capitalists are mutual customers for the remainder of the commodities—not to use them carelessly, but to use them for the extension of production, for accumulation. Then what else is accumulation but extension of capitalist production? Those goods which fulfill this purpose must not consist of luxurious articles for the private consumption of the capitalists, but must be composed of various means of production (new constant capital) and provisions for the workers [variable capital—Trans.].

All right, but such a solution only pushes the problem from this moment to the next. After we have assumed that accumulation has started and that the increased production throws an even bigger amount of commodities on to the market the following year, the same question arises again: where do we then find the consumers for this even greater amount of commodities? Will we answer: well, this growing amount of goods will again be exchanged among the capitalists to extend production again, and so forth, year after year? Then we have the roundabout that revolves around itself in empty space. That is not capitalist accumulation, i.e., the amassing of money capital, but its contrary: producing commodities for the sake of it; from the standpoint of capital an utter absurdity. If the capitalists as a class are the only customers for the total amount of commodities, apart from the share they have to part with to maintain the workers— if they must always buy the commodities with their own money, and

realize the surplus value, then amassing profit, accumulation for the capitalist class, cannot possibly take place.

They must find many other buyers who receive their means of purchase from an independent source, and do not get it out of the pocket of
the capitalist like the laborers or the collaborators of capital, the government officials, officers, clergy, and liberal professions. They have to be consumers who receive their means of purchase on the basis of commodity
exchange, i.e., also production of goods, but taking place outside of capitalist commodity production. They must be producers, whose means of
production are not to be seen as capital, and who belong to neither of the
two classes—capitalists or workers—but who still have a need, one way or
another, for capitalist commodities.

But where are those buyers? Apart from the capitalists with their en-
tourage of hangers-on, there are no other classes or strata in society today.

Here we get down to the heart of the problem. Marx, in the second
volume of *Capital*, as in the first, presupposes that capitalist production is
the sole and exclusive mode of production. He says in the first volume:

> Here we take no account of export trade, by means of which a nation
> can change articles of luxury either into means of production or means
> of subsistence, and vice versa. In order to examine the object of our
> investigation in its integrity, free from all disturbing subsidiary circum-
> stances, we must treat the whole world as one nation, and assume that
> capitalist production is everywhere established and has possessed itself of
> every branch of industry.[2]

And in the second volume: "Apart from this class, according to our
assumption—the general and exclusive domination of capitalist production—there is no other class at all except the working class."[3]

Under this condition, there are only capitalists cum hangers-on and
workers in society; other classes, other producers and consumers are
nowhere to be found. In that case, capitalist production is faced with the
insoluble question which I tried to point out above.

You can twist and turn it as you wish, but so long as we retain the
assumption that there are no other classes but capitalists and workers,
then there is no way that the capitalists as a class can get rid of the sur-

plus goods in order to change the surplus value into money, and thus accumulate capital.

But Marx's assumption is only a theoretical premise in order to simplify investigation. In reality, capitalist production is not the sole and completely dominant form of production, as everyone knows, and as Marx himself stresses in *Capital*. In reality, there are in all capitalist countries, even in those with the most developed large-scale industry, numerous artisan and peasant enterprises which are engaged in simple commodity production. In reality, alongside the old capitalist countries there are still those even in Europe where peasant and artisan production is still strongly predominant, like Russia, the Balkans, Scandinavia, and Spain. And finally, there are huge continents besides capitalist Europe and North America, where capitalist production has only scattered roots, and apart from that the people of these continents have all sorts of economic systems, from the primitive Communist to the feudal, peasantry and artisan. Not only do all these social and productive forms coexist, and coexist locally with capitalism, but there is a lively intercourse of a specific kind. Capitalist production as proper mass production depends on consumers from peasant and artisan strata in the old countries, and consumers from all countries; but for technical reasons, it cannot exist without the products of these strata and countries. So there must develop right from the start an exchange relationship between capitalist production and the noncapitalist milieu, where capital not only finds the possibility of realizing surplus value in hard cash for further capitalization, but also receives various commodities to extend production, and finally wins new proletarianized labor forces by disintegrating the noncapitalist forms of production.

This is only the bare economic content of the relationship. Its concrete design in reality forms the historic process of the development of capitalism on the world stage in all its colorful and moving variety.

First, the exchange relation of capital with its noncapitalist environment confronts the difficulties of a barter economy, secure social relations, and the limited demand of patriarchal peasant economy and artisan production. Here capital uses "heroic means," the axe of political violence. Its first act in Europe is the revolutionary conquest of the feudal barter economy. Overseas, it begins with the subjugation and destruction of traditional communities, the world historical act of the birth of capital, since then the constant epiphenomenon of accumulation. Through destruction of the primitive barter relations in these countries, European capital opens the doors to commodity exchange and production, transforms the population into customers of capitalist commodities and hastens its own accumulation by making mass raids on their natural resources and accumulated treasures. Since the beginning of the nineteenth century, accumulated capital from Europe has been exported along these lines to noncapitalist countries in other parts of the world, where it finds new customers and thus new opportunities for accumulation on the ruins of the native forms of production.

Thus capitalism expands because of its mutual relationship with noncapitalist social strata and countries, accumulating at their expense and at the same time pushing them aside to take their place. The more capitalist countries participate in this hunting for accumulation areas, the rarer the noncapitalist places still open to the expansion of capital become and the tougher the competition; its raids turn into a chain of economic and political catastrophes: world crises, wars, revolution.

But by this process capital prepares its own destruction in two ways. As it approaches the point where humanity only consists of capitalists and proletarians, further accumulation will become impossible. At the same time, the absolute and undivided rule of capital aggravates class struggle throughout the world and the international economic and political anarchy to such an extent that, long before the last consequences of economic development, it must lead to the rebellion of the international proletariat against the existence of the rule of capital.

This, in brief, is my conception of the problem and its solution. At first glance it may appear to be a purely theoretical exercise. And yet the practical meaning of the problem is at hand—the connection with the most outstanding fact of our time: imperialism. The typical external phenomena of imperialism: competition among capitalist countries to win colonies and spheres of interest, opportunities for investment, the international loan system, militarism, tariff barriers, the dominant role of finance capital, and trusts in world politics, are all well known. Its connection with the final phase of capitalism, its importance for accumulation, are so blatantly open that it is clearly acknowledged by its supporters as well as its enemies. But Social Democracy refuses to be satisfied with this empirical knowledge. It must search for the precise economic rules behind appearances, to find the actual roots of this large and colorful complex of imperialist phenomena. As always in these cases, only precise theoretical knowledge of the problem at its roots can provide our practical struggle against imperialism with security, aim, and force—essential for the politics of the proletariat. Before Marx's *Capital* appeared, the fact that there was exploitation, surplus labor, and profits, was well known. But only the precise theory of surplus value, the wage laws, and the industrial reserve army, as Marx bases them in his theory of value, have given a strong foundation for the practical class struggle, on which the German and, in its footsteps, the international labor movement developed until the World War [First World War—Trans.]. That theory alone is not enough; that one can sometimes connect the best theory with the worst practice is shown by the present collapse of German Social Democracy. This collapse did not occur as a result of Marxist theory, but in spite of it, and it can only be overthrown by bringing the practice of the labor movement into harmony with its theory. In the class struggle as a whole, as in each important part of it, we can only gain a secure foundation for our position from Marx's theory, from the buried treasures found in his fundamental works.

There is no doubt that the explanation for the economic roots of imperialism must be deduced from the laws of capital accumulation, since, according to common empirical knowledge, imperialism as a whole is nothing but a specific method of accumulation. But how is that possible, if one does not question Marx's assumptions in the second volume of *Capital* which are constructed for a society in which capitalist production is the only form, where the entire population consists solely of capitalists and wage laborers?

However one defines the inner economic mechanisms of imperialism, one thing is obvious and common knowledge: the expansion of the rule of capital from the old capitalist countries to new areas, and the economic and political competition of those countries for the new parts of the world. But Marx assumes, as we have seen in the second volume of *Capital*, that the whole world is one capitalist nation, that all other forms of economy and society have already disappeared. How can one explain imperialism in a society where there is no longer any space for it?

It was at this point that I believed I had to start my critique. The theoretical assumption of a society of capitalists and workers only—which is legitimate for certain aims of investigation (as in the first volume of *Capital*, the analysis of individual capital and its practice of exploitations in the factory)—no longer seems adequate when we deal with the accumulation of gross social capital. As this represents the real historical process of capitalist development, it seems impossible to me to understand it if one abstracts it from all conditions of historical reality. Capital accumulation as the historical process develops in an environment of various precapitalist formations, in a constant political struggle, and in reciprocal economic relations. How can one capture this process in a bloodless theoretical fiction, which declares this whole context, the struggle and the relations, to be nonexistent?

Here especially it seems necessary, in the spirit of Marxist theory, to abandon the premise of the first volume, and to carry out the inquiry into accumulation as a total process, involving the metabolism of capital and its historical environment. If one does this, then the explanation of the process follows freely from Marx's basic theories, and is consistent with the other portions of his major works on economics.

Marx himself only posed the question of the accumulation of gross capital, but his answer went no further. As a basis for his analysis, he first selected that pure capitalist society; but not only did he not take this analysis to its conclusion, he also broke off at just this central question. In order to illustrate his conception he constructed some mathematical models, but hardly had he started on their significance for practical social possibilities and their verification from this standpoint when sickness and death forced him to stop writing. It was clearly left to his pupils to solve this problem (like many others), and my *Accumulation* was intended as an attempt in this direction.

The solution I proposed might have been judged as correct or incorrect; it could have been criticized, contested, supplemented; or another solution could have been produced. None of this happened. What followed was quite unexpected: the "experts" explained that there was no problem to be solved! Marx's illustrations in the second volume of *Capital* were a sufficient and exhaustive explanation of accumulation; the models there proved quite conclusively that capital could grow excellently, and production could expand, if there was no other mode of production in the world than the capitalist one; it was its own market, and only my complete inability to understand the ABC of Marx's models could persuade me to see a problem here. . . .

Imperialism

. . . Of course, tactics and strategy in the practical struggle are not directly dependent on whether one considers the second volume of *Capital* to be a finished work or just a fragment, whether one believes in the possibility of accumulation in an "isolated" capitalist society or not, whether one interprets Marx's models of reproduction one way or the other. Thousands of proletarians are good and brave fighters for the aims of socialism without knowing about these theoretical problems—for the reasons of a common basic understanding of the class struggle, an incorruptible class instinct, and the revolutionary traditions of the movement. But there is the closest connection between the understanding and treatment of theoretical problems and the practice of political parties over long periods. In the decade before the World War, German Social Democracy, as the international metropolis of proletarian intellectual life, displayed total harmony in theoretical as well as practical areas; in both areas the same indecision and ossification appeared, and it was the same imperialism as the overwhelmingly dominant manifestation of public life which defeated the theoretical as well as the political general staff of Social Democracy. The proud monolithic edifice of official German Social Democracy was revealed at its first historical trial to be a Potemkin village.★ Similarly, the apparent theoretical "expert knowledge" and infallibility of official Marxism, which blessed every practice of the movement, turned out to be a grandiose façade hiding its inner insecurity and inability to act behind intolerant and insolent dogmatism. The sad routine moving along the old tracks of the "tried

---

★[Potemkin villages. Gregory Alexandrovich Potemkin (1724–91), the most outstanding personality of the time of Catherine the Great, and said to have been Catherine's lover, was authorized by the Empress to organize "New Russia" in the South. He brought old ports up to date, set up new villages, and founded Ekaterinislav (Catherine's Glory). His critics alleged that his villages were cardboard fronts, built to deceive the Empress when she toured the area.—Trans.]

and tested tactics," i.e., nothing but parliamentarianism, corresponded to
the theoretical epigons who clung to the master's formula whilst renounc-
ing the living spirit of his teachings. We have already noted in passing some
proof of this thoughtlessness in the "supreme court" of "experts."

But the connection with practice is in our case even more obvious
than it may seem at first sight. It basically means two different methods of
fighting imperialism.

Marx's analysis of accumulation was developed at a time when imperialism had not yet entered on to the world stage. The final and absolute
rule of capital over the world—the precondition on which Marx bases his
analysis—entails the *a priori* exclusion of the process of imperialism. But—
and here lies the difference between the errors of a Marx and the crass
blunders of his epigons—in this case even the error leads on to something
fruitful. The problem posed and left unanswered in the second volume of
Capital—to show how accumulation takes place under the exclusive rule
of capitalism—is insoluble. Accumulation is simply impossible under these
conditions. This apparently rigid theoretical contradiction has only to be
translated into historical dialectics, in that it conforms to the spirit of the
entire Marxist teaching and way of thinking, and the contradiction in
Marx's model becomes the living mirror of the global career of capitalism,
of its fortune and fall.

Accumulation is impossible in an exclusively capitalist environment.
Therefore, we find that capital has been driven since its very inception to
expand into noncapitalist strata and nations, ruin artisans and peasantry,
proletarianize the intermediate strata, the politics of colonialism, the politics of "opening-up" and the export of capital. The development of capitalism has been possible only through constant expansion into new
domains of production and new countries. But the global drive to expand
leads to a collision between capital and precapitalist forms of society,
resulting in violence, war, revolution: in brief, catastrophes from start to
finish, the vital element of capitalism.

Capital accumulation progresses and expands at the expense of noncapitalist strata and countries, squeezing them out at an ever faster rate.
The general tendency and final result of this process is the exclusive world
rule of capitalist production. Once this is reached, Marx's model becomes
valid: accumulation, i.e., further expansion of capital, becomes impossible.

Capitalism comes to a dead end, it cannot function any more as the historical vehicle for the unfolding of the productive forces, it reaches its objective economic limit. The contradiction in Marx's model of accumulation is, seen dialectically, only the living contradiction between the boundless expansionist drive and the limit capital creates for itself through progressive destruction of all other forms of production; it is the contradiction between the huge productive forces which it awakens throughout the world during the process of accumulation and the narrow basis to which it is confined by the laws of accumulation. Marx's model of accumulation—when properly understood—is precisely in its insolubility the exact prognosis of the economically unavoidable downfall of capitalism as a result of the imperialist process of expansion whose specific task it is to realize Marx's assumption: the general and undivided rule of capital.

Can this ever really happen? That is, of course, theoretical fiction, precisely because capital accumulation is not just an economic but also a political process.

> Imperialism is as much a historical method for prolonging capital's existence as it is the surest way of setting an objective limit to its existence as fast as possible. This is not to say that the final point need actually be attained. The very tendency of capitalist development towards this end is expressed in forms which make the concluding phase of capitalism a period of catastrophes.[4]

> The more ruthlessly capital uses militarism to put an end to noncapitalist strata in the outside world and at home, the more it depresses the conditions of existence of all working strata, the more the day-to-day history of capital accumulation on the world stage changes into an endless chain of political and social catastrophes and convulsions; these latter, together with the periodic economic catastrophes in the shape of crises, make continued accumulation impossible and the rebellion of the international working class against the rule of capital necessary, even before it has economically reached the limits it set for itself.[5]

Here, as elsewhere in history, theory is performing its duty if it shows us the *tendency* of development, the logical conclusion to which it is objectively heading. There is as little chance of this conclusion being reached as there was for any other previous period of social development to unfold itself completely. The *need* for it to be reached becomes less as social consciousness, embodied this time in the socialist proletariat, becomes more involved as an active factor in the blind game of forces. In this case, too, a correct conception of Marx's theory offers the most fruitful suggestions and the most powerful stimulus for this consciousness.

Modern imperialism is not the prelude to the expansion of capital, as in Bauer's model; on the contrary, it is only the last chapter of its historical process of expansion: it is the period of universally sharpened world competition between the capitalist states for the last remaining noncapitalist areas on earth. In this final phase, economic and political catastrophe is just as much the intrinsic, normal mode of existence for capital as it was in the "primitive accumulation" of its development phase. The discovery of America and the sea route to India were not just Promethean achievements of the human mind and civilization but also, and inseparably, a series of mass murders of primitive peoples in the New World and large-scale slave trading with the peoples of Africa and Asia. Similarly, the economic expansion of capital in its imperialist final phase is inseparable from the series of colonial conquests and World Wars which we are now experiencing. What distinguishes imperialism as the last struggle for capitalist world domination is not simply the remarkable energy and universality of expansion but—and this is the specific sign that the circle of development is beginning to close—the return of the decisive struggle for expansion from those areas which are being fought over back to its home countries. In this way, imperialism brings catastrophe as a mode of existence back from the periphery of capitalist development to its point of departure. The expansion of capital, which for four centuries had given the existence and civilization of all noncapitalist peoples in Asia, Africa, America, and Australia over to ceaseless convulsions and general and complete decline, is now plunging the civilized peoples of Europe itself into a series of catastrophes whose final result can only be the decline of civilization or the transition to the socialist mode of production. Seen in this light, the position of the proletariat with regard to imperialism leads to a general confrontation with the rule of capital. The specific rules of its conduct are given by that historical alternative.

According to official "expert" Marxism, the rules are quite different. The belief in the possibility of accumulation in an "isolated capitalist society," the belief that capitalism is conceivable even without expansion, is the theoretical formula of a quite distinct tactical tendency. The logical conclusion of this idea is to look on the phase of imperialism not as a historical necessity, as the decisive conflict for socialism, but as the wicked invention of a small group of people who profit from it. This leads to convincing the bourgeoisie that, even from the point of view of their capitalist interests, imperialism and militarism are harmful, thus isolating the alleged small group of beneficiaries of this imperialism and forming a bloc of the proletariat with broad sections of the bourgeoisie in order to "moderate" imperialism, starve it out by "partial disarmament" and "draw its claws"! Just as liberalism in the period of its decline appeals for a well-informed as against an ill-informed monarchy, the "Marxist center" appeals for the bourgeoisie it will educate as against the ill-advised one, for international disarmament treaties as against the disaster course of imperialism, for the peaceful federation of democratic nation states as against the struggle of the great powers for armed world domination. The final confrontation between proletariat and capital to settle their world-historical contradiction is converted into the utopia of a historical compromise between proletariat and bourgeoisie to "moderate" the imperialist contradictions between capitalist states.[6]

Otto Bauer concludes his criticism of my book with the following words:

> Capitalism will not collapse from the mechanical impossibility of realizing surplus value. It will be defeated by the rebellion to which it drives the masses. Not only then, when the last peasant and the last petty-bourgeois change into wage-workers, thus no longer providing a surplus market, will capitalism disintegrate: it will be cut down much earlier by the growing rebellion of the ever-rising working class, educated, united and organized by the mechanism of the capitalist mode of production itself.

In order to direct this advice to me specifically, Bauer, a master of abstraction, had to abstract not only from the entire meaning and direction of my conception of accumulation, but also from the clear text of my statements. His own brave words, however, can once again only be construed as a typical abstraction of "expert" Marxism, i.e., as the harmless but short-lived flickering of "pure thought." This is demonstrated by the position of this group of theoreticians towards the outbreak of the World War. The rebellion of the ever-rising, educated, and organized working class suddenly changed into the policy of "abstention" on epoch-making decisions of world history and "silence" until the bells of peace ring out. "The road to power," brilliantly illustrated down to the last detail in a period of serene peace, when there was still not a sound in the treetops,★ changed course straight to the "road to impotence" at the first gust of reality. The epigons who held the official theoretical leadership of the Labor movement in the last decade bankrupted themselves at the first outbreak of the world crisis and handed leadership over to imperialism. A clear understanding of these connections is one of the essential conditions for the reconstruction of a proletarian policy which would measure up to its historical tasks in the period of imperialism.

Once again, the self-pitying will bewail the fact that "Marxists are arguing amongst themselves," that tried and tested "authorities" are being contested. But Marxism is not a dozen people who ascribe the right to "expert knowledge" to each other and before whom the mass of faithful Moslems must prostrate themselves in blind trust.

Marxism is a revolutionary world outlook which must always strive for new discoveries, which completely despises rigidity in once-valid theses, and whose living force is best preserved in the intellectual clash of self-criticism and the rough and tumble of history. Thus, I agree with Lessing, who wrote to the young Reimarus:

"But what can one do! Let each man say what he thinks to be the truth, and leave truth itself to God."

Notes

1. Karl Marx, *Capital* (Moscow: Foreign Language Publishing House, 1965), vol. 1, p. 564.

★[*"In allen Wipfeln Ruh"*—quotation from Goethe.— Trans.]

2. *Capital*, vol. 1, p. 581, footnote 1.

3. Ibid., vol. 11, p. 348.

4. Luxemburg, *The Accumulation of Capital*, p. 425.

5. Ibid., p. 445.

6. Eckstein, who denounced me for the "catastrophe theory" in his review in *Vorwärts* of January 1913 by simply borrowing from the vocabulary of Kolb-Heine-David: ("The practical conclusion which Comrade Luxemburg constructs on the theory of necessity of noncapitalist consumers, *especially the catastrophe theory*, falls with the theoretical assumption")—is denouncing me now, since the swamp theoreticians have taken a "left" turn, for the opposite crime of aiding and abetting the right-wing Social Democracy. He points out eagerly that Lensch, the same Lensch who gravitated to Kolb-Heine-David in the World War, approved of my book and reviewed it favorably in the *Leipziger Volkszeitung*. Is the connection not obvious? Suspicious, highly suspicious! "For that very reason" Eckstein had felt himself obliged to destroy my book so thoroughly in *Vorwärts*. But the very same Lensch approved of Marx's *Capital* even more—before the war. Yes, and a man called Max Grunwald was for years an enthusiastic interpreter of Marx's *Capital* at the Berlin Workers' Education School. Is that not convincing proof that Marx's *Capital* directly leads one to cheer for England's destruction and write birthday articles for Hindenburg? But that sort of blunder happens to Eckstein, ruining his intentions. As is well known, already Bismarck complained often about the blind eagerness of his journalistic reptiles.

11

REBUILDING THE INTERNATIONAL

(1915)

Luxemburg's great critique of the socialist movement's massive and tragic failure in the face of World War I is her 1915 work, written from prison, The Junius Pamphlet: The Crisis of German Social Democracy. *It is one of the most eloquent of all her writings, and one that is available in whole or in part in other collections. Many of the same political points can be found in this more succinct article, published in 1915 in the first issue of the oppositional journal* Die Internationale.

I

On August 4th, 1914, German Social Democracy abdicated politically, and at the same time the Socialist International collapsed. All attempts at denying or concealing this fact, regardless of the motive on which they are based, tend objectively to perpetuate, and to justify, the disastrous self-deception of the socialist parties, the inner malady of the movement, that led to the collapse, and in the long run to make the Socialist International a fiction, a hypocrisy.

The collapse itself is without precedent in the history of all times. Socialism or Imperialism—this alternative summarizes completely the political orientation of the labor parties in the past decade. For in Germany it was formulated in innumerable program speeches, mass meetings, brochures, and newspaper articles as the slogan of Social Democracy, as the party's interpretation of the tendencies of the present historical epoch.

With the outbreak of the world war, word has become substance, the alternative has grown from a historical tendency into the political situation. Faced with this alternative, which it had been the first to recognize and bring to the masses' consciousness, Social Democracy backed down without a struggle and conceded victory to imperialism. Never before in the history of class struggles, since there have been political parties, has there been a party that, in this way, after fifty years of uninterrupted growth, after achieving a first-rate position of power, after assembling millions around it, has so completely and ignominiously abdicated as a political force within twenty-four hours, as Social Democracy has done. Precisely because it was the best-organized and best-disciplined vanguard of the International, the present-day collapse of socialism can be demonstrated by Social Democracy's example.

Kautsky, as the representative of the so-called "Marxist Center," or, in political terms, as the theoretician of the swamp, has for years degraded theory into the obliging handmaiden of the official practice of the party bureaucrats and thus made his own sincere contribution to the present collapse of the party. Already he has thought out an opportune new theory to justify and explain away the collapse. According to this theory, Social Democracy is an instrument for peace but not a means of combatting war. Or, as Kautsky's faithful pupils in the Austrian "struggle," sighing profusely at the present aberrations of German Social Democracy, decree: the only policy befitting socialism during the war is "silence"; only when the bells of peace peal out can socialism again begin to function.[1] This theory of a voluntarily assumed eunuch role, which says that socialism's virtue can be upheld only if, at the crucial moments, it is eliminated as a factor in world history, suffers from the basic mistake of all accounts of political impotence: it overlooks the most vital factor.

Faced with the alternative of coming out for or against the war, Social Democracy, from the moment it abandoned its opposition, has been forced by the iron compulsion of history to throw its full weight behind the war. The same Kautsky who in the memorable meeting of the parliamentary party of August 3rd pleaded for its consent to the war credits, the same "Austro-Marxists" (as they call themselves) who now see as self-evident the Social Democratic parliamentary party's consent to the war credits—even they now occasionally shed a few tears at the nationalistic excesses of the Social Democratic party organs and at their inadequate theoretical training, particularly in the razor-thin separation of the concept of "nationality" and of other "concepts" allegedly guilty of those aberrations. But events have their own logic, even when human beings do not. Once Social Democracy's parliamentary representatives had decided in favor of supporting the war, everything else followed automatically with the inevitability of historical destiny.

On August 4th, German Social Democracy, far from being "silent," assumed an extremely important historical function: the shield-bearer of imperialism in the present war. Napoleon once said that two factors decide the outcome of a battle: the "earthly" factor, consisting of the terrain, quality of the weapons, weather, etc., and the "divine" factor, that is, the moral constitution of the army, its morale, its belief in its own cause. The "earthly" factor was taken care of on the German side largely by the Krupp firm of Essen; the "divine" factor can be charged above all to Social Democracy's account. The services since August 4 that it has rendered and is rendering daily to the German war leaders are immeasurable: the trade unions that on the outbreak of war shelved their battle for higher wages and invested with the aura of "socialism" all the military authorities' security measures aimed at preventing popular uprisings; the Social Democratic women who withdrew all their time and effort from Social Democratic agitation and, arm in arm with bourgeois patriots, used these to assist the needy warriors' families; the Social Democratic press which, with a few exceptions, uses its daily papers and weekly and monthly periodicals to propagate the war as a national cause and the cause of the proletariat; that press which, depending on the turns the war takes, depicts the Russian peril and the horror of the Tsarist government, or abandons a perfidious Albion to the people's hatred, or rejoices at the uprisings and revolutions in foreign colonies; or which prophesies the restrengthening of Turkey after this war, which promises freedom to the Poles, the Ruthenians, and all peoples, which imparts martial bravery and heroism to the proletarian youth—in short, completely manipulates public opinion and the masses for the ideology of war; the Social Democratic parliamentarians and party leaders, finally, who not only consent to funds for the waging of war, but who attempt to suppress energetically any disquieting stirrings of doubt and criticism in the masses, calling these "intrigues," and who for their part support the government with personal services of a discreet nature, such as brochures, speeches, and articles displaying the most genuine German-national patriotism—when in world history was there a war in which anything like this happened?

Where and when has the suspension of all constitutional rights been accepted so submissively as a matter of course? Where has such a hymn of praise to the most severe press censorship been sung from the ranks of the opposition as it has in the individual newspapers of German Social Democracy? Never before has a war found such Pindars; never has a military dictatorship found such obedience; never has a political party so fervently sacrificed all that it stood for and possessed on the altar of a cause which it had sworn a thousand times before the world to fight to the last drop of blood. Judged against this metamorphosis, the National Liberals are real Roman Catos, *rochers de bronze* [bronze rocks—Trans.]. Precisely the powerful organization and the much-praised discipline of German Social Democracy were confirmed when the body of four million allowed a handful of parliamentarians to turn it around and harness it to a wagon heading in the opposite direction to its aim in life. The fifty years of preparatory work by Social Democracy have materialized in the present war. And the trade unions and party leaders can claim that the impetus and victorious strength of this war on the German side are in large measure the fruits of the "training" of the masses in the proletarian organizations. Marx and Engels, Lassalle and Liebknecht, Bebel and Singer trained the German proletariat so that Hindenburg might lead it. And the more advanced the training, the organization, the famous discipline, the consolidation of the trade unions and the workers' press in Germany, in comparison with France, the more effective is the assistance rendered to the war by German Social Democracy than that given by the French Social Democratic Party. The French socialists, together with their ministers, seem to be the merest dabblers in the unfamiliar trade of nationalism and the waging of war, when one compares their deeds with the services being rendered to patriotic imperialism by German Social Democracy and the German trade unions.

II

The official theory which misuses Marxism as it pleases for the current domestic requirements of the party officials in order to justify their day-to-day dealings, and whose organ is *Die Neue Zeit*, attempts to explain the minor discrepancy between the present function of the workers' party and its words of yesterday by saying that international socialism was much concerned with the question of doing something against the outbreak of war, but not with doing something after it had broken out.[2] Like a girl who obliges all, this theory assures us that the most wonderful harmony prevails between the present practice of socialism and its past, that none of the socialist parties need reproach themselves with anything which would call into question their membership in the International. At the same time, however, this conveniently elastic theory also has an adequate explanation at hand of the contradiction between the present position of international Social Democracy and its past, a contradiction that strikes even the most shortsighted of people. The International is said to have aired only the question of the prevention of war. Then, however, "the war was upon us," as the formula goes, and now it turns out that quite different standards of behavior apply to the socialists after the war had begun than before it. The moment war was upon us, the only question left for the proletariat of each country was: victory or defeat. Or, as another "Austro-Marxist," F. Adler, explained more in terms of natural science and philosophy: the nation, like any organism, must above all ensure its survival. In good German this means: for the proletariat there is not one vital rule, as scientific socialism has hitherto proclaimed, but rather there are two such rules: one for peace and one for war. In peacetime the class struggle applies within each country, and international solidarity vis-à-vis other countries; in wartime it is class solidarity within and the struggle between the workers of the various countries without. The global historical appeal of the *Communist*

Manifesto undergoes a fundamental revision and, as amended by Kautsky, now reads: proletarians of all countries, unite in peacetime and cut each other's throats in war! Thus today: "Every shell a Russian in Hell—every engagement a dead Frenchman" (*jeder Schuss ein Russ—jeder Stoss ein Franzos*), and tomorrow, after peace has been concluded: "We embrace the millions of the whole world." For the International is "essentially an instrument for peace" but not an "effective implement in war."[3]

This obliging theory does not merely open up charming perspectives for Social Democratic practice by elevating the fickleness of the parliamentary party, coupled with the Jesuitism of the Center Party, to virtually a fundamental dogma of the Socialist International. It also inaugurates a completely new "revision" of historical materialism compared with which all Bernstein's former attempts appear as innocent child's play. The proletarian tactics prior to and after the outbreak of the war are supposed to be based on different, indeed opposite, guiding principles. This presupposes that the social conditions, the foundations of our tactics, are also basically different in war than in peace. According to historical materialism as founded by Marx, all hitherto written history is the history of class struggles. According to Kautsky's revised materialism, the words, "except in time of war," must be added. Accordingly, social development, since for millennia it has been periodically interspersed with wars, takes its course according to the following scheme: a period of class struggle, then a pause in which there is a merger of the classes and a national struggle, then again a period of class struggles, again a pause and class merger, and so forth, in this charming pattern. Each time the foundations of social life in peacetime are turned upside down by the outbreak of war and those in periods of war are inverted the moment peace is concluded. This, as one can see, is no longer a theory of social development "in catastrophes," against which Kautsky once had to defend himself, this is a theory of development—in somersaults. According to this theory, society moves in somewhat the same manner as an iceberg driven by spring waters, which, when its base has melted away on all sides in the tepid stream, after a certain time does a nose dive, whereupon this cute game periodically repeats itself.

Now this revised historical materialism crudely affronts all the hitherto accepted facts of history. This freshly constructed antithesis between war and class struggle neither explains nor demonstrates that constant dialectical transition from war into class struggle and from class struggle into war, which reveals their essential inner unity. So it was in the wars between medieval cities, in the wars of the Reformation, in the Dutch war of liberation, in the wars of the great French Revolution, in the American War of Secession, in the uprising of the Paris Commune, in the great Russian Revolution of 1905. And this is not all; even in purely abstract-theoretical terms, Kautsky's theory of historical development completely wipes out the Marxist theory, as a moment's reflection would make clear. For if, as Marx assumes, both the class struggle and war do not fall from the sky, but originate in deeply rooted economic and social causes, then the two cannot disappear periodically unless their causes vanish into thin air. Now the proletarian class struggle is only a necessary consequence of the economic exploitation and of the political class rule of the bourgeoisie. But during a war, economic exploitation does not diminish in the least; on the contrary, its impetus is increased immensely by the speculative mania which flourishes in the exuberant atmosphere of war and industry, and by the pressure of the military dictatorship on the worker. Neither is the political class rule of the bourgeoisie diminished in wartime; on the contrary, it is raised to a stark class dictatorship by the suspension of constitutional rights. Since the economic and political sources of the class struggle in society inevitably increase tenfold in wartime, how then can the class struggle cease to exist? Conversely, in the present historical period, wars originate in the competitive interests of groups of capitalists and in capitalism's need to expand. Both motives, however, are operative not only while the cannons are roaring, but also during peacetime, which means that they prepare and make inevitable further outbreaks of war. War is indeed—as Kautsky is wont to quote from Clausewitz—only "the continuation of politics by other means." And the imperialist phase of the rule of capitalism has indeed made peace illusory by actually declaring the dictatorship of militarism—war—to be permanent.

For the exponents of the revised historical materialism, this results in the necessity of choosing between two alternatives. Either the class struggle is the paramount law of existence of the proletariat, and the party officials' proclamation of class harmony in its place during wartime is an outrage against the proletariat's vital interests; or the class struggle in both war and peace is an outrage against the "national interests" and "the security of the fatherland." Both in wartime and in peacetime, either the class struggle or class harmony is the fundamental factor of social life. In practice the alternative is even clearer: either Social Democracy must say *pater peccavi* to the patriotic bourgeoisie (as former young daredevils and present-day old devotees in our ranks are already proclaiming contritely) and thus have to revise fundamentally all its tactics and principles, in peacetime as well as in wartime, in order to adapt to its present social-imperialist position; or the party will have to say *pater peccavi* to the international proletariat and adapt its behavior during the war to its principles in peacetime. And what applies to the German labor movement of course also applies to the French.

Either the International will remain a refuse heap after the war, or its resurrection will begin on the basis of the class struggle from which alone it draws its vital forces. Not by retelling the same old story will it be revived after the war, not by returning fresh, cheerful, merry, and bold, as though nothing had happened, not by playing the old melodies that captivated the world until August 4th. Only by means of an "excruciatingly thorough denunciation of our own indecision and weakness," of our own moral fall since August 4th, can the rebuilding of the International begin. And the first step in this direction is to take action for the rapid termination of the war and for the preparation of a peace in accordance with the common interest of the international proletariat.

III

Until now, only two positions on the question of peace have been visible within the party. The first of these, advocated by a member of the Party Executive, Scheidemann, and by several other Reichstag deputies and party newspapers, echoes the government in its support of the slogan of "holding out," and opposes the movement for peace as inopportune and dangerous to the military interests of the fatherland. The proponents of this trend advocate the continuation of the war and are thus objectively ensuring that the war is continued according to the wishes of the ruling classes "until a victory is won which accords with the sacrifices made," until "a secure peace" is guaranteed. In other words, the supporters of the policy of "holding out" are ensuring that the actual development of the war approximates as closely as possible to the imperialist conquests which the *Post*, which Rohrbach, Dix, and other prophets of Germany's global dominance have openly declared to be the aim of the war. If all these wonderful dreams do not become reality, if the trees of youthful imperialism do not grow into the sky, it will not be through any fault of the *Post* people and their pacemakers in Social Democracy. It is apparently not the solemn "declarations" in parliament "against any policy of conquest" that are conclusive for the outcome of the war, but rather the affirmation of the policy of "holding out." The war, whose continuation is advocated by Scheidemann and others, has its own logic. Its real sponsors are those capitalist-agrarian elements that are in the saddle in Germany today, not the modest figures of the Social Democratic parliamentarians and editors who merely hold the stirrup for them. Among those propagating this trend, the social-imperialist attitude of the party is most clearly manifest.

While in France, too, the party leaders—admittedly in a completely different military situation—cling to the slogan, "hold out until victory," a movement for the speediest termination of the war is making itself gradually but increasingly felt in all countries. The greatest single characteristic of all these thoughts and desires for peace is the most cautious preparation of peace guarantees which are to be demanded before war is finished. Not only the universal demand for no annexations, but also a whole series of new demands are appearing: universal disarmament (or, more modestly, systematic limitation of the arms race), abolition of secret diplomacy, free trade for all nations in the colonies, and other such wonderful proposals. The admirable aspect of all these clauses calling for the future happiness of humanity and for the prevention of future wars is the irrepressible optimism with which, emerging intact from the terrible catastrophe of the present war, new resolutions are to be planted at the grave of the old aspirations. If the collapse of August 4th has proved anything, it is the lesson in world history that neither pious hopes nor cleverly devised utopian formulas addressed to the ruling class can provide effective guarantees of peace or build a wall against war.

The only real safeguard for peace depends on the resolution of the proletariat to remain faithful to its class politics and its international solidarity through all the storms of imperialism. There was no lack of demands and formulae on the part of the socialist parties in the crucial countries, above all in Germany; the deficiency was in their ability to back up these demands with a will and with deeds in the spirit of the class struggle and internationalism. If today, after all that we have experienced, we viewed the action for peace as a process of reasoning out the best formulae against war, this would be the greatest danger to international socialism. For this would mean that, despite its cruel lessons, it would have learnt nothing and forgotten nothing.

Here again we find the prime example of this in Germany. In a recent issue of *Die Neue Zeit*, the Reichstag deputy, Hoch, laid down a peace program which—as the party organ attested—he warmly supported. Nothing was missing from this program: neither a list of enumerated demands which was supposed to prevent future wars in the most painless and reliable manner, nor a very convincing statement that an impending peace was possible, necessary, and desirable. There was only one thing missing: an explanation of how one should work for this peace with acts, not with "desires"! For the author belongs to the compact majority in the parliamentary party that not only twice voted for war credits, but also on each occasion called its action a political, patriotic, socialist necessity. And, excellently drilled in its new role, this group is prepared to grant further credits for the continuation of the war as a matter of course. To support material means of continuing the war, and, in the same breath, to praise the desirability of an early peace with all its blessings, "to press the sword into the government's fist with one hand and with the other to wave the soft palm branch over the International"—this is a classical chapter in practical politics of the swamp as propagated theoretically in the same *Neue Zeit*. When the socialists of neutral countries, for example the Copenhagen Conference participants, seriously consider the preparation of demands and proposals for peace on paper as an action contributing to the speedy termination of the war, then this is a relatively harmless error. An understanding of this salient point in the present situation of the International and of the causes of its collapse can and must be the common property of all socialist parties. The redeeming deed for the restoration of peace and of the International can only emanate from the socialist parties of the belligerent countries. The first step towards peace and towards the International is the rejection of social imperialism. And if the Social Democratic parliamentarians continue to approve funds for the waging of the

war, then their desires and declarations for peace and their solemn procla-
mations "against any policy of conquest" are a hypocrisy and a delusion.
This is particularly true of Kautsky's International and its members who
alternately embrace one another fraternally and cut each other's throats,
declare that they "have nothing with which to reproach themselves." Here
again events have their own logic. When they grant war credits, people like
Hoch surrender the controlling reins and bring about the virtual opposite
of peace, namely, a policy of "holding out." When people like Scheidemann support the policy of "holding out," they in fact hand over the reins
to the *Post* people and thus accomplish the reverse of their solemn declarations against "any policy of conquest," i.e., the unleashing of the imperialist instincts—until the country bleeds to death. Here again there is only
one choice: either Bethmann-Hollweg—or Liebknecht. Either imperialism or socialism as Marx understood it.

Just as in Marx himself the roles of acute historical analyst and bold revolutionary, the man of ideas and the man of action were inseparably bound
up, mutually supporting and complementing each other, so for the first time
in the history of the modern labor movement the socialist teachings of
Marxism united theoretical knowledge with revolutionary energy, the one
illuminating and stimulating the other. Both are in equal measure part of
the essence of Marxism; each, separated from the other, transforms Marxism
into a sad caricature of itself. In the course of half a century, German Social
Democracy harvested the most abundant fruits from the theoretical knowledge of Marxism and, nurtured on its milk, grew into a powerful body. Put
to the greatest historical test—a test which, moreover, it had foreseen theoretically with scientific certainty and foretold in all its important features—
Social Democracy was found completely lacking in the second vital element
of the labor movement: the energetic will, not merely be to understand history, but to change it as well. With all its exemplary theoretical knowledge
and strength of organization, the party was caught in the vortex of the historical current, turned around in a trice like a rudderless hulk, and exposed
to the winds of imperialism against which it was supposed to work its way
forward to the saving island of socialism. Even without the mistakes of
others, the defeat of the whole International was sealed by this failure of its
"vanguard," its best trained and strongest élite.

It was an epoch-making collapse of the first order which enmeshes man and delays his liberation from capitalism. However if it comes down to it, Marxism itself is not completely without blame. And all attempts to adapt Marxism to the present decrepitude of socialist practice, to prostitute it to the level of the venal apologetics of social imperialism, are more dangerous than even all the open and glaring excesses of nationalistic errors in the ranks of the party; these attempts tend not only to conceal the real causes of the great failure of the International, but also to drain the sources of its future rebuilding. If the International, like the peace, is to correspond to the interests of the proletarian cause, it must be born of the self-criticism of the proletariat, of its reflection upon its own power, the same power that broke like a reed in a storm, but that, grown to its true size, is historically qualified to uproot thousand-year-old oaks of social injustice and to move mountains. The road to this power—one that is not paved with resolutions—is at the same time the road to peace and to the rebuilding of the International.

Notes

1. See the article by F. Adler in the January number of *Kampf* [1915—Ed.].
2. See Kautsky's article in *Die Neue Zeit* of October 2 of last year [1914 —Ed.].
3. See Kautsky's article in *Die Neue Zeit* of October 27 of last year [1914 —Ed.].

12

Letters from Prison

(1917–1918)

While in prison for opposing the imperialist slaughter that was then called The Great War, Luxemburg wrote many letters to her closest friends, among whom were Luise Kautsky (wife of Karl Kautsky) and Sophie Liebknecht (wife of Karl Liebknecht). They give us a vivid sense of many of this revolutionary's personal qualities as well as insights into her political thinking.

To Luise Kautsky (January 26, 1917)

Lulu beloved:

Yesterday (in my absence) I was arraigned in Berlin, where no doubt I earned a few more months of jail. Today it is exactly three months since my imprisonment in the Third Division. In celebration of two such memorial days—of a kind that for years have been pleasantly

From *Letters to Karl and Luise Kautsky from 1996 to 1918*, ed. Luise Kautsky, trans. Louis P. Lochner (New York: Robert M. McBride Co., 1925) and *Letters from Prison*, trans. Cedar and Eden Paul (London: The Socialist Book Centre, 1946).

interrupting my existence—you are to receive a letter. Pardon me, my dear, if I have kept you waiting for an answer; I have just passed through a short period of despicable cowardliness. We have had several days of icy wind and storm, and I felt myself so insignificant and weak that I would not leave my "pen" at all, for fear lest the cold weather might destroy me. When I am in such a frame of mind I naturally wait anxiously for a hearty, warm letter, but unfortunately my friends always wait for the initiative and the impulse to come from me. No one ever has the original and good idea to write to me of his own accord—excepting only Hänschen (Hans Diefenbach) who, however, evidently has grown somewhat tired of writing "letters that failed to reach her" and that remain unanswered. Finally a letter arrived from Sonia L.; the ring to her correspondence, however, is always that of a cracked glass. So that, as usual, I had to recover by my own willpower—and it is well thus. Now I am quite well again and in good spirits, only I miss you to gossip and laugh with, as only we two know how. I would certainly succeed in getting you to laugh soon again, although your last letters sounded alarmingly morose. Do you remember how on one occasion we returned from an evening at Bebel's, and at midnight the three of us staged a frog concert on the street? At that time you said that, when we were together, you were always intoxicated as it were—as though we had drunk champagne. That is what I like so much about you—that I can always bring you into a "champagne mood," when life seems to tickle one's fingers and one is ready for every tomfoolery. Supposing we do not see each other for three years: after half an hour it seems as though it had been but yesterday that we last met. And so I'd like suddenly to break in now upon Hans Naivus and to laugh at your family table as we did last June when Hänschen visited you (he wrote me afterward that on the whole way to the front he had to laugh right out in the railway compartment, to the surprise of his comrades, to whom he surely "seemed like an idiot"). The time for real champagne is over, for a long time at least, since poor Faisst fell as the first victim of the world war— over for champagne—over for Wolf songs. In that connection: I have a very pleasant memory of our last "spree." It took place last summer, when I was in the Black Forest. One Sunday he came with Costia* for a visit,

---

*[Clara Zetkin's younger son.—L. K.]

climbing up from Wildbad. It was a splendid day, and after the meal we grouped about a battery of "Mumm"* bottles. We reveled in the sun and were very happy. The "noble giver" naturally drank most himself. Once again he experienced an "unforgettable hour," laughed, gesticulated, shouted, and chased one effervescing glass after another down his broad Suabian "mug." He was especially amused at the Sunday picnickers who swarmed about us on the veranda. "Just look at those Philistines gaping at us," he kept exclaiming, enthusiastically, "if they only knew *who* is having a drinking bout here!" The funniest part about it all was the fact that it was we who were the real innocents, for the innkeeper, as he himself told me in the evening, had somehow unraveled the mystery of my unfortunate "incognito"† and had retailed the news of his discovery all his guests. The rogue served us with such peculiar smirks and pulled the corks with an extra loud report; the Philistines, however, as you might well imagine, were highly edified about this "social-democratic champagne-bout."

And now spring will let "its blue ribbon flutter" for the third time over Faisst's grave. (He sang this song‡ very beautifully—much better than Julia Culp, whom we—don't you remember?—heard together in the *Sin-gakademe.*) I suppose all inclination for music as for everything else has left you for quite a while. Your mind is preoccupied with worries about the wrong course history is taking, and your heart is full of sighs over the despicable conduct of—Scheidemann and comrades. And everybody who writes me, moans and sighs similarly. To me, nothing seems more ludicrous than that. Don't you understand that the general misery is altogether *too great* to bemoan it? I can give grieve if Mimi is taken down with sickness or when something is the matter with you. But when the whole world is out of sorts, then I try merely to *comprehend* what has happened and why it happened; and once I have done my duty I rest content and recover my good spirits. *Ultra posse nemo obligatur.* And besides, *everything* is still left that otherwise gave me joy: music and painting and cloud and botanical excursions in springtime and good books and Mimi and you and many other things besides—in short, I am immensely rich and intend to remain

---

*["Mumm" is a celebrated brand of champagne.—Trans.]

†[As has already been mentioned, Rosa never registered under the name of Luxemburg when travelling. At times even she went under the wildest faked names.—L.K.]

‡[Music by Hugo Wolf; words by Mörike.—L. K.]

so until the end. This complete yielding to the miseries of the day is something that I can't understand and bear at all. Just note how, for instance, a Goethe stood above events with his cool composure! Just think what he had to go through: the great French revolution which, seen at close range, certainly must have seemed like a bloody and entirely purposeless farce; and then from 1793 to 1815 an unbroken chain of wars, during which the world again looked like a madhouse let loose. And how quietly, with what mental equilibrium he at the same time pursued his studies about the metamorphosis of plants, about the theory of color, about a thousand and one things! I don't ask you to write poetry like Goethe; but his conception of life—the universality of interests, the inner harmony—is something that everybody can acquire for himself, or at least strive for. And if perchance you should say, "but Goethe was no fighter in the political realm," I reply: a fighter, more than anybody else, must try to rise above events, otherwise he will sink up to his nose into every little trifle. Of course, I am thinking of fighters of big caliber, not of weathervanes of the size of the "big men" who gather about your table and who, the other day, sent me a postcard greeting. Never mind—*your* greeting was the only one I really cared for among them all. And because of it, I am going to send you a little picture from my Turner collection one of these days. But don't you dare turn me down, as some one did recently! Just imagine, at Christmastime I sent a beautiful picture from this collection to Leo, when I received the message through Miss Jacob: declined with thanks—this would be "vandalism"—the picture must be returned to the collection! I was furious, for here, too, I agree with Goethe:*

> Hätt' ich irgend wohl Bedenken,—
> Balch, Bokhara, Samarkand—
> Süsses Liebchen, Dir zu schenken
> Dieser Städte Rausch und Tand?
> Aber frage Du den Kaiser
> Ob er Dir die Städte giebt?
> Er ist mächtiger und weiser,
> Doch er weiss nicht, wie man liebt. . . .

---

*[In the "West—Ostlicher Diwan."—L. K.]

Leo is neither Kaiser nor wiser, nor does he know "how one loves." But
we two, know how, don't we, Louise? And if in the near future I should
take a notion to snatch down a few stars in order to present them to some-
body as cuff buttons, I shouldn't want some cold pedant with raised finger
to object and say that I was throwing confusion into all the school-Atlantes
of astronomy!

The Grainer collection which you sent me gives me ever greater pleasure; I often turn its pages and thereby work up a constantly increasing
hunger for others. Would it not be possible for Robert★ to send me a few
of his latest pictures through the next human being that comes to visit me
here (as to whom the finger of Herr von Kessel will designate, you may
learn through Miss J.)? I would guarantee their safe return; and I would get
a thievish joy out of them! Anyway, couldn't Robert himself come to visit
me? In that event he could probably carry out his intention of painting me,
provided three or four sittings would suffice. My God, the idea appeals to
me! As long as I am "sitting" anyway, I might as well sit for him! In any case
the very sight of this dew-kissed youth with his beaming eyes would do me
good. I am quite sure that he, as the son of the court painter at the royal
theater, will get the permission, all the more so if Count Hülsen† will write
a line. . . . This, of course, merely in fun; Hans Naivus will rather die than
confess to the Count his friendship for the "firebrand." But I suppose
Robert will get permission even without a protector.

Above all, how about *you*? Have you put in your application as yet? I
should of course prefer that you come in spring when the country here looks
more hospitable; it is said to be quite beautiful, according to people who have
seen it. In view of the calamitous condition of the railroads and the rawness
of the weather it would be far too risky for you now. But I shall unconditionally order your visit for the spring. You will be surprised at all that you
will find about me: the black wrens attend me faithfully before the window;
they know my voice exactly and seem to like it when I sing. Not long ago I
was singing the "Countess" Aria from Figaro, when six of them squatted
down upon the bush before the window and listened motionless to the end—
it looked too "cute" for words. Then, too, every day two blackbirds come at

---

★[Robert Kautsky, painter, youngest son of Hans Kautsky.—L. K.]
†[Count Hülsen was then general manager of the court theater.—L. K.]

my call; I have never seen any as tame; they eat from the tin before the window. For that reason, though, I have ordered a cantata for April 1st that will be a stunner. Can't you send me some sunflower seeds for this little folk? And then—I also want to order one of those war cakes for my own "beak" that you sent several times before; it will give me a slight foretaste of Paradise.

Speaking of things high and most high: here is another matter that won't let me rest: it seems that even without any fault of mine the world of stars has got into disorder. I don't know whether, in the midst of all your anxiety about Scheidemann, you have noticed that an epoch-making discovery was made last year: an Englishman, Walkey, is said to have discovered the "center of the universe." This "center" is supposed to be the star Canopus in the sign of the zodiac Ship Argo (southern hemisphere), which is "only" 500 light-years away from us and is about one and a half million times larger than the sun. These dimensions don't impress me at all, I am quite *blasé*. But there is something else that worries me: a center about which "everything" moves, transforms the universe into a globe. Now, I find it the top notch of absurdity to imagine the universe as a globe as a sort of large potato dumpling or ball of ice cream. In this case above all others, where it is a question of the "whole," such symmetry of figure is a flat, petty-bourgeois conception. Besides, in that event nothing more nor less than the *infinity* of the universe goes by the boards. For, a "globelike infinity" is nonsense. And for my spiritual comfort I absolutely must have something more than human stupidity to think of as infinite! As you see, I literally have "the cares of Herr von Kant." What does Hans Naivus or his learned *filius* think about this?

Now do write a decent letter immediately *de omnibus rebus*, otherwise I shall eject you from the main chamber of my heart, where you have a place directly beside Mimi, and put you into a side chamber.

Good Lord! I forgot the main thing: I haven't finished the translation as yet—only seven printer's sheets are still missing, but these, too, I shall first have to copy. Can't the publisher judge from the twelve sheets?

The finish at last. I embrace you.

Your

R.

To Sophie Liebknecht (April 19, 1917)

Your card yesterday gave me a great deal of pleasure, although it was rather melancholy. If only I could be with you now to make you laugh once more as I did that time after Karl's arrest. Do you remember how we made everyone stare at us by the way we were laughing in the Café Fürstenhof? We had a jolly time then, in spite of everything. Think how we used to drive in a motor-car down Potsdamer Platz every morning, and on to the prison across the Tiergarten where the flowers were blooming, through the quiet Lehrter Strasse with its tall elms; then on the way back, we made it a point of honor to get out at the Fürstenhof: after that, you had always to come to my place in the South End, where everything was in its May glory; next came the pleasant hours in my kitchen, where you and my little Mimi sat patiently awaiting the achievements of my culinary skill. (Do you remember those runner beans I cooked after the French manner?)

Through all my memories of the time runs a vivid impression of the persistently brilliant and hot weather, the only sort of weather that gives a really joyful sense of spring.

In the evening, of course, I had to visit you in my turn, to go to your dear little room.—I love you as a housewife, it suits you to perfection, standing at the table with your girlish figure, as you pour out the tea. Finally, towards midnight we used to see one another home through the dimly lighted, flower-scented streets. Can you recall that wonderful moonlit night in the South End, when I saw you home, how the gables, steeply silhouetted in black against the lovely deep blue of the night sky, resembled the battlements of feudal I castles?

Sonyusha, if only I could always be with you, to take your mind off your troubles, sometimes talking and sometimes silent, so that I could keep you from unhappy brooding. In your card you ask: "Why do these things happen?" Dear child, life is like that, and always has been. Sorrow, and parting, and unsatisfied yearnings are just a part of life. We have to take everything as it comes, and to find beauty in everything. That's what I manage to do. Not from any profound wisdom, but simply because it is my nature. I feel instinctively that this is the only right way of taking life, and that is why I am truly happy in all possible circumstances. I would not spare anything out of my life, or have it different from what it has been and is. If only I could bring you to my way of looking at things. . . .

But I haven't thanked you yet for Karl's photograph. I was so delighted to get it. You could not possibly have thought of a more lovely birthday present. He is on the table in a fine frame and his eyes follow me about wherever I go. (You know how the eyes in some pictures seem to be looking at one wherever one is.) The likeness is excellent. How pleased Karl must be at the news from Russia. But you have good reason to rejoice, too, for now there is nothing to hinder your mother from coming to see you. Had you thought of that? For your sake I do so long for sunshine and I warmth. Here the buds have not opened yet, and yesterday we had sleet. How far is the spring advanced in my "southern landscape" in the South End of Berlin? Last year at this time we were standing together at the garden gate and you were admiring the wealth of flowers. . . .

Don't trouble about writing. I shall often write to you, but I shall be quite satisfied if you send me a postcard now and then.

Have you got my little *Botanist's Guide* with you? Don't worry, darling; everything will come out all right, you'll see.

Much love.
Always your
Rosa.

To Sophie Liebknecht (End of May 1917)

Sonyusha,

Where do you think I am writing this letter? In the garden! I have brought out a small table at which I am now seated, hidden among the shrubs. To the right is the currant bush smelling of cloves; to the left, a privet in flower; overhead, a sycamore and a young slender Spanish chestnut stretch their broad, green hands; in front is the tall, serious, and gentle white poplar, its silvery leaves rustling in the breeze.

On the paper, as I write, the faint shadows of the leaves are at play with the interspersed patches of sunlight; the foliage is still damp from a recent shower, and now and again drops fall on my face and hands.

Service is going on in the prison chapel; the sound of the organ reaches me indistinctly, for it is masked by the noise of the leaves, and by the clear chorus of the birds, which are all in a merry mood today; from afar I hear the call of the cuckoo.

How lovely it is; I am so happy. One seems already to have the midsummer mood—the full luxuriance of summer and the intoxication of life. Do you remember the scenes in Wagner's *Meistersinger*, the one in which the prentices sing "Midsummer Day! Midsummer Day!" and the folk scene where, after singing "St. Crispin! St. Crispin!" the motley crowd joins in a frolicsome dance?

Such days as these are well fitted to produce the mood of those scenes.

I had such an experience yesterday. I must tell you what happened. In the bathroom, before dinner, I found a great peacock-butterfly on the window. It must have been shut up there for two or three days, for it had almost worn itself out fluttering against the hard windowpane, so that there was now nothing more than a slight movement of the wings to show that it was still alive.

Directly I noticed it, I dressed myself, trembling with impatience, climbed up to the window, and took it cautiously in my hand. It had now ceased to move, and I thought it must be dead. But I took it to my own room and put it on the outside window sill, to see if it would revive. There was again a gentle fluttering for a little, but after that the insect did not move. I laid a few flowers in front of its antennae, so that it might have somethign to eat. At that moment the black-cap sang in front of the window so lustily that the echoes rang. Involuntarily I spoke out loud to the butterfly, saying: "Just listen how merrily the bird is singing; you must take heart, too, and come to life again!" I could not help laughing at myself for speaking like this to a half-dead butterfly, and I thought: " You are wasting your breath!" But I was not, for in about half an hour the little creature really revived; after moving about for a while, it was able to flutter slowly away. I was so delighted at this rescue. . . . In the afternoon, of course, I went out into the garden again. I am there always from eight in the morning till noon, when I am summoned to dinner; and again from three till six.

I was expecting the sun to shine, for I felt that it must really show itself once more. But the sky was overcast, and I grew melancholy.

I strolled about the garden. A light breeze was blowing, and I saw a remarkable sight. The overripe catkins on the white poplar were scattered abroad; their seed-down was carried in all directions, filling the air as if with snow-flakes, covering the ground and the whole courtyard; the silvery seed-down made everything look quite ghostlike. The white poplar blooms later than the catkin-bearing trees, and spreads far and wide thanks to this luxuriant dispersal of its seeds; the young shoots sprout like weeds, from all the crannies on the wall and from between the paving stones.

At six o'clock, as usual, I was locked up. I sat gloomily by the window with a dull sense of oppression in the head, for the weather was sultry. Looking upward I could see at a dizzy height the swallows flying gaily to and fro against a background; formed of white, fleecy clouds in a pastel-blue sky; their pointed wings seemed to cut the air like scissors.

Soon the heavens were overcast, everything became blurred; there was a thunder storm with torrents of rain, and two loud peals of thunder which shook the whole place. I shall never forget what followed. The storm had passed on; the sky had turned a thick monotonous grey; a pale, dull spectral twilight suddenly diffused itself over the landscape, so that it seemed as if the whole prospect were under a thick grey veil. A gentle rain was falling steadily upon the leaves; sheet lightning flamed at brief intervals, tinting the leaden sky with flashes of purple, while the distant thunder could still be heard rumbling like the declining waves of a heavy sea. There, quite abruptly, the nightingale began to sing in the sycamore in front of the window.

Despite the rain, the lightning, and the thunder, the notes rang out as clear as a bell. The bird sang as if intoxicated, as if possessed, as if wishing to drown the thunder, to illuminate the twilight.

Never have I heard anything so lovely. On the background of the alternately leaden and lurid sky, the song seemed to show like shafts of silver. It was so mysterious, so incredibly beautiful, that involuntarily I murmured the last verse of Goethe's poem,

"Oh, wert thou here."

Always your
Rosa.

To Sophie Liebknecht (Mid-November 1917)

My beloved Sonichka,

I hope soon to have a chance of sending you this letter at long last, so I hasten to take up my pen. For how long a time I have been forced to forbear my habit of talking to you—on paper at least. I am allowed to write a few letters, and I had to save up my chances for Hans D.★ who was expecting to hear from me. But now all is over. My last two letters to him were addressed to a dead man, and one has already been returned to me. His loss still seems incredible. But enough of this. I prefer to consider such matters in solitude. It only annoys me beyond expression when people try, as N. tried, to "break the news" to me, and to make a parade of their own grief by way of "consolation." Why should my closest friends understand me so little and hold me so cheaply as to be unable to realize that the best way in such cases is to say, quickly, briefly, and simply: "He is dead"?

. . . How I deplore the loss of all these months and years in which we might have had so many joyful hours together, notwithstanding all the horrors that are going on throughout the world. Do you know, Sonichka, the longer it lasts, and the more the infamy and monstrosity of the daily happenings surpasses all bounds, the more tranquil and more confident becomes my personal outlook. I say to myself that it is absurd to apply moral standards to the great elemental forces that manifest themselves in a hurricane, a flood, or an eclipse of the sun. We have to accept them simply as data for investigation, as subjects of study.

Manifestly, objectively considered, these are the only possible lines along which history can move, and we must follow the movement without losing sight of the main trend. I have the feeling that all this moral filth through which we are wading, this huge madhouse in which we live, may all of a sudden, between one day and the next, be transformed into its very opposite, as if by the stroke of a magician's wand; may become something stupendously great and heroic; must inevitable be transformed, if only the war lasts a few years longer. . . . Read Anatole France's *The Gods are Athirst*. My main reason for admiring this work so much is because the author, with the

---

★[Dr. Han's Dieffenbach, one of Rosa's closest friends, killed in the war.]

insight of genius into all that is universally human, seems to say to us: "Behold, out of these petty personalities, out of these trivial commonplaces, arise, when the hour is ripe, the most titanic events and the most monumental gestures of history." We have to take everything as it comes both in social life and in private life; to accept what happens, tranquilly, comprehensively, and with a smile. I feel absolutely convinced that things will take the right turn when the war ends, or not long afterwards; but obviously we have first to pass through a period of terrible human suffering.

What I have just written reminds me of an incident I wish to tell you of, for it seems to me so poetical and so touching. I was recently reading a scientific work upon the migrations of birds, a phenomenon which has hitherto seemed rather enigmatic. From this I learned that certain species, which at ordinary times live at enmity one with another (because some are birds of prey, whilst others are victims), will keep the peace during their great southward flight across the sea. Among the birds that come to winter in Egypt—come in such numbers that the sky is darkened by their flight, —are, besides hawks, eagles, falcons and owls, thousands of little song birds such as larks, golden-crested wrens, and nightingales, mingling fearlessly with the great birds of prey. A truce of God seems to have been declared for the journey. All are striving towards the common goal, to drop, half dead from fatigue, in the land of the Nile, and subsequently to assort themselves by species and localities. Nay more, during the long flight the larger birds have been seen to carry smaller birds on their backs, for instance, cranes have passed in great numbers with a twittering freight of small birds of passage. Is not that charming?

. . . In a tasteless jumble of poems I was looking at recently, I came across one by Hugo von Hoffmannsthal. As a rule I do not care for his writings, I consider them artificial, stilted, and obscure; I simply can't understand him. But this poem is an exception; it pleased me greatly and made a strong impression on me. I am sending you a copy of it, for I think you will like it, too.

I am now deep in the study of geology. Perhaps you will think that must be a dry subject, but if so, you are mistaken. I am reading it with intense interest and passionate enjoyment; it opens up such wide intellectual vistas and supplies a more perfectly unified and more comprehensive conception of nature than any other science. There are so many things I should like to tell you about it, but for that we should have to have a real talk—taking a morning stroll together through the country at the South End, or seeing one another home several times in succession on a calm moonlit night. What are you reading now? How are you getting on with the *Lessing Legende*?★ I want to know everything about you. Write at once, if you can, by the same route, or, failing that, by the official route, without mentioning this letter. I am already counting the weeks till I can hope to see you here again. I suppose it will be soon after the New Year?

What news have you from Karl? When do you expect to see him? Give him a thousand greetings from me. All my love to you, my dear, dear Sonichka. Write soon and copiously.

Your
Rosa.

To Luise Kautsky (November 24, 1917)

Dearest Lulu: I sent you a few lines recently. I am now seizing upon this opportunity, although it is difficult for me to write anything just now. With you, after all, I can speak of almost nothing except *him*, and on that topic there is nothing to say. I at least cannot formulate any words. Also, I must not think of it, otherwise I could not bear it. On the contrary, I continue to live in a dream as though he were still here. I see him alive before me, chat with him in my imagination about everything, *in me* he continues to live.

Yesterday my letter to him dated 21.10 was returned, that is the second one. Letters that failed to reach him!

From his sister† I received a dear letter; she must be a splendid woman, after all she is Hannes' sister.

And how are you? How do you manage to live without all the boys? It must be very quiet and empty in your house now. How do you spend your days? I still see you before me as you were in Wronke in May. You had such a dear look then, such a fearsomely pained expression in your eyes. You did

---

★[A book by Franz Mehring.]
†[Mrs. Margarete Miller, née Diefenbach, of Stuttgart.—L. K.]

not see me as I watched you from my hiding-place, you walked straight across the courtyard into our "house" and carried the little travelling bag with gifts in your hand. I looked upon your dear face and thought to myself: how young are these grey-blue eyes, in which there lies so much restless, unsatisfied searching and such helpless pain, these eyes are 20 years younger than your appearance otherwise; they betray the fact that in your innermost heart you are still the groping, searching, fearsome girl. How much I love you precisely for this inner uncertainty! . . . I should now like to be outside, to sit and chat with you. Dearest, do not be discouraged, don't live like a frog that has been stepped upon! Look, we now have—at least here—such wonderfully mild spring days; the evenings with their silvery moon are so beautiful. I cannot see enough of it, when in the dusk I go walking in the prison courtyard (I purposely go in the evening, so as not to see the walls, the whole surroundings). Read something beautiful! Have you good books now? Please do write me what you are reading, perhaps I shall send or at least recommend you something beautiful that will cheer you.

I am up to my neck in geology, which animates me extraordinarily and gives me much happiness. I am seized with fear when I remember how short a span of life still remains for me and how much there is still to be learned!

Are you happy about the Russians?* Of course they will not be able to maintain themselves in this witches' sabbath,—not because statistics show that economic development in Russia is too backward, as your clever husband has figured out, but because the social democracy in the highly developed west consists of pitifully wretched cowards who, looking quietly on, will let the Russians bleed themselves to death. But such a collapse is better than to "remain alive for the fatherland." It is an historical deed, the traces of which will not disappear in eons of time. I am expecting many other great things during the coming years, only I should prefer to admire history not merely from behind iron bars. . . .

Dearest, be calm and firm, be cheerful despite anything and write me soon. With an embrace,

Your Rosa.

When you write officially, do not make reference to this letter.

---

*[The Russian revolution of October 1917 is meant.—L. K.]

To Sophie Liebknecht (Mid-December 1917)

Karl has been in Luckau prison for a year now. I have been thinking of
that so often this month and of how it is just a year since you came to see
me at Wronke, and gave me that lovely Christmas tree. This time I
arranged to get one here, but they have brought me such a shabby little
tree, with some of its branches broken off—there's no comparison
between it and yours. I'm sure I don't know how I shall manage to fix the
eight candles that I have got for it. This is my third Christmas under lock
and key, but you needn't take it to heart. I am is tranquil and cheerful as
ever. Last night I lay awake for a long time. I have to go to bed at ten, but
can never get to sleep before one in the morning, so I lie in the dark, pon-
dering many things. Last night my thoughts ran this wise: "How strange
it is that I am always in a sort of joyful intoxication, though without sufficient cause. Here I am lying in a dark cell upon a mattress hard as stone;
the building has its usual churchyard quiet, so that one might as well be
already entombed; through the window there falls across the bed a glint of
light from the lamp which burns all night in front of the prison. At intervals I can hear faintly in the distance the noise of a passing train or close
at hand the dry cough of the prison guard as in his heavy boots, he takes
a few slow strides to stretch his limbs. The grind of the gravel beneath his
feet has so hopeless a sound that all the weariness and futility of existence
seems to be radiated thereby into the damp and gloomy night. I lie here
alone and in silence, enveloped in the manifold black wrappings of darkness, tedium, unfreedom, and winter—and yet my heart beats with an
immeasurable and incomprehensible inner joy, just as if I were moving in
the brilliant sunshine across a flowery mead. And in the darkness I smile at
life, as if I were the possessor of a charm which would enable me to transform all that is evil and tragical into serenity and happiness." But when I
search my mind for the cause of this joy, I find there is no cause, and can
only laugh at myself. I believe that the key to the riddle is simply life itself.
This deep darkness of night is soft and beautiful as velvet, if only one looks
at it in the right way. The grind of the damp gravel beneath the slow and
heavy tread of the prison guard is likewise a lovely little song of life—for
one who has ears to hear. At such moments I think of you, and would that

I could hand over this magic key to you also. Then, at all times and in all
places, you would be able to see the beauty and the joy of life; then you
also could live in the sweet intoxication, and make your way across a
flowery mead. Do not think that I am offering you imaginary joys, or that
I am preaching asceticism. I want you to taste all the real pleasures of the
senses. My one desire is to give you in addition my inexhaustible sense of
inward bliss. Could I do so, I should be at ease about you, knowing that
in your passage through life you were clad in a star-bespangled cloak which
would protect you from everything petty, trivial, or harassing.

I am interested to hear of the lovely bunch of berries, black ones and
reddish-violet ones you picked in Steglitz Park. The black berries may
have been elder—of course you know the elder berries which hang in
thick and heavy clusters among fan-shaped leaves. More probably, however, they were privet, slender and graceful, upright spikes of berries, amid
narrow, elongated green leaves. The reddish-violet berries, almost hidden
by small leaves, must have been those of the dwarf medlar; their proper
color is red, but at this late season, when they are overripe and beginning
to rot, they often assume a violet tinge. The leaves are like those of the
myrtle, small, pointed, dark green in color, with a leathery upper surface,
but rough beneath.

Sonyusha, do you know Platen's *Verhängnisvolle Gabel*? Could you send
it to me, or bring it when you come? Karl told me he had read it at home.
George's poems are beautiful. Now I know where you got the verse, "And
amid the rustling of ruddy corn," which you were fond of quoting when
we were walking in the country. I wish you would copy out for me "The
Modern Amades" when you have time. I am so fond of the poem (a
knowledge of which I owe to Hugo Wolf's setting) but I have not got it
here. Are you still reading the *Lessing Legende*? I have been rereading
Lange's *History of Materialism*, which I always find stimulating and invigorating. I do so hope you will read it some day.

Sonichka, dear, I had such a pang recently. In the courtyard where I
walk, army lorries often arrive, laden with haversacks or old tunics and
shirts from the front; sometimes they are stained with blood. They are sent
to the women's cells to be mended, and then go back for use in the army.
The other day one of these lorries was drawn by a team of buffaloes
instead of horses. I had never seen the creatures close at hand before. They

are much more powerfully built than our oxen, with flattened heads, and horns strongly recurved, so that their skulls are shaped something like a sheep's skull. They are black, and have huge, soft eyes. The buffaloes are war trophies from Rumania. The soldier-drivers said that it was very difficult to catch these animals, which had always run wild, and still more difficult to break them in to harness. They had been unmercifully flogged— on the principle of "vae victis." There are about a hundred head in Breslau alone. They have been accustomed to the luxuriant Rumanian pastures and have here to put up with lean and scanty fodder. Unsparingly exploited, yoked to heavy loads, they are soon worked to death. The other day a lorry came laden with sacks, so overladen indeed that the buffaloes were unable to drag it across the threshold of the gate. The soldier-driver, a brute of a fellow, belabored the poor beasts so savagely with the butt end of his whip that the wardress at the gate, indignant at the sight, asked him if he had no compassion for animals. "No more than anyone has compassion for us men," he answered with an evil smile, and redoubled his blows. At length the buffaloes succeeded in drawing the load over the obstacle, but one of them was bleeding. You know their hide is proverbial for its thickness and toughness, but it had been torn. While the lorry was being unloaded, the beasts, which were utterly exhausted, stood perfectly still. The one that was bleeding had an expression on its black face and in its soft black eyes like that of a weeping child—one that has been severely thrashed and does not know why, nor how to escape from the torment of ill-treatment. I stood in front of the team; the beast looked at me; the tears welled from my own eyes. The suffering of a dearly loved brother could hardly have moved me more profoundly than I was moved by my impotence in face of this mute agony. Far distant, lost forever, were the green, lush meadows of Rumania. How different there the light of the sun, the breath of the wind; how different there the song of the birds and the melodious call of the herdsman. Instead, the hideous at one with you in my pain, my weakness, and my street, the fetid stable, the rank hay mingled with moldy straw, the strange and terrible men—blow upon blow, and blood running from gaping wounds. Poor wretch, I am as powerless, as dumb, as yourself; I am longing.

Meanwhile the women prisoners were jostling one another as they busily unloaded the dray and carried the heavy sacks into the building. The driver,

hands in pockets, was striding up and down the courtyard, smiling to himself
as he whistled a popular air. I had a vision of all the splendor of war! . . .

Write soon, darling Sonichka.

Your
Rosa.

Never mind, my Sonyusha; you must be calm and happy all the same.
Such is life, and we have to take it as it is, valiantly, heads erect, smiling
ever—despite all.

To Luise Kautsky (December 19, 1917)

Dearest:

While still under the impression of your dear, long letter, which I received
today and which I have already read through several times, I hasten to answer
you at once, in the hope of being able in the near future to transmit my
epistle to you *sub rosa.* I was so happy about the letter! Not so much, however, about its undertone, which seemed somewhat cool and not very happy
to me. It is as though a shadow had been cast over you,—I suppose it is
Hannes' shadow. . . . I understood that, yet I felt hurt. Again and again I read
the letter through, in order to sense from it the impulsive, passionate, and
warm breath so familiar to me, which I always knew how to draw out of you
whenever I picked at your heartstrings, and which satisfies such a want in me.

How is it, you sheep, that you still doubt my friendship from time to
time? I was surprised, since I know that our relation is already founded as
upon a rock, especially and doubly so since our loss of Hannes. What is it
that again awakens doubts within you? Tell me, for I haven't the faintest
idea. I write but infrequently, it is true, but certainly you comprehend that
it is *exclusively* the constraint from outside that hinders me and that makes
me loathe to write. I cannot pour out my heart as I should like to, if I have
to reflect while writing as to whether the letter hasn't already gone beyond
the limits set, whether it isn't too long, etc. I must feel myself free, as now,
to write as much as I like to, then only can I chat unreservedly.

Visits, of course, are also only half as much fun considering my condition. Only now, for instance, I can explain to you why your visit to Wronke, when you came the first time, was such a fiasco. Just imagine, when I entered the room I was taken by surprise to find entirely new regulations governing the whole procedure. Until then only one person had usually been left there to watch me, and I sat close to my visitors, hand in hand, and chatted undisturbed; suddenly I found a stiff double guard placed over us and a long table between you and me! I felt as though cold water had been poured over me, all the more so since not a word had been told me about the reasons for this aggravation (afterwards, indeed, I learned about the suspicion which our good M. had awakened by her *naïveté*). I was so enraged over this treatment, which *you* of course could not judge, that I decided in my first excitement to decline entirely and wholly to receive any visitors. Of course I could not intimate to you just what had taken place, and therefore seemed so unreasonably moody to you. It was not till the next morning that I quieted down sufficiently to tell myself that I mustn't care a rap about the whole matter, but rather enjoy your visit with all my heart. Here this matter is arranged quite amicably and simply and I should therefore like to ask you: when are you thinking of coming? You say nothing about it in your letter and this gives me cause for uneasiness. Of course I don't want to vex you, but rather ask you to visit me only in case your health, time, humor, and other arrangements so permit and you really derive enjoyment from it. We could see each other about four times and I believe that faithful Igel would accompany you here, too. I recall even now how happy I was suddenly to espy him through the opening gate. Perhaps a similar impromptu could be arranged here, yes, I am sure of it. . . .

And now about Hannes, about our dear, tender, pure boy, like whom there is no second one on earth. That he left behind him something like notes or a diary or poems, I learned only the other day from a letter of our mutual friend Gerlach (you remember, he is one of the victims whom we dragged about with us at that carnival episode, when we ran about masked in Friedenau and stirred up sleeping burghers). G. was very close to Hannes and has collapsed completely over the blow. Now, this G. had many an opportunity at Stuttgart, where he is ill in a hospital, to chat with Hannes' "aunt," Miss Reich, who was his father's housekeeper, and, as it were, a second mother to Hannes. She told him quite a little about U.'s childhood and youth and also reported about H.'s literary legacy. Gerlach hopes to catch sight of the latter and of course to write me about it. And as for H.'s *poems*,—Julek's brother,* with whom, as you know, H. was on terms of friendship, wrote about these from Posen; it seems, therefore, that H. there spoke about his poems and possibly read some of them. I myself know nothing about this, except that he dedicated several poems in the style of Heine, humorous and light, to me. If I am not mistaken you are in correspondence with the Posen M.'s; perhaps you will be good enough to sound them along these lines and write me what positive information can be gained.

Hannes' sister had written me a dear letter, whereupon I replied to her just as heartily and in a manner that not only made it possible but almost imperative for her to get in touch with me again. But she remains quite silent. I don't know what to make of it. In any case the following occurs to me: when at last I am free, and assuming that the world is still standing, at least upon one leg, I should like to suggest to you that the two of us (Igel may of course accompany us) go to Stuttgart, in order to make the sister's acquaintance and possibly look around among the things left by him, and also to chat with his aunt. I should like very much to breathe with you the atmosphere of his closest surroundings among the things reminding us of him. Do you like the idea? There is something else I should like to undertake with you, that I had intended to do with Hannes. I don't know whether you know that H. was an enthusiastic admirer of Romain Rolland. Especially his last letters were filled with *Jean Christophe* [Romain Rolland's novel—Ed.]. He had persuaded me to read this work, had found therein a thousand mutual points of contact, devotion to Hugo Wolf, heartstrings between Germany and France, etc. I too learned to love him (Romain Rolland) and suggested to Hannes that we either travel to Paris together to make R. R.'s acquaintance, or else invite him to come to Germany.

After all, we live but once and good men of this caliber are few and far between; why should one forego the luxury of knowing them and of seeking spiritual contact with them?

The letter in which I offered the suggestion was returned with the black-rimmed notice of death. I am sure that H. would have agreed

---

*[A brother of Julius Marchlewski.—L. K.]

enthusiastically. Shall we not carry this idea out—"God willing?" Above all, you must of course read *Jean Christophe*—or have you already done so? In that case I am surprised that you mention nothing about it. Igel, too, *must* read it; that is something after his heart. Unfortunately only half of the work has as yet appeared in German, but these first volumes are the most beautiful ones.

This story of his youth and his life, written as it is so simply and genuinely, ought to stimulate you and awaken the firm desire at last to make a beginning of your own autobiography.

You are asking about Malvida Meysenburg.★ I had just received it in the last sending from Hannes, but find it so insipid that I did not get further than the middle of the first volume. I find this person somewhat sentimental and lacking in taste.

I have nibbled here and there at Ede's memoirs; you are quite right, they are an accurate reflection of the author.

But you must read Korolenko and give me your judgment about the whole thing. I have recently sent the balance (fifty pages of manuscript) to the chief command and am in hopes that they will soon be handed to Mathilde J. for copying on the typewriter. Let her then give you the entire work, read it as a connected story, and let me know your impression as quickly as possible. *Nota bene*: I have, though with a heavy heart, had to sacrifice the entire closing section of the original, since it partly contained untranslatable matter (such as long Ukrainian poems) and partly kept referring to the Russian literature of the seventies of which the German reader, of course, hasn't the faintest idea, and which, besides, is decidedly inferior from an artistic point of view. I therefore closed with the death of the father, which seemed like the best close to me, since the father is the real central figure of this volume.

I am otherwise opposed to such arbitrariness on the part of the translator, but I saw no other way out in this situation and hope that you, too, will agree. I am corresponding directly with Kestenberg. He merely insists upon his pound of flesh: a preface from me, and I am making a desperate effort to gather some material for it.

I have an idea for a translation for you. In Barnim street I had ordered

---

★["Memoirs of an Idealist."]

a book that seems very well adapted for publication in the German language: *Julie de l'Espinasse*, by Marquis de Ségur. It is a biographical-historical essay, an amazing story of a human life, and at the same time a most interesting cultural document. As you know, Mme. de l'Espinasse was the friend of d'Alembert and the central figure in the whole circle of Encyclopaedists; the story is charmingly told. If you like the idea, I shall have the book sent me (I gave mine away), for it is unfortunately not to be had anymore in bookstores. I am sure that Cassirer *vel* Kestenberg would gladly undertake to bring it out, only I haven't the faintest idea as to how the question of translation rights now stands, especially not now, during the war with France. In any case, however, I believe that it would be a good thing if you were to have the manuscript ready, so as to be able possibly to publish it after the war with the approval of the owners of the rights. I have no doubt but that you would find great enjoyment, in the task (greater than in the Eastern Question).

Your Job's post about the educational committee hurt and offended me very much, for I am not at all in touch with the Teltow-Beskow folk, as you can imagine. Nor can I comprehend how *they* came to drop you in the election. Had you been elected by the T.-B.'s originally? I thought you were a delegate from Greater Berlin. Evidently you were merely a victim of your name this time. Do you still remember the "recommending" speech of Comrade Wulff on the occasion of your first election? There you have the counterpart.* . . . Unfortunately I can't do anything about it and believe me, I should have found many other points besides, where I should like to take a hand.

Yes, the Bolsheviks! Of course they don't please me either with their

---

*[If my memory serves me right, I had complained to Rosa about the fact that I had been dropped in the elections for the educational committee, and had assumed that this was done at the instigation of the super-radicals from Teltow-Beskow (a district on the outskirts of Berlin), for whom the name of Kautsky then had no pleasant ring, as he was regarded by them as too "moderate."

Rosa's reference concerning the first election recalls the fact that, when in 1911 I was proposed by Comrade Heinrich Schulz for membership in the educational committee at the general meeting of the association, Mrs. Wulff supported his motion by referring to the fact that "as the wife of Comrade Kautsky I would be especially well qualified for this office."—L. K.]

peace-fanaticism. But after all—*they* are not to blame. They are in a strait-jacket, and have merely the choice between two beatings and are choosing the lesser. *Others* are responsible for the fact that the devil profits by the Russian revolution. . . . Therefore let us sweep before our own doors. On the whole events there are glorious and will have incalculable results. If only I could talk with you and Igel about all these things, and especially, if I could but stir! But complaining isn't my long suit; for the present I am following events and am in strong hopes of some day experiencing something myself. . . .

There were, of course, a thousand things about which I wanted to tell you, my present studies, etc., etc., now that the gates to my heart stand ajar, but I must nevertheless close for today.

Only a word about the funny dream last night. (I have been sleeping very restlessly of late, and have palpitation of the heart.) I dreamed that I was to sing Hugo Wolf's "Als ich auf dem Euphrat schiffte" at a concert arranged by Faisst, and that I was to play my own accompaniment on the piano. Suddenly I remembered at 7 o'clock in the evening that I couldn't play the piano at all, then how was I to accompany myself? Thereupon I cut myself in the finger, making it bleed so as to have an excuse, and you ventured the opinion that on account of my wounded finger I could send my regrets for not participating in the concert. No, for God's sake, I cried, Faisst would be so angry he'd break with me. I must hurry and persuade my niece to accompany me! Then I remembered that my niece didn't play the piano either, but rather the violin, and I awoke in terror. . . . I suppose it is the yearning for music that inspires such dreams. Laugh about it, as I did, and be embraced a thousand times.

Your R.

To Sophie Liebknecht (March 24, 1918)

My dearest Sonichka,

It is such a terribly long time since I last wrote, but you have been often in my mind. One thing after another seems to take away my wish to write. . . . If we could only be together, strolling through the countryside and talking of whatever might come into our heads—but there is no chance of it at present. My petition for release was rejected, to the accompaniment of a detailed description of my incorrigible wickedness; a request for a brief furlough had no better fate. I shall have to stay here, apparently, till we have conquered the whole world!

Sonyusha, when a long time passes without my having any news from you, I always get the impression that in your loneliness—uneasy, miserable, and even desperate—you must be as helpless as a leaf driven before the wind. The idea makes me very unhappy. But just think, spring has come again, the days are growing so long and so light; there must already be a great deal to see and to listen to in the country. Go out as much as you can; the sky is now so interesting and so variegated with the clouds restlessly chasing one another, the chalky soil, where none of the crops have yet begun to show, must be lovely in the changing lights. Feast your eyes on it all, so that I can see it through you.

That is the only thing of which one never tires, the only thing which perpetually retains the charm of novelty and remains inviolably faithful. For my sake, too, you positively must go to the Botanical Gardens, so that you can tell me all about them. Something exceedingly strange is happening this spring. The birds have come north four to six weeks earlier than usual. The nightingale arrived here on March 10th; the wryneck, which is not due till the end of April, was heard laughing as early as March 15th; the golden oriole, which is sometimes called "the Whitsun bird," and which is never seen till May, was already uttering its flutelike note in the grey sky before dawn fully a week ago. I can hear them all from a distance when they sing in the grounds of the lunatic asylum. I can't think what the meaning or this premature migration is. I wonder sometimes whether the same thing is happening in other places, or whether the influence of the lunatic asylum is responsible for the early return to the particular spot. Do go to the Botanical Gardens, Sonichka, towards noon when the sun is shining brightly, and let me know all you can hear. Over and above the issue of the battle of Cambrai, this really seems to me the most important thing in the world.

The pictures you have sent me are lovely. Needless to say a word about the Rembrandt. As for the Titian, I was even more struck by the horse than by the rider; I should not have thought it possible to depict so much power, so much majesty, in an animal. But the most beautiful of all is Bartolommeo Veneziano's *Portrait of a Lady*. I knew nothing of the work of this artist. What a frenzy of color, what delicacy of line, what a mysterious charm of expression! In a vague sort of way the Lady reminds me of Mona Lisa. Your pictures have brought a flood of joy and light into my prison cell.

Of course you must keep Hans Dieffenbach's book. It grieves me that all his books should not have come into our hands. I would rather have given them to you than to anyone. Did the Shakespeare reach you in good time? What news from Karl, and when do you expect him again? Give him a thousand greetings from me, and a message: "This, too, will pass." Keep your spirits up; enjoy the spring; when the next one comes, we shall all enjoy it together. Best love. Happy Easter!

Love, too, to the children,

Your
Rosa.

13

THE OLD MOLE

(1917)

> *The overthrow of Russia's autocratic monarchy by mass strikes and working-class street actions in March 1917 had obvious relevance for the war-weary masses in Germany and other European nations. Luxemburg's keen analytical mind was drawn to the task of trying to make sense of the complex and fluid realities, at the same time shrewdly comparing them to developments and possibilities in Germany. This article, written from prison, appeared in the May 1917 issue of the oppositional paper* Spartacus.

The outbreak of the Russian Revolution has broken the stalemate in the historical situation created by the continuation of the world war and the simultaneous failure of the proletarian class struggle. For three years Europe has been like a musty room, almost suffocating those living in it. Now all at once a window has been flung open, a fresh, invigorating gust of air is blowing in, and everyone in the room is breathing deeply and freely of it. In particular the "German liberators" are anxiously watching

the theater of the Russian Revolution. The grudging respect of the
German and Austro-Hungarian governments for the "cadgers and con-
spirators" and the nervous tension with which our ruling classes receive
every utterance by Cheidze★ and by the workers' and soldiers' Soviet concerning the question of war and peace are now a tangible confirmation of
the fact which only yesterday met the uncomprehending opposition of the
socialists from the A.G.† This was the fact that the way out of the blind
alley of the world war led not through diplomatic "agreements" and
Wilsonian messages, but solely and exclusively through the revolutionary
action of the proletariat. The victors at Tannenberg and Warsaw now trem-
blingly await their own "liberation" from the choking noose of war by the
Russian proletariat, by the "mob in the street"!

Of course even with the greatest heroism the proletariat of one single
country cannot loosen this noose. The Russian Revolution is growing of
its own accord into an international problem. For the peace efforts of the
Russian workers bring them into acute conflict not only with their own
bourgeoisie, but also with the English, French, and Italian bourgeoisie.
The rumblings of the bourgeois press in all the Entente countries—*The
Times, Malin, Corriere della Sera*, etc.—show that the capitalists of the West,
these stout-hearted champions of "democracy" and of the rights of the
"small nations," are watching, with gnashing teeth and hourly mounting
rage, the advances made by the proletarian revolution that has checked the
glorious era of the undivided rule of imperialism in Europe. The capitalists of the Entente now provide the strongest support for the Russian
bourgeoisie against whom the Russian proletariat is revolting in its struggle
for peace. In every way—diplomatically, financially, commercially—the
Entente capitalists can exert the greatest pressure on Russia, and are surely
doing so already. A liberal revolution? A provisional government of the
bourgeoisie? How nice! These would be immediately recognized officially
and welcomed as a guarantee of Russia's military fitness, as an obedient
instrument of international imperialism. But not one step further! If the
Russian Revolution were to show its proletarian essence, if it were to turn

---

★[The Menshevik President of the Soviet.]
†[The *Arbeitergemeinschaft*, as the centrist opposition which formed the USPD was
then known.]

logically against war and imperialism, then its cherished allies would bare their teeth and attempt to curb it by all possible means. Thus the socialist proletariat of England, France, and Italy has now a bounden duty to raise the banner of revolt against war. Only through vigorous mass action in their own countries, against their own ruling classes, can they avoid openly betraying the Russian revolutionary proletariat, and prevent it bleeding to death in its unequal struggle against not only the Russian bourgeoisie, but also the Western bourgeoisie. The Entente powers' intervention in the internal affairs of the Russian Revolution, which has already taken place, demands of the workers of these countries, as a matter of honor, that they cover the Russian Revolution by attacking the flank of their own ruling classes in order to compel them to make peace.

And now the German bourgeoisie! Torn between smiling sourly and weeping bitterly, they are watching the actions and growing power of the Russian proletariat. Lulled into habitually regarding its own working masses as merely military and political cannon fodder, the German bourgeoisie might well like to utilize the Russian proletariat to get itself out of the war as soon as possible. The hard-pressed German imperialism, which at this very moment is in extremely difficult straits both in the West and in Asia Minor, and at its wits' end at home because of food problems, would like to extricate itself from the affair as quickly as possible and with some semblance of decorum in order to repair and arm itself calmly for further wars. Because of its proletarian-socialist tendency to peace, the Russian Revolution is intended to serve this purpose. Thus both German imperialism and the Entente powers are speculating on how they can profit by the revolution, only from opposite sides. The Western powers want to harness the wagon of imperialism to the bourgeois-liberal tendency of the revolution in order to carry on the war until the defeat of the German competitor. German imperialism would like to avail itself of the proletarian tendency of the revolution in order to extricate itself from the imminent threat of military defeat. Well, why not, gentlemen? German Social Democracy has served so excellently in masking your uncontrolled genocide as an "act of liberation" against Russian Tsarism. Why shouldn't Russian Social Democracy help free the stranded "liberators" from the thorny situation of a war gone awry? The German workers helped wage war when it suited imperialism; the Russian workers are expected to make peace for the same reason.

However, Cheidze is not such an easy man to deal with as Scheide-mann.* Despite a hasty "announcement" by the *Norddeutsche Allgemeine* and hurriedly dispatching Scheidemann to Stockholm for "negotiations," they can expect at best a kick in the pants from the Russian socialists of all shades. And as for a hastily managed "put-up job," a separate peace with Russia, concluded at the eleventh hour, which the German "liberators" would so like to see, and which they are hard pressed to make, the matter definitely cannot be arranged. If the Russian proletariat is to see the victory of its peaceful tendency, it must acquire an increasingly decisive overall position in the country, so that its class action grows to colossal proportions in scope, ardor, profundity and radicalism, and so that Social Democracy can either sweep along or cast aside all the still undecided classes who have been duped by bourgeois nationalism. With barely concealed horror, the German "liberation" find themselves face to face with this clearly visible and inevitable, but so formidable, aspect of the peace tendency in Russia. They fear—and with good reason—that the Russian Moor, unlike his German counterpart, having done his work, will not want to "go," and they fear the sparks which could fly from the neighboring fire on to the East Prussian barns. They readily understand that only the deployment of the most extreme revolutionary energy in a comprehensive class struggle for political power in Russia is capable of effectively carrying through the struggle for peace. But at the same time they long for the good old days of Tsarism, for the "centuries-old faithful friendship with their Eastern neighbor," Romanov absolutism. *Tua res agitur!* Your interests are at stake! This warning by a Prussian minister against the Russian Revolution endures in the soul of the German ruling classes, and the heroes of the Königsberg Trial† are all "as magnificent as the day they were born." It would be expecting too much of the East Prussian police and military State to think it would allow a republic—and a republic freshly constructed and controlled by the revolutionary-socialist proletariat—to exist on its flank. And this East Prussian police spirit is

---

*[In the original the author refers to the SPD leader as *Scheidemännchen*, implying that he is an incomplete or little man, or a mannekin.]

†[The trial in 1904 of a number of German Social Democrats charged with assisting in the smuggling of revolutionary literature into Russia.]

compelled to acknowledge its secret aversion in the open marketplace. The German "liberators" today must publicly raise their right hands and swear that they have no intention of throttling the revolution and restoring dear pug-nosed Nicholas on the Tsarist throne! It was the Russian Revolution that forced the German "liberators" to give themselves this resounding slap before the whole world. With this the Russian Revolution suddenly wiped from the slate of history the whole infamous lie which German Social Democracy and the official mythology of German militarism had lived on for three years. This is how the storm of revolution acts to cleanse, to eradicate lies, to sterilize; this is how it suddenly sweeps away with ruthless broom all the dung-heaps of official hypocrisy that have been accumulating since the outbreak of the world war and the silencing of the class struggle in Europe. The Russian Revolution tore away the mask of "democracy" from the face of the Entente bourgeoisie, and from German militarism it tore away the mask of the would-be liberator from Tsarist despotism.

Nevertheless the question of peace is not quite as simple for the Russian proletariat as it would suit the purposes of Hindenburg and Bethmann to believe. The victory of the revolution, as well as its further tasks, requires more secure backing for the future. The outbreak of the revolution and the commanding position assumed by the proletariat has immediately transformed the imperialist war in Russia into that which the mendacious claptrap of the ruling classes would have us believe it is in every country: a war of national defense. The beautiful dreams of Constantinople and the "national-democratic" plans for reapportionment, which were to make the world so happy, were thrust back down the throats of Milyukov and his associates by the masses of workers and soldiers, and the slogan of national defense was put into practice. However, the Russian proletariat can end the war and make peace with a clear conscience only when their work—the achievement of the revolution and its continued unhampered progress—has been secured! They, the Russian proletariat, are today the only ones who really have to defend the cause of freedom, progress, and democracy. And these things must today be preserved not only against the chicanery, the pressure and the war mania of the Entente bourgeoisie, but tomorrow above all—against the "fists" of the German "liberators." A semiabsolutist police and military state is not a good neighbor for a young republic shaken by internal struggles, and an imperialist soldiery schooled in blind obedience is not a good neighbor for a revolutionary proletariat which is making ready for the most intrepid class struggles of unforeseeable significance and duration.

Already the German occupation of an unfortunate "Independent Poland" is a heavy blow against the Russian Revolution. The operational basis of the revolution is indeed limited when a country which was always one of the most explosive centers of the revolutionary movement, and which in 1905 marched at the head of the Russian Revolution, is completely eliminated and transformed socially into a graveyard, politically into a German barracks. Where then is the guarantee that tomorrow, when peace has been concluded, once German militarism has pried itself loose from the burden of war and resharpened its claws, it will not strike at the Russian proletariat's flank in order to prevent the German semi-absolutist regime from being shaken?

The strangled "assurances" of yesterday's heroes of the Königsberg Trial—these are not enough to put our minds at rest. We still remember only too well the example of the Paris Commune. After all, the cat cannot leave the mouse alone. The world war has unleashed such an orgy of reaction in Germany, has revealed such a degree of militaristic omnipotence, has so stripped away the façade of greatness of the German working class as such, and has shown the foundations of so-called political freedom in Germany to be so empty and flawed, that the prospects from this point of view have become a tragic and serious problem. The "danger of German militarism" to imperialist England or France is of course humbug, war mythology, the cry of Germany's rivals. The danger of German militarism to revolutionary, republican Russia, by contrast, is a very real fact. The Russian proletariat would be very careless politicians if they failed to ask themselves whether the German cannon fodder that allows imperialism to lead it to the slaughterhouse on every battlefield today would not tomorrow obey the command to fight against the Russian Revolution. Of course Scheidemann, Heilmann, and Lensche will already have a "Marxist" theory to hand for it, and Legien and Schlicke will prepare a treaty for this slave-trade, all faithful to the patriotic tradition of the German princes who sold their native subjects as cannon fodder abroad.

There is only one serious guarantee against these natural concerns for the future of the Russian Revolution: the awakening of the German proletariat, the attainment of a position of power by the German "workers and soldiers" in their own country, a revolutionary struggle for peace by the German people. To make peace with Bethmann and Hindenburg would be a hideously difficult and hazardous enterprise with a dubious outcome. With the German "workers and soldiers," peace would be concluded immediately and would rest upon solid foundations.

Thus the question of peace is in reality bound up with the unimpeded, radical development of the Russian Revolution. But the latter is in turn bound up with the parallel revolutionary struggles for peace on the part of the French, English, Italian, and, especially, the German proletariat.

Will the international proletariat shift the responsibility for coming to terms with the European bourgeoisie on to the Russian workers' shoulders, will it surrender this struggle to the imperialist mania of the English, French, and Italian bourgeoisie? At the moment this is how the question of peace should really be formulated.

The conflict between the international bourgeoisie and the Russian proletariat thus reveals the dilemma of the last phase of the global situation: either world war to the verge of universal ruin or proletarian revolution—imperialism or socialism.

And here again we are confronted by our old betrayed slogans of revolution and socialism, words which we repeated a thousand times in our propaganda and which we failed to put into practice when, on the outbreak of war, the time came to give substance to them. They again presented themselves to every thinking socialist as the futile genocide dragged on. They presented themselves once more in an obviously negative form as a result of the wretched fiasco of the attempts of bourgeois pacifism at achieving a diplomatic agreement. Today we again see them in a positive light; they have become the substance of the work, the destiny and the future of the Russian Revolution. Despite betrayal, despite the universal failure of the working masses, despite the disintegration of the Socialist International, the great historical law is making headway—like a mountain stream which has been diverted from its course and has plunged into the depths, it now reappears, sparkling and gurgling, in an unexpected place.

Old mole. History, you have done your work well! At this moment the slogan, the warning cry, such as can be raised only in the great period of global change, again resounds through the International and the German proletariat. That slogan is: Imperialism or Socialism! War or Revolution! There is no third way!

14

Speech to the Founding Convention of the German Communist Party

(1918; excerpts)

Luxemburg was in agreement with many revolutionary socialists who concluded that the German Social Democratic Party, and the Socialist International, had been discredited by World War I. The perspectives animating her political activity were—despite important differences—also very much in harmony with the orientation animating those who made the Bolshevik Revolution of 1917. It is hardly surprising, therefore, to find her in the forefront of the German Communist Party's founding convention in late 1918, where she gave this speech. The sweep of her critical intelligence, and her deeply revolutionary-democratic commitments, stand in stark contrast to the sectarianism and bureaucratic deterioration which so severely damaged that organization after her death. This was her final speech. It first appeared in the December 31, 1918, issue of Die Rote Fahne.

Comrades! Our task today is to discuss and adopt a program. In undertaking this task we are not actuated solely by the consideration that yesterday we founded a new party and that a new party must formulate a program. Great historical movements have been the determining

From Mary-Alice Waters, ed., *Rosa Luxemburg Speaks* (New York: Pathfinder Press, 1970).

causes of today's deliberations. The time has arrived when the entire socialist program of the proletariat has to be established upon a new foundation. We are faced with a position similar to that which was faced by Marx and Engels when they wrote the *Communist Manifesto* seventy years ago. As you all know, the *Communist Manifesto* dealt with socialism, with the realization of the aims of socialism, as the immediate task of the proletarian revolution. This was the idea represented by Marx and Engels in the Revolution of 1848; it was thus, likewise, that they conceived the basis for proletarian action in the international field. In common with all the leading spirits in the working-class movement, both Marx and Engels then believed that the immediate introduction of socialism was at hand. All that was necessary was to bring about a political revolution, to seize the political power of the state, and socialism would then immediately pass from the realm of thought to the realm of flesh and blood.

Subsequently, as you are aware, Marx and Engels undertook a thoroughgoing revision of this outlook. In the joint preface to the reissue of the *Communist Manifesto* in the year 1872, we find the following passage: "No special stress is laid on the revolutionary measures proposed at the end of section two. That passage would, in many respects, be differently worded today. In view of the gigantic strides of modern industry during the last twenty-five years and of the accompanying improved and extended organization of the working class, in view of the practical experience gained, first in the February Revolution, and then, still more, in the Paris Commune, where the proletariat for the first time held political power for two whole months, this program has in some details become antiquated. One thing especially was proved by the Commune, viz., that the 'working class cannot simply lay hold of the ready-made state machinery and wield it for its own purposes.' "

What is the actual wording of the passage thus declared to be out of date? It runs as follows:

The proletariat will use its political supremacy: to wrest, by degrees, all capital from the bourgeoisie; to centralize all instruments of production in the hands of the state, i.e., of the proletariat organized as the ruling class; and to increase the total of productive forces as rapidly as possible.

Of course, in the beginning, this cannot be effected except by means of despotic inroads on the rights of property, and on the conditions of bourgeois production; by measures, therefore, which appear economically insufficient and untenable, but which, in the course of the movement, outstrip themselves, necessitate further inroads upon the old social order, and are unavoidable as a means of entirely revolutionizing the mode of production.

The measures will, of course, be different in different countries.

Nevertheless, in the most advanced countries, the following will be pretty generally applicable:

1. Abolition of property in land and application of all land rents to public purposes.

2. A heavy progressive or graduated income tax.

3. Abolition of the right of inheritance.

4. Confiscation of the property of all emigrants and rebels.

5. Centralization of credit in the hands of the state, by means of a national bank with state capital and an exclusive monopoly.

6. Centralization of the means of communication and transport in the hands of the state.

7. Extension of factories and instruments of production owned by the state: the bringing into cultivation of waste lands, and the improvement of the soil generally, in accordance with a concerted plan.

8. Equal obligation upon all to labor. Establishment of industrial armies, especially for agriculture.

9. Coordination of agriculture with manufacturing industries: gradual abolition of the distinction between town and country, by a more equable distribution of the population throughout the rural areas.

10. Free education for all children in public schools. Abolition of children's factory labor in its present form. Combination of education with industrial production, etc., etc.

With a few trifling variations, these, as you know, are the tasks that confront us today. It is by such measures that we shall have to realize socialism. Between the day when the above program was formulated, and the present hour, there have intervened seventy years of capitalist development, and the historical evolutionary process has brought us back to the standpoint which Marx and Engels had in 1872 abandoned as erroneous. At that time there were excellent reasons for believing that their earlier views had been wrong. The further evolution of capital has, however, resulted in this, that what was error in 1872 has become truth today, so that it is our immediate objective to fulfill what Marx and Engels thought they would have to fulfill in the year 1848. But between that point of development that beginning in the year 1848, and our own views and our immediate task, there lies the whole evolution, not only of capitalism, but in addition of the socialist labor movement. Above all, there have intervened the previously mentioned developments in Germany as the leading land of the modern proletariat.

This working-class evolution has taken a peculiar form. When, after the disillusionments of 1848, Marx and Engels had given up the idea that the proletariat could immediately realize socialism, there came into existence in all countries socialist parties inspired with very different aims. The immediate objective of these parties was declared to be detail work, the petty daily struggle in the political and industrial fields. Thus, by degrees, would proletarian armies be formed, and these armies would be ready to realize socialism when capitalist development had matured. The socialist program was thereby established upon an utterly different foundation, and in Germany the change took a peculiarly typical form. Down to the collapse of August 4, 1914, the German social democracy took its stand upon the Erfurt program, and by this program the so-called immediate minimal aims were placed in the foreground, while socialism was no more than a distant guiding star. . . .

The fourth of August did not come like thunder out of a clear sky; what happened on the fourth of August was not a chance turn of affairs, but was the logical outcome of all that the German socialists had been doing day after day for many years. [*Hear! hear!*] Engels and Marx, had it been possible for them to live on into our own time, would, I am convinced, have protested with the utmost energy, and would have used all the forces at their disposal to keep the party from hurling itself into the abyss. But after Engels's death in 1895, in the theoretical field the leadership of the party passed into the hands of Kautsky. The upshot of this change was that at every annual congress the energetic protests of the left wing against a purely parliamentarist policy, its urgent warnings against the sterility and the danger of such a policy, were stigmatized as anarchism, anarchizing socialism, or at least anti-Marxism. What passed officially for Marxism became a cloak for all possible kinds of opportunism, for persistent shirking of the revolutionary class struggle, for every conceivable half measure. Thus the German social democracy, and the labor movement, the trade-union movement as well, were condemned to pine away within the framework of capitalist society. No longer did German socialists and trade unionists make any serious attempt to overthrow capitalist institutions or to put the capitalist machine out of gear.

But we have now reached the point, comrades, when we are able to say that we have rejoined Marx, that we are once more advancing under his flag. If today we declare that the immediate task of the proletariat is to make socialism a living reality and to destroy capitalism root and branch, in saying this we take our stand upon the ground occupied by Marx and Engels in 1848; we adopt a position from which in principle they never moved. It has at length become plain what true Marxism is, and what substitute Marxism has been. [*Applause.*] I mean the substitute Marxism which has so long been the official Marxism of the social democracy. You see what Marxism of this sort leads to, the Marxism of those who are the henchmen of Ebert, David, and the rest of them. These are the official representatives of the doctrine which has been trumpeted for decades as Marxism undefiled. But in reality Marxism could not lead in this direction, could not lead Marxists to engage in counterrevolutionary activities side by side with such as Scheidemann. Genuine Marxism turns its weapons against those also who seek to falsify it. Burrowing like a mole beneath the foundations of capitalist society, it has worked so well that the larger half of the German proletariat is marching today under our banner, the storm-riding standard of revolution. Even in the opposite camp, even where the counterrevolution still seems to rule, we have adherents and future comrades-in-arms. . . .

What has the war left of bourgeois society beyond a gigantic rubbish-heap? Formally, of course, all the means of production and most of the instruments of power, practically all the decisive instruments of power, are still in the hands of the dominant classes. We are under no illusions here. But what our rulers will be able to achieve with the powers they possess, over and above, frantic attempts to reestablish their system of spoliation through blood and slaughter, will be nothing more than chaos. Matters have reached such a pitch that today mankind is faced with two alternatives: It may perish amid chaos; or it may find salvation in socialism. As the outcome of the great war it is impossible for the capitalist classes to find any issue from their difficulties while they maintain class rule. We now realize the absolute truth of the statement formulated for the first time by Marx and Engels as the scientific basis of socialism in the great charter of our movement, in the *Communist Manifesto*. Socialism, they said, will become a historical necessity. Socialism is inevitable, not merely because proletarians are no longer willing to live under the conditions imposed by the capitalist class, but further because, if the proletariat fails to fulfill its duties as a class, if it fails to realize socialism, we shall crash down together to a common doom. [*Prolonged applause.*]

Here you have the general foundation of the program we are officially adopting today, a draft of which you have all read in the pamphlet *Was will der Spartakusbund?* [What Does Spartacus Want?—Trans.]. Our program is deliberately opposed to the leading principle of the Erfurt program; it is deliberately opposed to the separation of the immediate and so-called minimal demands formulated for the political and economic struggle, from the socialist goal regarded as a maximal program. It is in deliberate opposition to the Erfurt program that we liquidate the results of seventy years' evolution, that we liquidate, above all, the primary results of the war, saying we know nothing of minimum and maximal programs; we know only one thing, socialism; this is the minimum we are going to secure. [*Hear! hear!*]

I do not propose to discuss the details of our program. This would take too long, and you will form your own opinions upon matters of detail. The task that devolves upon me is merely to sketch the broad lines in which our program is distinguished from what has hitherto been the official program of the German social democracy. I regard it, however, as of the utmost importance that we should come to an understanding in our estimate of the concrete circumstances of the hour, of the tactics we have to adopt, of the practical measures which must be undertaken, in view of the course of the revolution down to the present time, and in view of the probable lines of further development. We have to judge the political situation from the outlook I have just characterized, from the outlook of those who aim at the immediate realization of socialism, of those who are determined to subordinate everything else to that end.

Our congress, the congress of what I may proudly call the only revolutionary socialist party of the German Proletariat, happens to coincide in point of time with a crisis in the development of the German revolution. "Happens to coincide," I say; but in truth the coincidence is no chance matter. We may assert that after the occurrences of the last few days the curtain has gone down upon the first act of the German revolution. We are now in the opening of the second act and it is our common duty to undertake self-examination and self-criticism. We shall be guided more wisely in the future, and we shall gain additional impetus for further advances, if we study all that we have done and all that we have left undone. Let us, then, carefully scrutinize the events of the first act in the revolution.

The movement began on November 9. The revolution of November 9 was characterized by inadequacy and weakness. This need not surprise us. The revolution followed four years of war, four years during which, schooled by the social democracy and the trade unions, the German proletariat had behaved with intolerable ignominy and had repudiated its socialist obligations to an extent unparalleled in any other land. We Marxists, whose guiding principle is a recognition of historical evolution, could hardly expect that in the Germany which had known the terrible spectacle of August 4, and which during more than four years had reaped the harvest sown on that day, there should suddenly occur on November 9, 1918, a glorious revolution, inspired with definite class-consciousness, and directed towards a clearly conceived aim. What happened on November 9 was to a very small extent the victory of a new principle; it was little more than collapse of the extant system of imperialism. [*Hear! hear!*]

The moment had come for the collapse of imperialism, a colossus with feet of clay, crumbling from within. The sequel of this collapse was a more or less chaotic movement, one practically devoid of reasoned plan. The only source of union, the only persistent and saving principle, was the watchword, "Form workers' and soldiers' councils." Such was the slogan of the revolution, whereby, in spite of the inadequacy and weakness of the opening phases, it immediately established its claim to be numbered among proletarian socialist revolutions. To those who participated in the revolution of November 9, and who nonetheless shower calumnies upon the Russian Bolshevists, we should never cease to reply with the question: "Where did you learn the alphabet of your revolution? Was it not from the

Russians that you learned to ask for workers' and soldiers' councils?" [*Applause.*]

Those pygmies who today make it one of their chief tasks, as heads of what they falsely term a socialist government, to join with the imperialists of Britain in a murderous attack upon the Bolsheviks, were then taking their seats as deputies upon the workers' and soldiers' councils, thereby formally admitting that the Russian Revolution created the first watchwords for the world revolution. A study of the existing situation enables us to predict with certainty that in whatever country, after Germany, the proletarian revolution may next break out, the first step will be the formation of workers' and soldiers' councils. [*Murmurs of assent.*]

Herein is to be found the tie that unites our movement internationally. This is the motto which distinguishes our revolution utterly from all earlier revolutions, bourgeois revolutions. On November 9, the first cry of the revolution, as instinctive as the cry of a newborn child, was for workers' and soldiers' councils. This was our common rallying-cry, and it is through the councils that we can alone hope to realize socialism. But it is characteristic of the contradictory aspects of our revolution, characteristic of the contradictions which attend every revolution, that at the very time when this great, stirring, and instinctive cry was being uttered, the revolution was so inadequate, so feeble, so devoid of initiative, so lacking in clearness as to its own aims, that on November 10 our revolutionists allowed to slip from their grasp nearly half the instruments of power they had seized on November 9. We learn from this, on the one hand, that our revolution is subject to the prepotent law of historical determinism, a law which guarantees that, despite all difficulties and complications, notwithstanding all our own errors, we shall nevertheless advance step by step towards our goal. On the other hand, we have to recognize, comparing this splendid battle cry with the paucity of the results practically achieved, we have to recognize that these were no more than the first childish and faltering footsteps of the revolution, which has many arduous tasks to perform and a long road to travel before the promise of the first watchwords can be fully realized.

The weeks that have elapsed between November 9 and the present day have been weeks filled with multiform illusions. The primary illusion of the workers and soldiers who made the revolution was their belief in the possibility of unity under the banner of what passes by the name of socialism. What could be more characteristic of the internal weakness of the revolution of November 9 than the fact that at the very outset the leadership passed in no small part into the hands of persons who a few hours before the revolution broke out had regarded it as their chief duty to issue warnings against revolution—[*Hear! hear!*]—to attempt to make revolution impossible—into the hands of such as Ebert, Scheidemann, and Haase. One of the leading ideas of the revolution of November 9 was that of uniting the various socialist trends. The union was to be effected by acclamation. This was an illusion which had to be bloodily avenged, and the events of the last few days have brought a bitter awakening from our dreams; but the self-deception was universal, affecting the Ebert and Scheidemann groups and affecting the bourgeoisie no less than ourselves.

Another illusion was that affecting the bourgeoisie during this opening act of the revolution. They believed that by means of the Ebert-Haase combination, by means of the so-called socialist government, they would really be able to bridle the proletarian masses and to strangle the socialist revolution. Yet another illusion was that from which the members of the Ebert-Scheidemann government suffered when the believed that with the aid of the soldiers returned from the front they would be able to hold down the workers and to curb all manifestations of the socialist class struggle. Such were the multifarious illusions which explain recent occurrences. One and all, they have now been dissipated. It has been plainly proved that the union between Haase and Ebert-Scheidemann under the banner of "socialism" serves merely as a fig leaf for the decent veiling of a counterrevolutionary policy. We ourselves, as always happens in revolutions, have been cured of our self-deceptions.

There is a definite revolutionary procedure whereby the popular mind can be freed from illusion, but, unfortunately, the cure involves that the people must be blooded. In revolutionary Germany, events have followed the course characteristic of all revolutions. The bloodshed in Chaussee Street on December 6, the massacre of December 24, brought the truth home to the broad masses of the people. Through these occurrences they came to realize that what passes by the name of a socialist government is a government representing the counterrevolution. They came to realize that anyone who continues to tolerate such a state of affairs is working against the proletariat and against socialism. [*Applause.*]

Vanished, likewise, is the illusion cherished by Messrs. Ebert, Scheidemann & Co., that with the aid of soldiers from the front they will be able forever to keep the workers in subjection. What has been the effect of the experiences of December 6 and 24? There has been obvious of late a profound disillusionment among the soldiery. The men begin to look with a critical eye upon those who have used them as cannon fodder against the socialist proletariat. Herein we see once more the working of the law that the socialist revolution undergoes a determined objective development, a law in accordance with which the battalions of the labor movement gradually learn through bitter experience to recognize the true path of revolution. Fresh bodies of soldiers have been brought to Berlin, new detachments of cannon fodder, additional forces for the subjection of socialist proletarians with the result that, from barrack after barrack, there comes a demand for the pamphlets and leaflets of the Spartacus Group.

This marks the close of the first act. The hopes of Ebert and Scheidemann that they would be able to rule the proletariat with the aid of reactionary elements among the soldiery, have already to a large extent been frustrated. What they have to expect within the very near future is an increasing development of definite revolutionary trends within the barracks. Thereby the army of the fighting proletariat will be augmented, and correspondingly the forces of the counterrevolutionists will dwindle. In consequence of these changes, yet another illusion will have to go, the illusion that animates the bourgeoisie, the dominant class. If you read the newspapers of the last few days, the newspapers issued since the incidents of December 24, you cannot fail to perceive plain manifestations of disillusionment conjoined with indignation, both due to the fact that the henchmen of the bourgeoisie, those who sit in the seats of the mighty, have proved inefficient. [*Hear! hear!*]

It had been expected of Ebert and Scheidemann that they would prove themselves strong men, successful lion tamers. But what have they achieved? They have suppressed a couple of trifling disturbances, and as a sequel the hydra of revolution has raised its head more resolutely than ever. Thus disillusionment is mutual, nay universal. The workers have completely lost the illusion which had led them to believe that a union between Haase and Ebert-Scheidemann would amount to a socialist government. Ebert and Scheidemann have lost the illusion which had led them to imagine that with the aid of proletarians in military uniform they could permanently keep down proletarians in civilian dress. The members of the middle class have lost the illusion that, through the instrumentality of Ebert, Scheidemann, and Haase, they can humbug the entire socialist revolution of Germany as to the ends it desires. All these things have a merely negative force, and there remains from them nothing but the rags and tatters of destroyed illusions. But it is in truth a great gain for the proletariat that naught beyond these rags and tatters remains from the first phase of the revolution, for there is nothing so destructive as illusion, whereas nothing can be of greater use to the revolution than naked truth.

I may appropriately recall the words of one of our classical writers, a man who was no proletarian revolutionary, but a revolutionary spirit nurtured in the middle class. I refer to Lessing, and quote a passage which has always aroused my sympathetic interest: "I do not know whether it be a duty to sacrifice happiness and life to truth. . . . But this much I know, that it is our duty, if we desire to teach truth, to teach it wholly or not at all, to teach it clearly and bluntly, unenigmatically, unreservedly, inspired with full confidence in its powers. . . . The cruder an error, the shorter and more direct is the path leading to truth. But a highly refined error is likely to keep us permanently estranged from truth, and will do so all the more readily in proportion as we find it difficult to realize that it is an error. One who thinks of conveying to mankind truth masked and rouged, may be truth's pimp, but has never been truth's lover." Comrades, Messrs. Haase, Dittmarnn, etc., have wished to bring us the revolution, to introduce socialism, covered with a mask, smeared with rouge; they have thus shown themselves to be the pimps of the counterrevolution. Today these concealments have been discarded, and what was offered is disclosed in the brutal and sturdy lineaments of Messrs. Ebert and Scheidemann. Today the dullest among us can make no mistake. What is offered is the counterrevolution in all its repulsive nudity. . . .

In order to secure support from the only class whose class interests the government really represents, in order to secure support from the bourgeoisie—a support which has in fact been withdrawn owing to recent occurrences—Ebert and Scheidemann will be compelled to pursue an increasingly counterrevolutionary policy. The demands of the South German states, as published today in the Berlin newspapers, gave frank expressions to the wish to secure "enhanced safety" for the German realm. In plain language, this means that they desire the declaration of a state of siege against "anarchist, disorderly, and Bolshevist" elements; that is to say, against socialists. By the pressure of circumstances, Ebert and Scheidemann will be constrained to the expedient of dictatorship, with or without the declaration of a state of siege. Thus, as an outcome of the previous course of development, by the mere logic of events and through the operation of the forces which control Ebert and Scheidemann, there will ensue during the second act of the revolution a much more pronounced opposition of tendencies and a greatly accentuated class struggle. [*Hear! hear!*] This intensification of conflict will arise, not merely because the political influences I have already enumerated, dispelling all illusions, will lead to a declared hand-to-hand fight between the revolution and the counterrevolution; but in addition because the flames of a new fire are spreading upward from the depths, the flames of the economic struggle.

It was typical of the first period of the revolution down to December 24 that the revolution remained exclusively political. Hence the infantile character, the inadequacy, the halfheartedness, the aimlessness, of this revolution. Such was the first stage of a revolutionary transformation whose main objective lies in the economic field, whose main purpose it is to secure a fundamental change in economic conditions. Its steps were as uncertain as those of a child groping its way without knowing where it is going; for at this stage, I repeat, the revolution had a purely political stamp. But within the last two or three weeks a number of strikes have broken out quite spontaneously. Now, I regard it as the very essence of this revolution that strikes will become more and more extensive, until they constitute at last the focus of the revolution. [*Applause.*] Thus we shall have an economic revolution, and therewith a socialist revolution. The struggle for socialism has to be fought out by the masses, by the masses alone, breast to breast against capitalism; it has to be fought out by those in every occupation, by every proletarian against his employer. Thus only can it be a socialist revolution.

The thoughtless had a very different picture of the course of affairs. They imagined it would merely be necessary to overthrow the old government, to set up a socialist government at the head of affairs, and then to inaugurate socialism by decree. Another illusion? Socialism will not be and cannot be inaugurated by decrees; it cannot be established by any government, however admirably socialistic. Socialism must be created by the masses, must be made by every proletarian. Where the chains of capitalism are forged, there must the chains be broken. That only is socialism, and thus only can socialism be brought into being. What is the external form of struggle for socialism? The strike, and that is why the economic phase of development has come to the front in the second act of the revolution. This is something on which we may pride ourselves, for no one will dispute with us the honor. We of the Spartacus Group, we of the Communist Party of Germany, are the only ones in all Germany who are on the side of the striking and fighting workers. [*Hear! hear!*] You have read and witnessed again and again the attitude of the Independent Socialists towards strikes. There was no difference between the outlook of *Vorwärts* and the outlook of *Freiheit*. Both journals sang the same tune: Be diligent, socialism means hard work. Such was their utterance while capitalism was still in control! Socialism cannot be established in that way, but only by carrying on an unremitting struggle against capitalism. Yet we see the claims of the capitalists defended, not only by the most outrageous profit-snatchers, but also by the Independent Socialists and by their organ, *Freiheit*; we find that our Communist Party stands alone in supporting the workers against the exactions of capital. This suffices to show that all are today persistent and unsparing enemies of the strike, except only those who have taken their stand with us upon the platform of revolutionary communism.

The conclusion to be drawn is, not only that during the second act of the revolution, strikes will become increasingly prevalent; but, further, that strikes will become the central feature and the decisive factors of the revolution, thrusting purely political questions into the background. The inevitable consequence of this will be that the struggle in the economic field will be enormously intensified. The revolution will therewith assume aspects that will be no joke to the bourgeoisie. The members of the capitalist class are quite agreeable to mystifications in the political domain, where masquerades are still possible, where such creatures as Ebert and Scheidemann can pose as socialists; but they are horror-stricken directly profits are touched.

To the Ebert-Scheidemann government, therefore, the capitalists will present these alternatives. Either, they will say, you must put an end to the strikes, you must stop this strike movement which threatens to destroy us; or else, we have no more use for you. I believe, indeed, that the government has already damned itself pretty thoroughly by its political measures. Ebert and Scheidemann are distressed to find that the bourgeoisie no longer reposes confidence in them. The capitalists will think twice before they decide to cloak in ermine the rough upstart, Ebert. If matters go so far that a monarch is needed, they will say: "It does not suffice a king to have blood upon his hand; he must also have blue blood in his veins." [*Hear! hear!*] Should matters reach this pass, they will say: "If we needs must have a king, we will not have a parvenu who does not know how to comport himself in kingly fashion." [*Laughter.*]

It is impossible to speak positively as to details. But we are not concerned with matters of detail, with the question precisely what will happen, or precisely when it will happen. Enough that we know the broad lines of coming developments. Enough that we know that, to the first act of the revolution, to the phase in which the political struggle has been the leading feature, there will succeed a phase predominantly characterized by an intensification of the economic struggle, and that sooner or later the government of Ebert and Scheidemann will take its place among the shades.

It is far from easy to say what will happen to the National Assembly during the second act of the revolution. Perhaps, should the assembly come into existence, it may prove a new school of education for the working class. But it seems just as likely that the National Assembly will never come into existence. Let me say parenthetically, to help you to understand the grounds upon which we were defending our position yesterday, that our only objection was to limiting our tactics to a single alternative. I will not reopen the whole discussion, but will merely say a word or two lest any of you should falsely imagine that I am blowing hot and cold with the same breath. Our position today is precisely that of yesterday. We do not propose to base our tactics in relation to the National Assembly upon what is a possibility but not a certainty. We refuse to stake everything upon the belief that the National Assembly will never come into existence. *We wish to be prepared for all possibilities, including the possibility of utilizing the National Assembly for revolutionary purposes should the assembly ever come into being.* Whether it comes into being or not is a matter of indifference, for whatever happens the success of the revolution is assured.

What fragments will then remain of the Ebert-Scheidemann government or of any other alleged social-democratic government which may happen to be in charge when the revolution takes place? I have said that the masses of the workers are already alienated from them, and that the soldiers are no longer to be counted upon as counterrevolutionary cannon fodder. What on earth will the poor pygmies be able to do? How can they hope to save the situation? They will still have one last chance. Those of you who have read today's newspapers will have seen where the ultimate reserves are, will have learned whom it is that the German counterrevolution proposes to lead against us should the worst come to the worst. You will all have read how the German troops in Riga are already marching shoulder to shoulder with the English against the Russian Bolsheviks. . . .

To resume the thread of my discourse, it is clear that all these machinations, the formation of Iron Divisions and, above all, the before-mentioned agreement with British imperialists, must be regarded as the ultimate reserves, to be called up in case of need in order to throttle the German socialist movement. Moreover, the cardinal question, the question of the prospects of peace, is intimately associated with the affair. What can such negotiations lead to but a fresh lighting-up of the war? While these rascals are playing a comedy in Germany, trying to make us believe that they are working overtime in order to arrange conditions of peace, and declaring that we Spartacists are the disturbers of the peace whose doings are making the Allies uneasy and retarding the peace settlement, they are themselves kindling the war afresh, a war in the East to which a war on German soil will soon succeed.

Once more we meet with a situation the sequel of which cannot fail to be a period of fierce contention. It devolves upon us to defend, not socialism alone, not revolution alone, but likewise the interests of world peace. Herein we find a justification for the tactics which we of the Spartacus Group have consistently and at every opportunity pursued throughout the four years of the war. Peace means the worldwide revolution of the proletariat. In one way only can peace be established and peace be safeguarded—by the victory of the socialist proletariat! [*Prolonged applause.*]

What general tactical considerations must we deduce from this? How can we best deal with the situation with which we are likely to be confronted in the immediate future? Your first conclusion will doubtless be a hope that the fall of the Ebert-Scheidemann government is at hand, and that its place will be taken by a declared socialist proletarian revolutionary government. For my part, I would ask you to direct your attention, not on the apex, but to the base. We must not again fall into the illusion of the first phase of the revolution, that of November 9; we must not think that when we wish to bring about a socialist revolution it will suffice to overthrow the capitalist government and to set up another in its place. There is only one way of achieving the victory of the proletarian revolution.

We must begin by undermining the Ebert-Scheidemann government by destroying its foundations through a revolutionary mass struggle on the part of the proletariat. Moreover, let me remind you of some of the inadequacies of the German revolution, inadequacies which have not been overcome with the close of the first act of the revolution. We are far from having reached a point when the overthrow of the government can ensure the victory of socialism. I have endeavored to show you that the revolution of November 9 was, before all, a political revolution; whereas the revolution which is to fulfill our aims, must in addition, and mainly, be an economic revolution. But further, the revolutionary movement was confined to the towns, and even up to the present date the rural districts remain practically untouched. Socialism would prove illusory if it were to leave our present agricultural system unchanged. From the broad outlook of socialist economics, manufacturing industry cannot be remodelled unless it be quickened through a socialist transformation of agriculture. The leading idea of the economic transformation that will realize socialism is an abolition of the contrast and the division between town and country. This separation, this conflict, this contradiction, is a purely capitalist phenomenon, and it must disappear as soon as we place ourselves upon the socialist standpoint.

If socialist reconstruction is to be undertaken in real earnest, we must direct attention just as much to the open country as to the industrial centers, and yet as regards the former we have not even taken the first steps. This is essential, not merely because we cannot bring about socialism without socializing agriculture; but also because, while we may think we have reckoned up the last reserves of the counterrevolution against us and our endeavors, there remains another important reserve which has not yet been taken into account. I refer to the peasantry. Precisely because the peasants are still untouched by socialism, they constitute an additional reserve for the counterrevolutionary bourgeoisie. The first thing our enemies will do when the flames of the socialist strikes begin to scorch their heels, will be to mobilize the peasants, who are fanatical devotees of private property. There is only one way of making headway against this threatening counterrevolutionary power. We must carry the class struggle into the country districts; we must mobilize the landless proletariat and the poorer peasants against the richer peasants. [*Loud applause.*]

From this consideration we may deduce what we have to do to ensure the success of the revolution. First and foremost, we have to extend in all directions the system of workers' councils. What we have taken over from November 9 are mere weak beginnings, and we have not wholly taken over even these. During the first phase of the revolution we actually lost extensive forces that were acquired at the very outset. You are aware that the counterrevolution has been engaged in the systematic destruction of the system of workers' and soldiers' councils. In Hesse, these councils have been definitely abolished by the counterrevolutionary government; elsewhere, power has been wrenched from their hands. Not merely, then, have we to develop the system of workers' and soldiers' councils, but we have to induce the agricultural laborers and the poorer peasants to adopt this system. We have to seize power, and the problem of the seizure of power assumes this aspect; what, throughout Germany, can each workers' and soldiers' council achieve? [*Bravo!*] There lies the source of power. We must mine the bourgeois state, and we must do so by putting an end everywhere to the cleavage in public powers, to the cleavage between legislative and executive powers. These powers must be united in the hands of the workers' and soldiers' councils.

Comrades, we have here an extensive field to till. We must build from below upwards, until the workers' and soldiers' councils gather so much strength that the overthrow of the Ebert-Scheidemann or any similar government will be merely the final act in the drama. For us the conquest of power will not be effected at one blow. It will be a progressive act, for we shall progressively occupy all the positions of the capitalist state, defending tooth and nail each one that we seize. Moreover, in my view and in that of my most intimate associates in the party, the economic struggle, likewise, will be carried on by the workers' councils. The settlement of economic affairs, and the continued expansion of the area of this settlement, must be in the hands of the workers' councils. The councils must have all power in the state. To these ends must we direct our activities in the immediate future, and it is obvious that, if we pursue this line, there cannot fail to be an enormous and immediate intensification of the struggle. For step by step, by hand-to-hand fighting, in every province, in every town, in every village, in every commune, all the powers of the state have to be transferred bit by bit from the bourgeoisie to the workers' and soldiers' councils.

But before these steps can be taken, the members of our own party and the proletarians in general must be schooled and disciplined. Even where workers' and soldiers' councils already exist, these councils are as yet far from understanding the purposes for which they exist. [*Hear! hear!*] We must make the masses realize that the workers' and soldiers' council has to be the central feature of the machinery of state, that it must concentrate all power within itself, and must utilize all powers for the one great purpose of bringing about the socialist revolution. Those workers who are already organized to form workers' and soldiers' councils are still very far from having adopted such an outlook, and only isolated proletarian minorities are as yet dear as to the tasks that devolve upon them. But there is no reason to complain of this, for it is a normal state of affairs. The masses must learn how to use power, by using power. There is no other way. We have, happily, advanced since the days when it was proposed to "educate" the proletariat socialistically. Marxists of Kautsky's school are, it would seem, still living in those vanished days. To educate the proletarian masses socialistically meant to deliver lectures to them, to circulate leaflets and pamphlets among them. But it is not by such means that the proletarians will be schooled. The workers, today, will learn in the school of action. [*Hear! hear!*]

Our scripture reads: In the beginning was the deed. Action for us means that the workers' and soldiers' councils must realize their mission and must learn how to become the sole public authorities throughout the realm. Thus only can we mine the ground so effectively as to make everything ready for the revolution which will crown our work. Quite deliberately, and with a dear sense of the significance of our words, did some of us say to you yesterday, did I in particular say to you, "Do not imagine that you are going to have an easy time in the future!" Some of the comrades have falsely imagined me to assume that we can boycott the National Assembly and then simply fold our arms. It is impossible, in the time that remains, to discuss this matter fully, but let me say that I never dreamed of anything of the kind. My meaning was that history is not going to make our revolution an easy matter like the bourgeois revolutions. In those revolutions it sufficed to overthrow the official power at the center, and to replace a dozen or so persons in authority. But we have to work from beneath. Therein is displayed the mass character of our revolution, one which aims at transforming the whole structure of society. It is thus characteristic of the modern proletarian revolution, that we must effect the conquest of political power, not from above, but from beneath.

The ninth of November was an attempt, a weakly, halfhearted, half-conscious, and chaotic attempt, to overthrow the existing public authority and to put an end to ownership rule. What is now incumbent upon us is that we should deliberately concentrate all the forces of the proletariat for an attack upon the very foundations of capitalist society. There, at the root, where the individual employer confronts his wage slaves; at the root, where all the executive organs of ownership rule confront the objects of this rule, confront the masses; there, step by step, we must seize the means of power from the rulers, must take them into our own hands. Working by such methods, it may seem that the process will be a rather more tedious one than we had imagined in our first enthusiasm. It is well, I think, that we should be perfectly clear as to all the difficulties and complications in the way of revolution. For I hope that, as in my own case, so in yours also, the description of the great difficulties we have to encounter, Of the augmenting tasks we have to undertake, will neither abate zeal nor paralyze energy. Far from it, the greater the task, the more fervently will you gather up your forces. Nor must we forget that the revolution is able to do its work with extraordinary speed. I shall make no attempt to foretell how much time will be required. Who among us cares about the time, so long only as our lives suffice to bring it to pass? Enough for us to know clearly the work we have to do; and to the best of my ability I have endeavored to sketch, in broad outline, the work that lies before us. [*Tumultuous applause.*]

15

WHAT ARE THE LEADERS DOING?

(1919)

As Germany moved toward a devastating defeat in the First World War, the authority of the monarchy was collapsing and there was an upwelling of revolutionary expectations. The leaders of the German Social Democratic Party in 1918 were Friedrich Ebert and Philipp Scheidemann, who made a deal with leading representatives of the German military and upper classes: prevent a working-class socialist revolution, and then a moderately democratic Weimar Republic would be created along with a package of social reforms. The two men became respectively President and Prime Minister of the new government, and another Social Democrat, Gustav Noske, became the regime's Defense Minister, directing the brutal measures to crush revolutionary currents among the working class. In addition to the Spartakusbund, *the larger breakaway of radicalized workers from the Social Democratic Party of Germany (SPD) had formed the Independent Social Democratic Party of Germany (USPD), and the SPD leadership aligned itself with the German military and the right-wing paramilitary* Freikorps *for the purpose of establishing "order." The ill-fated Spartacist uprising—led by*

From *Rosa Luxemburg: Selected Political Writings*, edited by Robert Looker, translated by William D. Graf. Copyright © 1972 by Jonathan Cape Ltd. Used by permission of Grove/Atlantic, Inc.

some of her more impatient comrades (and against her opposition)—was developing as Luxemburg herself sought to advance a radicalizing awareness and revolutionary spirit among broader layers within the workers' movement. Luxemburg was one of many murdered in the savage repression. This article first appeared in the January 7, 1919, issue of the German Communist daily Die Rote Fahne.

In the fiery atmosphere of the revolution, people and things mature with incredible rapidity. Only three short weeks ago, when the conference of the workers' and soldiers' councils ended, it seemed that Ebert and Scheidemann were at the zenith of their power. The representatives of the masses of revolutionary workers and soldiers throughout Germany had surrendered blindly to their leaders. The convocation of the National Assembly from which the "people in the streets" were barred, the degradation of the Executive Council, and with it the councils, to impotent mock-figures—what a triumph for the counterrevolution all along the line! The fruits of November 9th seemed to be squandered and thrown away, the bourgeoisie once more breathed a sigh of relief, and the masses were left perplexed, disarmed, embittered, and, indeed, doubting. Ebert and Scheidemann fancied themselves at the peak of power.

The blind fools! Not even twenty days have gone by since then, and their illusory power has overnight begun to totter. The masses are the real power, the actual power, by virtue of the iron compulsion of history. One may put them in chains for the time being, one may formally deprive their organizations of any power—but they need only stir, only straighten their backs obstinately, and the earth will tremble under the feet of the counterrevolution.

Anyone who witnessed yesterday's mass demonstration in the Siegesallee, who felt this adamant revolutionary conviction, this magnificent mood, this energy that the masses exuded, must conclude that politically the proletarians' have grown enormously through their experience of recent weeks, in the latest events. They have become aware of their power, and all that remains is for them to avail themselves of this power.

Ebert-Scheidemann and their customers, the bourgeoisie, who incessantly cry *putsch*, are at this moment experiencing the same disillusionment felt by the last Bourbon when his minister replied to his outraged cry about the "rebellion" of the people of Paris with the words, "Sir, this is no rebellion, it is a revolution!"

Yes, it is a revolution with all its externally chaotic development, with its alternating ebb and flow, with momentary surges towards the seizure of power and equally momentary recessions of the revolutionary breakers. And the revolution is making its way step by step through all these apparent zigzag movements and is marching forward irresistibly.

The mass must learn to fight, to act in the struggle itself. And today one can sense that the workers of Berlin to a large extent have learned to act; they thirst for resolute deeds, clear situations, sweeping measures. They are not the same as they were on November 9th; they know what they want and what they should do.

However, are their leaders, the executive organs of their will, well informed? Have the revolutionary chairmen and delegates of the large-scale concerns, have the energy and resolve of the radical elements of the USPD grow in the meanwhile? Has their capacity for action kept pace with the growing energy of the masses?

We are afraid that we cannot answer these questions with a straight-forward yes. We fear that the leaders are still the same as they were on November 9th, that they have learned little more. Twenty-four hours have gone by since the Ebert government's attack on Eichhorn.* The masses enthusiastically followed the appeal of their leaders; spontaneously and on their own strength they brought about the reappointment of Eichhorn. On their own spontaneous initiative they occupied *Vorwärts* and seized the bourgeois editors and the WTB [Wolff's Telegraphic Bureau] and, so far as possible, they armed themselves. They are waiting for further instructions and moves from their leaders.

And meanwhile, what have these leaders done? What have they decided? Which measures have they taken to safeguard the victory of the revolution in this tense situation in which the fate of the revolution will be decided, at least for the next epoch? We have seen and heard nothing!

---

*[Emil Eichhorn, a USPD deputy who became Chief of Police in Berlin in the November Revolution, was dismissed from his post by the SPD provisional government on January 4th because of his sympathies with the revolutionary Left.]

Perhaps the delegates of the workers are conferring profoundly and productively. Now, however, the time has come to act.

Ebert, Scheidemann, et al., are surely not frittering away their time with conferences. Most certainly they are not asleep. They are quietly preparing their intrigues with the usual energy and circumspection of the counterrevolutionary; they are sharpening their swords to catch the revolution unawares, to assassinate it.

Other spineless elements are already industriously at work paving the way for "negotiations," bringing about compromises, throwing a bridge across the abyss which has opened up between the masses of workers and soldiers and the Ebert government, inducing the revolution to make a "compromise" with its mortal enemies.

Now there is no time to lose. Sweeping measures must be undertaken immediately. Clear and speedy directives must be given to the masses, to the soldiers faithful to the revolution. Their energy, their bellicosity must be directed towards the right goals. The wavering elements among the troops can be won for the sacred cause of the people by means of resolute and clear actions taken by the revolutionary bodies.

Act! Act! Courageously, resolutely, consistently—that is the "accursed" duty and obligation of the revolutionary chairmen and the sincerely socialist party leaders. Disarm the counterrevolution, arm the masses, occupy all positions of power. Act quickly! The revolution obliges. Its hours count as months, its days as years, in world history. Let the organs of the revolution be aware of their high obligations!

BIBLIOGRAPHY

Works by Rosa Luxemburg

Bronner, Stephen Eric, ed. *The Letters of Rosa Luxemburg.* New Edition. Amherst, N.Y.: Humanity Books, 1993.

Davis, Horace B., ed. *The National Question: Selected Writings by Rosa Luxemburg.* New York: Monthly Review Press, 1976.

Ettinger, Elizbieta, ed. *Comrade and Lover: Rosa Luxemburg's Letters to Leo Jogiches.* Cambridge, Mass.: MIT Press, 1981.

Howard, Dick, ed. *Selected Political Writings of Rosa Luxemburg.* New York: Monthly Review Press, 1971.

Looker, Robert, ed. *Rosa Luxemburg: Selected Political Writings.* New York: Grove Press, 1974.

Luxemburg, Rosa. *The Accumulation of Capital.* Translated by Agnes Schwarzchild. New York: Monthly Review Press, 1968.

———. *The Accumulation of Capital—An Anti-Critique* (with Nikolai Bukharin, *Imperialism and the Accumulation of Capital*). Edited by Kenneth Tarbuck. New York: Monthly Review Press, 1972.

———. *Letters from Prison* [to Sophie Liebknecht]. Translated by Cedar and Eden Paul. London: The Socialist Book Centre, 1946.

269

————. *Letters to Karl and Luise Kautsky from 1896 to 1918*. Edited by Luise Kautsky, translated by Louis P. Lochner. New York: Robert M. McBride Co., 1925.

Waters, Mary-Alice, ed. *Rosa Luxemburg Speaks*. New York: Pathfinder Press, 1970.

Works About Rosa Luxemburg

Arendt, Hannah. "Rosa Luxemburg, 1871–1919." *Men in Dark Times*. New York: Harcourt, Brace and World, 1968.

Basso, Lelio. *Rosa Luxemburg, A Reappraisal*. New York: Praeger, 1975.

Bronner, Stephen E. *Rosa Luxemburg: A Revolutionary for Our Time*. New York: Columbia University Press, 1987.

Cliff, Tony. *Rosa Luxemburg*. London: Bookmarks, 1983.

Dunayevskaya, Raya. *Rosa Luxemburg, Women's Liberation, and Marx's Philosophy of Revolution*. Urbana: University of Illinois Press, 1991.

Frölich, Paul. *Rosa Luxemburg: Her Life and Work*. New York: Monthly Review Press, 1972.

Geras, Norman. *The Legacy of Rosa Luxemburg*. London: Verso, 1983.

Löwy, Michael. "Rosa Luxemburg's Conception of 'Socialism or Barbarism.'" *On Changing the World, Essays in Political Philosophy, from Karl Marx to Walter Benjamin*. Atlantic Highlands, N.J.: Humanities Press, 1993.

Lukacs, Georg. "The Marxism of Rosa Luxemburg" and "Critical Observations on Rosa Luxemburg's 'Critique of the Russian Revolution.'" *History and Class Consciousness: Studies in Marxist Dialectics*. Cambridge, Mass.: MIT Press, 1971.

Mandel, Ernest. "Rosa Luxembrg and German Social Democracy." *Revolutionary Marxism and Social Reality in the Twentieth Century*. Edited by Steve Bloom. Amherst, N.Y.: Humanity Books, 1994.

Martin, Jean-Paul [Michel Pablo (Raptis)]. "Democracy and Workers' Rule." *Fourth International*, January–February, 1953.

Nettl, J. P. *Rosa Luxemburg*. 2 vols. London: Oxford University Press, 1966.

Nye, Andrea. *Philosophia: The Thought of Rosa Luxemburg, Simone Weil, and Hannah Arendt*. New York: Routledge, 1994.

Related Works

Abendroth, Wolfgang. *A Short History of the European Working Class.* New York: Monthly Review Press, 1972.

Anderson, Evelyn. *Hammer or Anvil: The Story of the German Working-Class Movement, 1875–1945.* London: Gollanz, 1945.

Anderson, Kevin. *Lenin, Hegel, and Western Marxism: A Critical Study.* Urbana: University of Illinois Press, 1995.

Berghahn, V. R. *Modern Germany.* Cambridge: Cambridge University Press, 1982.

Bernstein, Eduard. *Evolutionary Socialism: A Criticism and Affirmation.* Translated by Edith Harvey. New York: Schocken Books, 1961.

———. *Selected Writings of Eduard Bernstein, 1900–1921.* Edited and translated by Manfred Steger. Amherst, N.Y.: Humanity Books, 1996.

Blobaum, Robert. *Feliks Dzierzhinski and the SDKPIL: A Study of the Origins of Polish Communism.* New York: Columbia University Press, 1984.

Bottomore, Tom, with Laurence Harris, V. G. Kiernan, and Ralph Miliband, eds. *A Dictionary of Marxist Thought.* Oxford: Basil Blackwell, 1991.

Braunthal, Julius. *History of the International, 1864–1943.* 2 vols. New York: Frederick A. Praeger, 1967.

Evans, Richard J. *Proletarians and Politics: Socialism, Protest, and the Working Class in Germany Before the First World War.* New York: St. Martin's Press, 1990.

Fletcher, Roger, ed. *Bernstein to Brandt: A Short History of German Social Democracy.* London: Edward Arnold, 1987.

Gay, Peter. *The Dilemma of Democratic Socialism: Eduard Bernstein's Challenge to Marx.* New York: Collier Books, 1962.

Gruber, Helmut, ed. *International Communism in the Era of Lenin.* Greenwich, Conn.: Fawcett, 1967.

Guttsman, W. L. *The German Social Democratic Party, 1875–1933.* London: Geroge Allen and Unwin, 1981.

Harman, Chris. *The Lost Revolution: Germany, 1918 to 1923.* London: Bookmarks, 1982.

Haupt, Georges. *Aspects of International Socialism: 1871–1914.* Cambridge: Cambridge University Press, 1986.

Hunt, Richard N. *The Political Ideas of Marx and Engels.* 2 vols. Pittsburgh: University of Pittsburgh Press, 1974 and 1984.

Kautsky, Karl. *The Road to Power: Political Reflections on Growing Into the Revolution.* Edited by John H. Kautsky, translated by Raymond Meyer. Amherst, N.Y.: Humanities Press, 1996.

————. *Selected Political Writings*. Edited and translated by Patrick Goode. London: Macmillan Press, 1983.

Le Blanc, Paul. *From Marx to Gramsci: An Introduction to Revolutionary Marxist Politics*. Amherst, N.Y.: Humanity Books, 1996.

Levine-Meyer, Rosa. *Levine: The Life of a Revolutionary*. Farnsborough, England: Saxon House, 1973.

Lidtke, Vernon. *The Alternative Culture: Socialist Labor in Imperial Germany*. New York: Oxford University Press, 1985.

Mandel, Ernest. *The Place of Marxism in History*. Amherst, N.Y.: Humanity Books, 1994.

Mayer, Arno J. *Why Did the Heavens Not Darken? The "Final Solution" in History*. New York: Pantheon Books, 1990.

Mecklenburg, Frank, and Manfed Stassen, eds. *German Essays on Socialism in the Nineteenth Century: Theory, History, and Political Organization, 1844–1914*. New York: Continuum, 1990.

Nolan, Mary. *Social Democracy and Society: Working-Class Radicalism in Dusseldorf, 1890–1920*. Cambridge: Cambridge University Press, 1981.

Pelz, William. *The Spartakusbund and the German Working-Class Movement, 1914–1919*. Lewiston, N.Y.: Edwin Mellen Press, 1987.

Riddel, John, ed. *The German Revolution and the Debate on Soviet Power: Documents, 1918–1919*. New York: Pathfinder Press, 1986.

Rowbotham, Sheila. *Women, Resistance and Revolution*. New York: Vintage Books, 1972.

Salvadori, Massimo. *Karl Kautsky and the Socialist Revolution*. London: New Left Books, 1976.

Schorske, Carl. *German Social Democracy, 1905–1917*. Cambridge, Mass.: Harvard University Press, 1955.

Steenson, Gary P. *Karl Kautsky, 1854–1938: Marxism in the Classical Years*. Pittsburgh: University of Pittsburgh Press, 1978.

————. *"Not One Man! Not One Penny!": German Social Democracy, 1863–1914*. Pittsburgh: University of Pittsburgh Press, 1981.

Trotnow, Helmut. *Karl Liebknecht: A Political Biography*. Hamden, Conn.: Archon Books, 1984.

Tudor, H., and J.M. Tudor, eds. *Marxism and Social Democracy: The Revisionist Debate, 1896–1898*. Cambridge: Cambridge University Press, 1988.

Weitz, Eric D. *Creating German Communism, 1890–1990: From Popular Protests to Socialist State*. Princeton: Princeton University Press, 1997.